# THE STRATEGIC CORPORAL REVISITED

# THE STRATEGIC CORPORAL REVISITED

CHALLENGES FACING COMBATANTS IN
21ST-CENTURY WARFARE

Edited by
David W Lovell
Deane-Peter Baker

*The Strategic Corporal Revisited: Challenges facing combatants in 21st-century warfare*

First published 2017

by UCT Press, an imprint of
Juta and Company (Pty) Ltd
PO Box 14373, Lansdowne 7779, Cape Town, South Africa
www.uctpress.co.za

© 2017 The Authors

ISBN 978 1 77582 220 2 (Print)
ISBN 978 1 77582 231 8 (Web PDF)

All rights reserved. No part of this publication may be reproduced or transmitted in any form or by any means, electronic or mechanical, including photocopying, recording, or any information storage or retrieval system, without prior permission in writing from the publisher. Subject to any applicable licensing terms and conditions in the case of electronically supplied publications, a person may engage in fair dealing with a copy of this publication for his or her personal or private use, or his or her research or private study. See section 12(1)(a) of the Copyright Act 98 of 1978.

Project manager: Edith Viljoen
Editor: Alfred LeMaitre
Proofreader: Leigh Daniels
Cover designer: Zach Viljoen
Typesetter: Nazli Jacobs
Indexer: Sanet le Roux

Typeset in 10,5 on 14pt Minion

Printed in South Africa by Idigital

The author and the publisher believe, on the strength of due diligence exercised, that this work does not contain any material that is the subject of copyright held by another person. In the alternative, they believe that any protected pre-existing material that may be comprised in it has been used with appropriate authority or has been used in circumstances that make such use permissible under the law.

# Contents

| | |
|---|---:|
| Acknowledgements | vi |
| List of Contributors | vii |
| Foreword – *Charles D Melson* | xi |
| **1** The 'Strategic Corporal' Revisited – *David W Lovell* | 1 |
| **2** Shared Leadership and the Strategic Corporal Metaphor: Some Considerations – *Nick Jans* | 19 |
| **3** The Strategic Corporal: Suffocated by Bureaucracy – *Richard Adams* | 32 |
| **4** The Strategic Contractor – *Deane-Peter Baker and David Pfotenhauer* | 55 |
| **5** The Strategic Civilian: Challenges for Non-Combatants in 21st-century Warfare – *Alan Ryan* | 73 |
| **6** Protection of Civilians: Challenges for the 'Strategic Corporal' in Peacekeeping Missions – *Siobhán Wills* | 92 |
| **7** The Strategic Corporal and the Challenge of Cyber Warfare – *Russell Buchan* | 111 |
| **8** Creating Strategic Corporals? Preparing Soldiers for Future Conflict – *David W Lovell* | 131 |
| **9** Strategic Gains without the Strategic Corporal: The Singapore Armed Forces in Afghanistan (2007–2013) – *Samuel Chan* | 147 |
| Epilogue: A Strategic Corporal's Perspective – *Anthony Moffitt* | 172 |
| References | 183 |
| Index | 200 |

# Acknowledgements

IN 2012, WITH THE CENTENARY of the outbreak of the First World War in prospect, David Lovell conceived the idea of a project to explore the future of warfare by considering how the role of the soldier had changed as distinct from (in particular) changes in the causes, weaponry and scale of conflict, on which much has already been written in the past two decades. The entry-point into these issues was provided by Charles C Krulak's notion of the 'strategic corporal', on which we asked a number of colleagues from our own university, and colleagues and associates from the Centre for Military and Security Law (CMSL) at the Australian National University (ANU), to reflect. The result—the volume before you—has taken some time to construct, but its thought-provoking breadth is, we believe, worth the wait. This co-operation between University of New South Wales (UNSW) Canberra at the Australian Defence Force Academy, where we help to teach Australia's future military officers, and our colleagues at ANU, is the continuation of a long-standing research partnership, and we are grateful for the support that CMSL provided for the discussions where the arguments of the chapters herein were first tested. Our special thanks to David Letts, Hitoshi Nasu and Rob McLaughlin. Thanks also to the University of New South Wales for providing the support required for us to complete the book. Finally, we thank the editors of the *ADF Journal* for permission to republish David Lovell's essay, which appears here as Chapter 8, and the editors of *Small Wars Journal* for permission to republish Alan Ryan's paper (Chapter 5).

*David W Lovell*
*Deane-Peter Baker*
Canberra, April 2017

# List of Contributors

Richard ADAMS, a former Australian Fulbright Scholar to Yale University, holds doctoral, master's and first-class degrees from the University of Western Australia, and a master's degree from the University of New South Wales (UNSW). His professional interests involve the relationship of the soldier to the state, the nature of public responsibility and the changing character of war. He is a researcher in the School of Humanities and Social Sciences at UNSW Canberra.

Deane-Peter BAKER joined UNSW Canberra in August 2012. He came to Canberra from Annapolis, Maryland, where he was an assistant professor of ethics in the Department of Leadership, Ethics and Law at the United States Naval Academy for two and a half years. Prior to that, Dr Baker was an associate professor of ethics at the University of KwaZulu-Natal in South Africa, where he taught for 11 years. His PhD was awarded by Macquarie University. Dr Baker has served in both the British Army and the South African Army. A specialist in both epistemology and the ethics of armed conflict, Dr Baker's research straddles philosophy, ethics and security studies. From 2006 to 2008 Dr Baker was chair of the Ethics Society of South Africa. He has held visiting fellowships at the Triangle Institute for Security Studies in North Carolina and the Strategic Studies Institute of the US Army War College, and was a 2010/11 academic fellow of the Foundation for the Defense of Democracies. From 2007 to 2010 Dr Baker was editor of the *African Security Review*. He is currently a researcher at the Australian Centre for the Study of Armed Conflict and Society, where he coordinates the Special Operations Studies Group, and a member of the International Panel on the Regulation of Autonomous Weapons.

Russell BUCHAN is a senior lecturer in international law at the University of Sheffield. Russell sits on the editorial board of the *Journal of the Use of Force in International Law* and the *International Community Law Review*.

His monograph *International Law and the Construction of the Liberal Peace* (Hart Publishing, 2013) was the recipient of the American Society of International Law's Francis Lieber Prize for an outstanding monograph in the field of the law of armed conflict for 2014. He co-edited, with Professor Nicholas Tsagourias, the edited collection *A Research Handbook on International Law and Cyberspace* (Edward Elgar: 2015). Russell is Co-Rapporteur for the International Law Association's Study Group on Cybersecurity, Terrorism and International Law.

**Samuel CHAN** is an adjunct lecturer at UNSW Canberra at the Australian Defence Force Academy. His academic background includes a BSc (Honours Class 1) in Statistics (UNSW), an MSc in Russian and East European Studies from St Antony's College, University of Oxford, and a PhD in Political and International Studies (UNSW). He is the beneficiary of the British Chevening Scholarship, the Tan Kah Kee Postgraduate Scholarship and the Australian Postgraduate Award. Dr Chan was formerly the Jebsen Fellow at the Centre for Conflict and Peace Studies in Kabul, Afghanistan, and also attended the summer seminar in military history at the United States Military Academy, West Point. He rendered Operationally Ready National Service as an army officer in the Singapore Armed Forces.

**Nick JANS, OAM** is a soldier, a scholar and a management consultant. He is a visiting fellow at both UNSW Canberra and the Centre for Defence Leadership and Ethics. He served in the Australian Army for 25 years in field artillery, training and personnel policy development, including active service in Vietnam, before leaving to pursue careers in consultancy and academic activities. He has published widely in the fields of organisational behaviour, human resource management and military sociology, and is currently on the editorial board of the journal *Armed Forces and Society*. He was lead author on *The Chiefs: A Study of Strategic Leadership* (Australian Defence College: 2013).

**David W LOVELL** is a Professor in International and Political Studies and Associate Dean (International) at UNSW Canberra at the Australian Defence Force Academy. His PhD was in the field of the history of ideas. He co-edits *The European Legacy* and is a member of the Australian Committee of the Council for Security Cooperation in the Asia-Pacific. He participated in a Human Rights Commission dialogue in Beijing in 1999, and in 2001 he was a member of the Australian delegation to the Second Global Forum on Fighting Corruption, and now regularly contributes to the International Association of Anti-Corruption Authorities. In 2005, he was the only non-European to be invited to the EU's 'A Soul for Europe' initiative in Budapest, and in 2006 he spoke on harmony and governance at the Beijing Forum. He has written or edited more than 15 books on topics including military ethics, Asia-Pacific security, Australian politics, communist and post-communist systems, and the history of ideas.

Anthony MOFFITT is a sergeant in the Australian Army and a career soldier with 25 years' experience and 11 operational deployments in army special operations. He is a passionate advocate of Human Performance (HP) initiatives in the military, and founded the first HP programme in the Australian Defence Force in 2013. He is a registered Provisional Psychologist, completing his Master of Psychology degree.

David PFOTENHAUER is a PhD student at UNSW Canberra, where his research explores the utility of Private Military Service Providers as viable options for surge capacity in expeditionary operations within a regional context. Australia and South Africa are employed as case studies in this project. He was formerly a Project Officer with the South African National Defence Force, where he participated in the general planning and research of the South African Army's post-conflict and reconstruction and development strategy.

Alan RYAN is the executive director of the Australian Civil-Military Centre. He was previously the principal of the Centre for Defence and Strategic Studies at the Australian Defence College. Prior to this appointment he was the senior adviser to the Minister for Defence, Senator the Hon Robert Hill. In that role, he was responsible for advising the minister on intelligence, operations, strategic and international issues. He has also worked as a consultant, providing consultancy services on strategy, security and crisis management to clients which have included Australian government departments, the United States Joint Chiefs of Staff and the Department of Peacekeeping Operations in the United Nations. From 1999 to 2003, he was the senior research fellow in the Australian Army's principal conceptual research institution, the Land Warfare Studies Centre. Prior to that, Dr Ryan was a senior lecturer at the

University of Notre Dame, Australia, where he was also Assistant Dean in the College of Arts and Sciences and the College of Law. He was director of the university's Politics and Law programme. He previously worked as a contract manager in intellectual property commercialisation for the University of Melbourne and the University of New England. Dr Ryan has a PhD from the Centre for International Studies at Cambridge University and a BA (Hons)/LLB from the University of Melbourne. He served with the Australian Army Reserve between 1981 and 1994 and on attachment with the British Territorial Army from 1987 to 1991. He has an extensive record of publication on historical, defence and strategic issues. He is an adjunct professor in the Graduate School of Management at La Trobe University.

**Siobhán WILLS** joined the Transitional Justice Institute at the University of Ulster in 2013. Prior to this, she held the Ariel Sallows Visiting Chair in Human Rights at the University of Saskatchewan. She has also taught at University College Cork, where she was co-director of the Centre for Criminal Justice and Human Rights. She has been a visiting fellow at the School of Advanced Studies, University of London, and a Fulbright Fellow at New York University and on the Harvard Human Rights Program. She is a member of the International Law Association Committee on the Use of Force and has published widely on international humanitarian law issues, peacekeeping, and the protection of civilians. She obtained her LLB from the National University of Ireland Galway in 2000, her LLM from Yale in 2001, and her DPhil from Oxford in 2007. Professor Wills's primary research and teaching area is Public International Law. Her areas of specialisation are the International Law of Armed Conflict, International Human Rights Law and International Criminal Law. She has published widely in these fields. Her work to date has focused on the protection role of peacekeeping missions, the legal characterisation of armed conflict, the law applicable to Chapter VII peacekeeping missions, accountability for peacekeepers' conduct, and the extent to which peacekeepers' acts or omissions have contributed to preventable 'harmful social outcomes' that cause widespread suffering.

# Foreword

## *Charles D Melson*
Chief Historian (Retired)
US Marine Corps Headquarters and University

> 'The Strategic Corporal Defined: The strategic corporal is a Marine who has mastered Marine basic skills, is tactically and technically proficient, is morally and ethically adept, savvy in both language and culture, mentally agile, physically fit, prepared to act and lead in a decentralized environment and is empowered by the trust and confidence of his seniors and subordinates.'
> Lt Gen George J Flynn (USMC), Deputy Commandant for Combat Development and Integration[1]

THIS COLLECTION OF ESSAYS, by a group of diverse and distinguished authors, indicates how far the concept of the 'strategic corporal' has travelled since it was first articulated in 1999. At that time, then-Commandant of the US Marine Corps General Charles C Krulak put forward observations on modern warfare that made conflicting demands on junior leaders to survive and solve the problems encountered in what he termed the 'three block war'. While rooted in contemporary problems, the background came from Krulak's personal experience in an institution the purpose of which he felt was to make Marines and to succeed in battle.

Krulak was born on 4 March 1942 in Quantico, Virginia. He graduated from the US Naval Academy in 1964. After commissioning, he served two tours in Vietnam, where he commanded a platoon and two rifle companies. In 1970, he ran the Counter-Guerrilla Warfare School in Okinawa, and following

---

1  USMC Concept and Plans Division, 'The strategic corporal', 1 September 2009.

duty at the Naval Academy in Annapolis, he commanded Marine Barracks at North Island, California, from 1973 to 1976. After a variety of staff postings, he assumed command of 3rd Battalion, 3rd Marine Regiment, in 1983. From there he moved on to serve with the 1st Marine Expeditionary Brigade, after which he became the military assistant to the Assistant Secretary of Defense. Subsequently, while the deputy director of the White House Military Office, he received his promotion to Brigadier General on 5 June 1989. He then served as Commanding General, 10th Marine Expeditionary Brigade, and 2nd Marine Division's assistant division commander. On 1 June 1990, he assumed command of the 6th Marine Expeditionary Brigade and the 2nd Force Service Support Group, which he took to the Gulf War in 1991. Promoted to Major General in March 1992, he commanded the Marine Corps Combat Development Command at Quantico, Virginia, and there received his third star and was assigned Commanding General of Fleet Marine Force, Pacific. General Krulak was thereafter promoted to full General, becoming the thirty-first Commandant of the US Marine Corps from 30 June 1995 through 30 June 1999. Famous for his notions of the 'strategic corporal' and the 'three block war', developed from the lessons of operations in Somalia, Haiti and Bosnia, he also added 'The Crucible'—a gruelling 54-hour final graduation exercise—to recruit training at Parris Island. General Krulak retired on 30 June 1999.

The utility of force appeared to be simpler in the past. In the 1960s and 1970s, I recall military training and education was focused on being able to seize, occupy and defend an assigned objective using fire, manoeuvre and close combat. Hearts and minds were recognised with the combined action programme for the South Vietnamese, but did not seem to apply to North Vietnamese regulars in open combat. Cold War orthodox warfare and irregular conflicts needs were often mixed together and mingled with civil disturbance, humanitarian service and non-combat evacuations in a confused manner. Manoeuvre warfare and fourth-generation theories were put forward as solutions to the muddle, but it took General Krulak to provide a needed degree of clarity.

While still used in Marine Corps colleges and schools for training and education, as far as I know the 'strategic corporal' has not been seen as a metaphor by a service that is not primarily recognised for military thought or theory. The focus was on the who, what, when, where and, to some extent, why of previous events, but not the 'what if' as presented here. It is

## Foreword

perhaps a measure of the concept's utility that it was used for this purpose to consider the challenges of this century that have been highlighted with the recent conflicts in Afghanistan, Iraq and elsewhere.[2] Editor and contributor David W Lovell provides an excellent introduction which puts these chapters within the context of the metaphor and the purpose of this anthology, which covers the ground of leadership, gender roles, education, training, international law, civilian participation, non-government agencies, private contractors, cyber warfare, employee relations, tactical colonels and strategic corporals on not-so-far-off battlefields.

As this volume shows, the challenges facing military senior and junior leaders are significant. I hope that leaders of all stripes will take the time to reflect on the complexities they may or will meet. This needs to be undertaken with mindfulness to change and situational awareness as defined by their mission. As it used to be said using the 'old school' concept of METT, it all depends upon the mission, enemy, troops and terrain.

---

2   Daniel Marston and Carter Malkasian (eds) (2008), *Counterinsurgency in modern warfare* (Oxford: Osprey Publishing); Mark Moyar (2009), *A question of command: counterinsurgency from the Civil War to Iraq* (New Haven, CT: Yale University Press).

# 1

# The 'Strategic Corporal' Revisited

## *David W Lovell*

OF ALL THE CHANGES in the fighting of wars over the past century, the one that is perhaps the most profound—at least for technologically advanced militaries, even though it most affects advanced 'Western' militaries thus far—is the rising expectation of the role of the soldier (and by the shorthand term 'soldier' the contributors to this volume generally mean to include, throughout, Marines, sailors, aircrew and other uniformed military personnel). We might take rising expectations around the levels of technical competence of the soldier for granted, as they operate ever more sophisticated weapons, communications and intelligence systems (though we may wonder, parenthetically, about the narrowing effects of, and dependencies caused by, technical specialisation, both to the specialist and to a military operation). But it is striking that for the ordinary soldier, for the non-commissioned officer, and for the junior officer—that is, for an increasing proportion of the lower strata in military organisations traditionally noted for their rigidly observed hierarchies—the expectations of levels of responsibility are rapidly increasing in the areas of decision-making in the field (for action and restraint) and communication to their superiors, non-combatants and outsiders such as the media. No longer must the soldier simply accept and obey orders; within many operations they have a level of autonomy to carry out the mission that those who breasted the trenches on the Western Front during the First World War could not even conceive.

Though this description might not have been exactly the sort of thing that US Marine Corps General Charles C Krulak had in mind when he published his essay on the 'strategic corporal' in 1999, Krulak served to draw our attention to a phenomenon that had been developing for some time and which would assume an increasing importance. Indeed, it has subsequently helped to drive further the expectations of senior defence officials about what their soldiers should be trained for and are capable of. One of the key points that General Krulak made was that the decisions soldiers made in the field, at some distance from their more senior officers, could have very significant—including disastrous—strategic and political consequences. This is particularly, but not only, the case where success in the larger conflict hinges on the perceptions of those populations who are directly affected by military operations, notably those conflicts in the early twenty-first century we have come to know as 'asymmetric',[1] where modern armies confront far-less powerful adversaries who nevertheless rely to some extent on popular support or neutrality as well as unconventional weapons and tactics. Such situations are closely allied with Krulak's notion of the 'three block war', where a range of operations (fighting, peace works and humanitarian assistance) might occur simultaneously within a very limited precinct.

It is worth remembering that General Krulak's reflections on the role of junior leaders in the US Marine Corps were driven as much by the increasing complexity of the tasks that faced contemporary military operations as by the potential for mistaken decisions to be rapidly communicated around the world and thus to damage an entire campaign. In his much-cited essay, 'The strategic corporal: leadership in the three block war',[2] Krulak outlined both the notion of the 'three block war'—'contingencies in which Marines may be confronted by the entire spectrum of tactical challenges in the span of a few hours and within the space of three contiguous city blocks'—and, critically for this discussion, that the outcome of military operations 'may hinge on decisions made by small unit leaders, and by actions taken at the *lowest* level'. 'Most importantly', he adds, the decisions thus taken

---

1   See, for example, Max G Manwaring (2012), *The complexity of modern asymmetric warfare* (Norman: University of Oklahoma Press); Martin Ewans (2005), *Conflict in Afghanistan: studies in asymmetric warfare* (London: Routledge); Rod Thornton (2007), *Asymmetric warfare: threat and response in the twenty-first century* (Cambridge: Polity); Josef Schröfl, Sean Cox and Thomas Pankratz (2009), *Winning the asymmetric war: political, social and military responses* (Frankfurt: Peter Lang).

2   Gen Charles C Krulak, 'The strategic corporal: leadership in the three block war', *Marines Magazine* (January 1999). Available at www.au.af.mil/au/awc/awcgate/usmc/strategic_corporal.htm, accessed on 11 April 2017.

*will likely be subject to the harsh scrutiny of both the media and the court of public opinion. In many cases, the individual Marine will be the most conspicuous symbol of American foreign policy and will potentially influence not only the immediate tactical situation, but the operational and strategic levels as well.*[3]

Krulak's notion of the 'three block war' has not found its way into doctrine, or been the subject of much detailed analysis.[4] The 'strategic corporal', by contrast, remains a popular expression, though it, too, remains to be more fully explored; that is the aim of this book.

The chapters herein seek to use the metaphor of the 'strategic corporal' as a way to focus on the demands facing junior leaders in contemporary military operations, and what might be done to enhance their ability to respond to them. While the foundation of the metaphor is to be found in the capacity of soldiers to make appropriate decisions under stress and in real time, the circumstances in which these decisions are made (and not simply the physical circumstances) need to be better understood, both by soldiers and their critical onlookers, be they villagers on the scene, senior military or political leaders remote from the operation, or anti-war activists thousands of miles away. This involves a host of considerations, which helps to explain why this collection covers so many diverse topics. It is not just about a soldier's professional mastery, though the ability to take command when required is basic to all the rest. Increasingly, it also means a genuine familiarity with legal and ethical issues, and an ability in low-intensity conflict to understand local culture and communicate with those in villages and neighbourhoods whose goodwill, or at least neutrality, are vital to ultimate success. In the non-war circumstances in which many Western militaries operate, such as humanitarian assistance and disaster relief as well as peacekeeping operations, it means dealing with civil authorities in the distribution of aid or even the administration of justice if local institutions have broken down. Sometimes it

---

3   Ibid.
4   As distinct, for example, from NATO's Peace Support Operations Doctrine. See A Walter Dorn and Michael Varey, 'Fatally flawed: the rise and demise of the "three-block war" concept in Canada', *International Journal* (Autumn 2008), 967–978. Available at walter-dorn.net/pdf/ThreeBlockWar-FatallyFlawed_Dorn-Varey_IJ_Aut2008.pdf, accessed on 9 April 2017.

involves negotiation and mediation. It may even mean having an understanding of the ways pervasive modern media works, and its potential to surveil—and sometimes derail—a mission. Sometimes it also means having a better understanding of the challenges that face one's own defence force, including the malign effects of bureaucratic inertia and the outsourcing of key capabilities to private contractors. This is the complex world in which the modern soldier now operates.

In part, the notion of the 'strategic corporal' is a way of saying that modern defence forces want their soldiers to think about the broader context and consequences of their actions. Military operations are increasingly played out in front of a worldwide audience. The choices soldiers make can often have far-reaching consequences, and the conflicts into which they will be sent in the twenty-first century promise to offer some new features. David Kilcullen, for example, has cited 'globalization and the backlash against it, the rise of nonstate actors with capabilities comparable to some nation-states, US conventional military superiority that forces all opponents to avoid its strengths and migrate toward unconventional approaches, and a global information environment based on the internet and satellite communications' as factors that seem to announce a new era of conflict, and demand adaptive responses.[5] Key to them all is the notion that the terrorist enemies of recent times rapidly mutate to counter our counter-measures and we need to respond—at all levels—by continuously updating our responses. Clear thinking is vital. Instead of an international relations approach, Kilcullen urges us to think through anthropology; think long-term, even in generational terms; and do not always think of military capacity or solutions, but also of diplomacy, aid and strategic communication.

The 'strategic corporal' provides us with a useful lens through which to view the diverse challenges of contemporary military operations, especially as they relate to the increasing responsibilities of junior leaders. Just as, it might reasonably be said, the expectations of the responsibilities of junior leaders in most aspects of human endeavour, especially in corporate and professional life, are constantly increasing. This is the common pool of human resources from which a modern defence force with a volunteer, as distinct from conscript, force must draw, train and retain its soldiers.

---

5   David J Kilcullen, 'New paradigms for 21st-century conflict', *eJournal USA: Foreign Policy Agenda* 12, 5 (May 2007), 39–45.

# The 'Strategic Corporal' Revisited

The 'strategic corporal' metaphor seems to have such a resonance in our language because, in military operations, developed states are increasingly trying to do more with less 'manpower', and, consequently, operational units are much smaller than entire divisions that went 'over the top' of muddy trenches on the Western Front, even though such small units have greater killing power than ever before and can summon devastatingly powerful airborne and other reinforcements at very short notice. With a reduction in size comes agility and speed, but these have the best effects when the intelligence leading the operation is astute and alive to the possibilities and pitfalls. But there are also large structural dangers that might arise from relying on the 'strategic corporal' or, to be more precise, on an armed force where decision-making is highly devolved. The distribution of tactical nuclear weapons, for example, to ground and air and naval units that have a large degree of autonomy risks the danger of an unintended escalation of conflict, whether by accident or poor decision-making. Such a suggestion certainly seems quite far from the intention of Krulak's contribution. Yet it shows the utility of the metaphor that we can quickly imagine diverse consequences of relatively autonomous decision-making, especially when allied with extraordinary destructive power.

## Issues

The chapters in this collection take a broad view of the challenges facing contemporary combatants, and how that influences the roles and responsibilities of the junior ranks. None denies or downplays the extension of autonomy to the lower levels of an advanced military force. Some think that important strategic gains can be made in certain circumstances without reliance on the initiative of the lower ranks, and that is indeed an important reminder. Some think that there is more that can be done to enable the development of strategic corporals, or, more precisely, the culture of responsibility and autonomy. In my own chapter, I reflect on the ways that soldiers should be educated to make the best of their potential roles during a career in the defence forces. Richard Adams, by contrast, powerfully argues that 'Defence'—or, depending on your country, 'Defense'—as an organisation exercises powerful bureaucratic constraints on budding strategic corporals. He asks, in effect, whether this is a command climate that can empower junior leaders. His message, if I can borrow from the cry of Diogenes of Sinope to Alexander the Great that has echoed for more than 2000 years, is: 'get out of my sun'.

Others insist that all ranks need to be properly apprised of the requirements of international law, especially as it concerns the *jus in bello* injunctions around proportionality and discrimination. On this latter issue, there seems to be little argument: some of the key examples of soldiers endangering the allied mission in Iraq and Afghanistan derive from indiscipline and breaking the rules of engagement in ways that have, understandably, infuriated locals. Desecrating dead bodies and defacing or destroying holy books, to name two issues that have been raised in the past decade: these quickly bring dishonour upon the allied forces and damage the *raison d'être* of their mission. Likewise, a high degree of legal and political complexity surrounds military decision-making today. Missions often have aims other than winning a war, and indeed few armed conflicts nowadays are declared wars. How does this complexity affect the protection of civilians, which has become a strategic issue as well as a legal one, especially since the endorsement of the responsibility-to-protect principle by the United Nations (UN) Security Council in April 2006?

Nick Jans, in the first substantive chapter, examines the strategic corporal metaphor from the perspective of organisational behaviour. Jans reflects on the long-standing reliance in the Australian Army on small group operations, but argues that we should not focus excessively on the most junior levels of command but look also at the general issues in leadership. Jans's emphasis on an organisational culture of shared leadership—where all, without consideration of rank, contribute to the leadership process—is tied to benefits for decision-making and operational outcomes. But it also has sometimes unsettling implications for professional behaviour throughout the armed forces, including the idea that leaders need intelligence, confidence and team-building skills, not just a reliance on rank or authoritatively delivered orders. To get the best from all members of the team and build 'strategic corporals', military leaders at all levels need to confront their leadership style and adopt what Jans and others have called 'officership'.

Richard Adams is clear that the dictum of counterinsurgency doctrine— the loss of moral legitimacy entails loss of the war—confirms that modern battle is as much about ideas as it is about territory. Counterinsurgency doctrine thus points to the ways in which the responsibilities of individual soldiers have expanded. Soldiers are no longer unquestioning pawns in a geo-strategic game played by political *padrones*. Revisiting the strategic corporal, Adams's chapter considers how soldiers might find strategic relevance, and how the military organisation might foster soldiers whose strategic relevance

## The 'Strategic Corporal' Revisited

is real rather than rhetorical. Recognising strategic value in the autonomous judgements of individual soldiers, this chapter resoundingly concludes that to cultivate strategic corporals there must be institutional reform of the military bureaucracy. Inherited, perpetuated and endemic, bureaucratic habit operates to stifle the independent responsibility that is foundational to the strategic corporal. More than the restructure of training courses, he argues that institutional reform of the bureaucracy is necessary to cultivate independently responsible soldiers.

Baker and Pfotenhauer focus on the roles of, and challenges around, the increasing use of private military contractors in conflict zones. They agree that when General Krulak first described the concept of the 'strategic corporal' in print in early 1999, his description of the likely combat environment of the future (nominally in 2020) was remarkably prescient. But they argue that Krulak did not, however, foresee the dramatic growth in the role that contractors have come to play in contemporary conflict zones (though nor did any significant analyst writing at that time). They offer a brief description of the strategic impact that contractors have had in the recent conflicts in Iraq and Afghanistan. Their chapter then asks how we might expect contractors to operate in environments where the tactical environment will be fluid and complex, where strategic success will sometimes hinge on tactical decisions taken at the lowest level, where operations will be conducted far from the 'flagpole', and where the media is omnipresent. Each factor is systematically examined. They conclude by examining the roles contractors could undertake as strategic enablers to less-capable military forces by augmenting, supporting, training and advising them.

Alan Ryan goes on to make the point that just as relatively junior military personnel are expected to demonstrate strategic levels of awareness, flexibility and leadership, so civilians are increasingly playing critical roles within contemporary combat zones. Many of these civilians are junior in rank, but when deployed into conflict areas carry enormous responsibility for decisions and as representatives of their agencies and countries. Although the division of roles between civilians and the military is generally clear, what is perhaps less well understood is the strategic role of civilian diplomats, aid personnel, police and advisers. While in a 'three block war' public servants should not be involved in fighting, they share that danger and will likely be engaged in mediating between warring parties and delivering aid. Ryan's chapter discusses the necessity of preparing civilian and military personnel to work together to understand what each brings to conflict termination and resolution. It also considers the challenges faced by civilians in-theatre. The 'strategic corporal' cannot do everything required of modern military operations; they need, and need to appreciate, the role of their 'strategic civilian' counterpart.

The following two chapters, by Siobhán Wills and Russell Buchan, bring to the fore two complex issues that 'strategic corporals', and those of us interested in the practical and ethical challenges facing contemporary soldiers, will have to confront: respectively, the role of soldiers in peacekeeping missions, and the question of whether those involved in cyber warfare are direct participants in hostilities and thus 'targets'. Wills concedes that although non-commissioned officers are sometimes required to take decisions that influence the strategic level of missions, they often do not have the broad-spectrum knowledge, both political and legal, or the training, or the experience, that should underpin decision-making in peacekeeping operations. Peacekeeping is difficult: peacekeepers face very different situations from armed conflicts; they are often buffeted by conflicting local forces; and recent history demonstrates that they have sometimes acquiesced in human rights violations, and sometimes even initiated them. Whole missions, and the bodies that initiate them, have become subject to significant criticisms. These problems are starting to be addressed by better training, and also by the UN's Rights Up Front plan of action adopted in 2014. Above all, Wills argues, missions need to be viewed by all their personnel from the perspective of the local people. All personnel need training in human rights protection, a supportive hierarchy, and thorough and consistent reporting.

Russell Buchan focuses on the rise of cyber warfare, and what this means for who can be targeted. During times of armed conflict, he reminds us, the principle of distinction imposes significant restrictions upon the conduct of combatants. A core feature of this principle is that combatants are precluded from directly targeting civilians until such time as they directly participate in hostilities (DPH). Indeed, combatants who directly target civilians commit a war crime under international criminal law. In order to comply with both international humanitarian law and international criminal law, it is therefore extremely important that combatants be able to accurately determine the circumstances in which a civilian directly participates in hostilities. In 2008, the International Committee of the Red Cross sought to clarify the matter by publishing interpretive guidance on the meaning of the concept of DPH.

## The 'Strategic Corporal' Revisited

However, the content of this guidance has been subject to considerable disagreement, and uncertainty remains as to how it is to be interpreted and applied to the physical battlefield. Perhaps unsurprisingly, disagreement and uncertainty are only enhanced in the context of the virtual battlefield. This is worrying given the increasing tendency of Western armed forces to outsource responsibility for cyber operations during times of armed conflict to civilian contractors. By interrogating various hypothetical and real-life examples, Buchan's chapter sheds light on whether, and under what circumstances, civilians who are involved in the creation and deployment of cyber weapons can be regarded as direct participants in hostilities, and assesses the implications that this has for the temporal and geographic scope of the armed conflict.

Lovell's chapter, on preparing soldiers for future conflict, begins by positing the inevitability of future conflict and, at the same time, the uncertainty of its contours. 'New' and 'old' wars are both still possibilities (at the risk of caricature: small-scale counterinsurgencies and unconventional wars on the one hand, and state-on-state wars on the other); not to forget the constabulary and emergency responder roles that most contributors agree further increase the demands on soldiers. How, then, to prepare soldiers for this range of challenges, to convince them that violence alone rarely solves the causes of conflict, and to stress that human factors during the course and resolution of conflict are ultimately more important than technological fixes? When we anticipate future conflicts, and prepare for them, we should think less of the development of incipient, and even imagined, technologies of killing—however ingenious, effectual and precise—and more of the qualities and attitudes that are required for the successful prosecution of the war and resolution of the issues that led to it. Lovell deploys the well-known distinction between training and education to argue for more emphasis on developing an all-round soldier than a specialist. The soldiers who put their lives at risk for their country need a complex set of intellectual strengths and insights to take with them into battle along with their weapons. They need a considered commitment to their cause; a capacity for courage, initiative and teamwork in its prosecution; an awareness of the cultural, religious, national or ideological dimensions of the struggle; an appreciation that the outcomes of battles are influenced by chance and its close companion, daring; and the self-awareness to monitor the psychological and not just the physical trauma of battle. A study of disciplines in the humanities and social sciences—politics, law, anthropology, history, literature, languages, and so on—will help to prepare soldiers for operations and for the return to civilian norms. A prepared soldier is more effectual and more resilient.

Chan's chapter offers a valuable reflection on the strategic use of military forces, which is not always the same depending on where a nation sits in the pecking order of military power. He examines Operation Blue Ridge (2007–2013), during which 492 members of the Singapore Armed Forces (SAF) contributed to the US-led military operations in Afghanistan. The initial section establishes that Washington, and not Kabul, was at the heart of Singapore's realpolitik decisions, underpinned by geostrategic and economic reasons. The remaining sections then systematically advance the notion that the 'strategic corporal' was a non-issue for the SAF—from force composition and preparation, to the specific niche areas where personnel were deployed, and how wide-ranging benefits (such as experience, heraldry, recruitment publicity and domestic communications) were conspicuously harvested while contributing to strategic goals. Operation Blue Ridge will enter Singapore's annals as a resounding success and serve as one tested model for future SAF deployments. But it also demonstrates that 'strategic corporals' are not a necessary focus of every military operation.

The final contribution to this volume comes from a practitioner, a real 'strategic corporal', an Australian non-commissioned officer with almost 20 years' operational experience, and some 11 operational deployments as a Special Operations soldier. Picking up on themes from Adams and Lovell in particular, Anthony Moffitt offers a passionate argument for enabling the strategic corporal through the breaking down of what he sees as obsolete and elitist hierarchies within military forces, a breaking down he argues will come in large part through the opening up of educational opportunities for soldiers across the board. Moffitt pulls no punches, and many will disagree with some or all of what he has to say, but it is a perspective that no one can afford to ignore.

## Defence as a learning organisation

Historically, one of the notable characteristics of (successful) fighting forces, or what we now know as defence forces, has been their ability and willingness to take up the latest thinking and advances in technology and organisation. They are, perforce, learning organisations. They learn from operating with their allies; they learn from hard experience what works and what does not; they learn from communities of practice; and they learn from their enemies.

The logic is compelling: those that do not innovate lose, and that often means losing their lives or other things they value as much (from property to identity). Nowadays, this historical reality has been formalised into an aspiration, or even a demand, that defence organisations should be learning organisations. Whether it is transitioning from the use of battering rams, or trebuchets, or cannons, or the replacement of sabre by musket, or the tank replacing horse-mounted cavalry, or the incremental practices of counterinsurgency, armed forces have long been ready adopters of new tactics and new technologies. It may be argued whether in the modern world the use of new technologies by armed forces was the driver of technological development, or whether the technology evolved and was taken up for military purposes; certainly the contemporary experience since at least the Second World War is that defence is a significant driver and innovator in technology,[6] often with large research and development organisation, and a brief to utilise appropriate commercial technological advances.[7] Likewise, armed forces have taken up measures of training and organising forces in novel ways to get the best out of their troops. The intelligence testing developed by Alfred Binet was adopted in the US during the First World War and adapted in order to place large numbers of people of different abilities into tasks that best suited their capacities.[8] It may also be said that the military has been a leader in one key characteristic of modernity: a career open to talents. (Which is not to say that social privilege has not also played its role—and those armed forces that most quickly removed their social elite from positions of officer command have tended to be those that have done well. Napoleon Bonaparte, the son of a minor, impoverished Corsican aristocrat, and a second lieutenant in the French Army

---

6     See Martin van Creveld (1991), *Technology and war: from 2000 BC to the present*, revised edition (New York: The Free Press), based on the central premise that 'war is completely permeated by technology and governed by it' (p 1).

7     The former US Secretary of Defense, Ashton B Carter, argued that the Defense Department needed to take up more readily the commercial innovations in technology that might have defence applications: see, for example, Ashton B Carter, 'Running the Pentagon right: how to get the troops what they need', *Foreign Affairs* 93, 1 (January/February 2014), 101–112.

8     Frederick L McGuire (1994), 'Army alpha and beta tests of intelligence', in RJ Sternberg (ed), *Encyclopedia of intelligence* (New York: Macmillan), 125–129.

who ultimately crowned himself Emperor in 1804, is a case in point.)[9] Armed forces also remain a field where social prejudice can be systematically addressed (as it has in the US, where it has allowed a pathway out of disadvantage for many African Americans).[10] We are currently witnessing a concerted effort by many defence leaders to capture the benefits of their diverse workforce, especially by addressing sexism.[11]

The question nevertheless remains whether this tradition of adaptation by armed forces to new technologies, tactics and organisational forms has, or can, become the central feature of their approach so as to rapidly understand and counter threats to the nation-state. In 2003 the US Army Corps of Engineers published *Learning Organization Doctrine: Roadmap for Transformation*, in which their commander, Lieutenant General Robert B Flowers declared that 'Organizational learning must be embedded in all that we do'. The aspiration as well as the understanding of what is to be built—'A learning organization is a nonthreatening, empowering culture where leadership,

---

9 Rothenberg argues that the Napoleonic wars, in terms of their tactics and strategy and their mass mobilisation, introduced modern warfare to the world: 'Alors que tous les conflits majeurs mêlent tradition et innovation, les guerres de la Révolution française, et plus encore les guerres napoléoniennes, en rupture très nette avec le passé, constituent l'origine des pratiques de la guerre moderne ... En 1809, les puissances européenes commençaient à rattraper leur retard sur les méthodes guerrières de Napoléon. Toutes augmentèrent leurs effectifs et adoptèrent le corps d'armée comme principale unité de manoeuvre, améliorèrent leur encadrement et se dotèrent d'une importante artillerie.' Gunther E Rothenberg (2000), *Atlas des guerres napoleoniennes: 1796–1815*, trans. G Brzustowski (Paris: Editions Autrement), 16–17.

10 Colin Powell wrote of the US Army after the end of official segregation in 1948: 'I was in a profession that would allow me to go as far as my talents would take me. And for a black, no other avenue in American society offered so much opportunity.' Colin L Powell, with Joseph E Persico (2011), *A soldier's way: an autobiography* (New York: Random House), 61. But the US forces' experience in Vietnam (see, for example, James E Westheider [2008], *The African American experience in Vietnam: brothers in arms* [Lanham, MD: Rowman & Littlefield]) was crucial in leading to a more integrated and meritocratic force.

11 Sometimes based on, or supporting, work done at UNSW Canberra. See, for example, Elizabeth A Thomson (2014), *Battling with words: a study of language, diversity and social inclusion in the Australian Department of Defence* (Canberra: Department of Defence), and Dee Gibbon, 'Unexpected turbulence: the cultural, gender-based challenges facing female pilots in the Australian Defence Force', in DAJ Mills, DJ Neil-Smith and DD Bridges (eds) (2014), *Absent Aviators* (Farnham: Ashgate), 115–146.

management, and the workforce focus on continuously developing organizational competence'[12]—are in key respects uncontroversial, and widely shared.[13] Nor should the effects of Hurricane Katrina in 2005 on Lake Pontchartrain's levee system be held against them in this discussion. What is problematic, however, in discussing the Corps of Engineers or any other Western military organisation, is whether the list of key characteristics required for a learning organisation are, or can be, developed. Such a list includes, from the Australian case: 'Inculcate leadership behaviours at all levels that reinforce learning'; 'Establish robust learning processes and practices'; 'Generate and reflect on a shared vision and understanding'; and 'Encourage collaboration and team learning', among others.[14] The fear is that such aspirations, and associated reports and workshops, tick the appropriate bureaucratic boxes, with little consequent change: less, perhaps, from hostility to the aspirations themselves than because of inertia or the overwhelming demands of everyday work. As early as 2002, Lieutenant Colonel Stephen J Gerras of the US Army War College questioned whether the US Army could yet meet its aspiration to develop the competencies of twenty-first-century leaders, outlined in Joint Vision 2020, including 'an ability to deal with cognitive complexity, tolerance of ambiguity, intellectual flexibility, a meaningful level of self-awareness, and an enhanced understanding of the relationships among organizational sub-systems that collectively construct the prevailing organizational climate'.[15] The cultural change to enable the development of a learning organisation for which Gerras advocated is arguably still required.

---

12  US Army Corps of Engineers (2003), *Learning organization doctrine: roadmap for transformation*, 2. Available at www.au.af.mil/au/awc/awcgate/army/learningdoctrine.pdf, accessed on 18 April 2017.

13  In the Australian Army, for example, an agreed definition of the Army Learning Organisation was devised in 2009: 'Army has the people, processes and culture that enable it to learn, share and apply knowledge to quickly meet Australia's strategic goals'; Steven Talbot, Denise McDowall, Christina Stothard and Maya Drobnjak, The Army Learning Organisation Workshop (Canberra: Australian Government, Defence Science Technical Organisation, 2013). Available at www.dtic.mil/cgi-bin/GetTRDoc?AD=ADA591410, accessed on 18 April 2017.

14  Ibid.

15  Stephen J Gerras (2002), *The army as a learning organization*, US Army War College, May 2002. Available at www.carlisle.army.mil/orgs/SSL/DCLM/pubs/Learning%20Organization.doc, accessed on 11 April 2017.

The ability to learn takes place at the organisational level, and at the unit and individual levels. Not to take up this challenge is high risk: for the organisation as a whole, it risks the security, or integrity of the nation, which is the highest duty for the modern state; at the individual level, it may mean death. As US Brigadier General Fastabend has argued, 'in the volatile, uncertain, complex, and ambiguous environment we face for the foreseeable future, if we were to choose merely one advantage over adversaries it would certainly be this: to be superior in the art of learning and adaptation'.[16]

Some have responded to the 'strategic corporal' by asking: what does this mean for education and training? Major Lynda Liddy of the Australian Regular Army asks this question, as does my chapter in this collection. But whereas Liddy feels confident that a type of strategic corporal 'has been a feature of the Australian Regular Army's small-unit military culture since the 1950s', Adams, as I have outlined earlier, argues in this volume that the type of initiative we expect from such small units is being stifled by defence bureaucracy. In this, his chapter reinforces a message made earlier by Major Pastel of the USMC, who argued—on a theme that Krulak himself mentioned—that the 'strategic corporal' was critical to the future success of the Corps, but that the Marine Corps leadership limited the development of such soldiers. Nurturing a more developed sense of personal responsibility, Pastel argues, requires that the USMC approach of 'zero-defects mentality' and 'micromanagement' be scrapped.[17]

That the 'strategic corporal' must be developed, through training and education, is a logical consequence of what has gone before. Where does that development happen; when—in relation both to a military career as a whole and to pre-deployment—does it happen; and, finally, what exactly needs to be developed? These are key questions. There are already, in Western countries, a large number of training and education institutions for early- and mid-career

---

16   David A Fastabend and Robert H Simpson, 'Adapt or die: the imperative for a culture of innovation in the United States Army', *ARMY Magazine* 54, 2 (February 2004), 16.
17   Major Teague A Pastel (2008), USMC, *Marine Corps leadership: empowering or limiting the strategic corporal?*, unpublished MMS dissertation, US Marine Corps Command and Staff College, Quantico, VA. Available at www.dtic.mil/get-tr-doc/pdf?AD=ada490868, accessed on 18 April 2017.

officers, and in some such countries parallel institutions for non-commissioned officers (NCOs).[18] Whether and how the content of such curricula should be harmonised is a worthy issue. Clearly, all soldiers need some knowledge of the Law of Armed Conflict, some appreciation of the cultural and linguistic differences between their own communities and those of their enemies, an improvement in communication and especially media skills, and an adaptability to the demands of very different operations in which they are likely to find themselves.[19] How deep this understanding should go is a legitimate question. Academic study of *jus in bello*, for example, need not always be required. The difficulty—as with all education—is to know how to develop the *judgement* of students, for judgement is crucial to operational problem-solving.

The metaphor of the 'strategic corporal' should be seen as arising from this context, in an era in which—from necessity—the individual soldier's actions have potentially wide ramifications. Not all of the learnings from the current era of the 'war on terrorism' point in this same direction. But all of them support the notion that the better educated a soldier can be, in other words, the more adaptable, the more likely is the complex threat of terrorism to be addressed and countered; and the more likely it is that senior positions will increasingly be filled by those who are open to new ideas and approaches, and new techniques and technologies.

One of the areas in which the adaptability of the military in general, and the soldier in particular, will increasingly be challenged is the area known as 'big data'. We are increasingly able to collect vast masses of data on the actions, beliefs and preferences of people who are going about their otherwise ordinary

---

18   Stringer has argued that the non-commissioned officer education system (NCOES) is undergoing a fundamental shift from training to education, with the opportunity to add 'essential language training, cultural education, and interagency exchange opportunities to the NCO educational portfolio'; his article makes recommendations for adapting the NCOES using best practices from other areas of the US officer education system. Kevin D Stringer, 'Educating the strategic corporal: a paradigm shift', *Military Review* 89, 5 (September–October 2009), 87–95.

19   See, for example, the discussion in TM Scott (2006), *Enhancing the future strategic corporal* ('Future War Paper'), unpublished MMS dissertation, USMC Marine Corps University, Quantico, VA. Available at www.dtic.mil/dtic/tr/fulltext/u2/a507697.pdf, accessed on 18 April 2017.

business, because those actions are monitored, recorded and stored by electronic means. Big data will increasingly be used by business to identify consumer needs and preferences, by governments to determine needs and monitor behaviour, and by militaries to identify and anticipate threats and shape effectual counter-measures. Vast amounts of such information are in the public domain on social media, for example, and we are increasingly able to correlate and make sense of that information in order to make decisions. This is a new frontier for military organisations, but one that they will rapidly master or risk defeat. Precisely how that will be done is not a key focus of this volume, though it arises from the thinking here, but it is a topic for further consideration. Scholarship will have to catch up with the developments in military organisations themselves, which contain very smart people.

But the metaphor of the 'strategic corporal' has larger implications, in so far as it emphasises the responsibility of all soldiers, from the lowest to the highest ranks, to make decisions with an understanding of their consequences for the conflict in which they participate. This includes not just understanding the enemy and his cultural and other contexts, and not just understanding the potential electronic and other spread of his actions onto the world's consciousness; it also includes an understanding of the armed force within which he—and, increasingly, she—operates. And this is precisely the point: integrating men and women into an effectual armed force takes understanding and cultural change on the part of the 'strategic corporals' themselves. If women are not effectively integrated into such a force, it limits the effectiveness of the fighting force, increases the incidence and depth of post-conflict trauma, and creates a poor image for the forces of freedom, especially when they are fighting bigotry and exclusiveness.

## Conclusion

The contributors' reactions to Krulak's notion suggest that it is a fruitful way to think about contemporary military operations. Krulak's own reluctance to give a strict definition has been a factor in this productiveness, though Liddy has made a very useful attempt to make precise what is germane in the 'strategic corporal' by offering the following definition:

# The 'Strategic Corporal' Revisited

> *A strategic corporal is a soldier that possesses technical mastery in the skill of arms while being aware that his judgment, decision-making and action can all have strategic and political consequences that can affect the outcome of a given mission and the reputation of his country.*[20]

Such a definition does not focus on a particular rank, but rather suggests—as I believe is useful—that the actions of junior leaders, including non-commissioned officers as well as ordinary 'diggers', as we would say in Australia, can have consequences far beyond the immediate. The understanding of potential consequences, and the personal responsibility that consequently arises, are critical elements in the process of developing all soldiers for their operational tasks.

While the 'strategic corporal' is a useful way to focus on the manifold challenges facing combatants in the twenty-first century, it leaves us with a number of central questions. We might question explicitly, as I have done so far implicitly, whether the *corporal* is the right level at which these capabilities and a substantial level of potential autonomy should be located. This is in no way to diminish the importance, or capabilities, of corporals, but rather to suggest—as I do in my later chapter—that all soldiers should be given the opportunity to develop their decision-making skills. Granted that the rank of corporal is in many armies regarded as the first crucial level of leadership, and corporals are often quite experienced in their roles, but the development of leadership needs to be a part of every modern defence force at all levels.[21]

The other element of Krulak's formulation that bears closer scrutiny is the idea of a relatively junior soldier being *strategic*. In ordinary parlance, we can quite legitimately say that being strategic means deploying the appropriate means to produce the desired outcomes. But what are the 'desired outcomes'? For a soldier on a particular operation, the goals will be clear and—in the

---

20  Lynda Liddy, 'The strategic corporal: some requirements in training and education', *Australian Army Journal* 2, 2 (2005), 140.

21  A somewhat different point is made by Simon King: 'The preferable solution to the mismatch identified by General Krulak ... surely lies with the concept of the tactical colonel, as this produces an altogether more realistic training objective. In short, the solution is to anchor the mission, not the unit size.' ('Strategic corporal or tactical colonel? Anchoring the right variable', *Defence & Security Analysis* 19, 2 (2003), 190.) In my view, by contrast, it is preferable to expand the training objective.

scheme of things—necessarily limited. We trust (or, perhaps, they trust) that those limited goals will fit with other operations' goals to form a complex mosaic that will ultimately lead to 'victory'. But this is where the requirement to be 'strategic' becomes more problematic. The soldier, be they a corporal or a lieutenant, can demonstrate all the preparedness, leadership and cultural acuity that a fine education and extensive training can develop, but if the grand strategy that puts them on a particular battlefield at a particular time is flawed, their efforts—in a strategic sense—will be counterproductive, or will have been squandered. The battle may be won, but the war is destined to be lost. We should not lose sight of the fact that 'strategic corporals' cannot compensate for strategic failure at the most senior levels. A misconceived project will likely turn out a disaster no matter how professional the soldiers who prosecute it. I think we have enough evidence of a decade of disappointment in Iraq and Afghanistan to substantiate this point. The corollary of the 'strategic corporal' is the 'strategic leader', but that is a topic for a far more familiar body of literature.

# 2

# Shared Leadership and the Strategic Corporal Metaphor: Some Considerations

## Nick Jans

IN THE OPERATIONAL ACTIVITIES variously labelled as 'war amongst the people', 'the three block war', 'asymmetric warfare' or 'fourth generation warfare', the local often becomes the strategic. This is because the consequences of front-line actions by very junior commanders in such situations

> can vary from the embarrassment of adverse media attention, the alienation of the local populace, or the outbreak of war with a neighbouring country. Conversely, the fruits of success can range from the projection of positive images of military intervention to viewers and commentators around the world, to the defeat of hostile groups thereby granting downtrodden and traumatized families hope for the future.[1]

Such situations reward a leadership process in which responsibility devolves lower and lower down the chain of command, ultimately landing on the corporal. This phenomenon has become known as the 'strategic corporal' effect.

Although the world had to wait for a US Marine Corps general, Charles Krulak, to coin the term in 1999, the strategic corporal phenomenon is

---

1   Robert Breen and Greg McCauley (2008), *The world looking over their shoulders: Australian strategic corporals on operations in Somalia and East Timor*, Land Warfare Studies Centre Papers 314, vii.

hardly a novel practice for the Australian Army. Its expertise in small-group operations has long been so well established that it was regarded as 'normal business' and, as such, scarcely deserving of a special label. Australian junior leaders have consistently performed creditably in a range of operational areas over the past few decades (Somalia, East Timor, Iraq and Afghanistan), contributing significantly to the success of Australian operations, while at the same time avoiding the damaging operational and ethical scandals experienced by Canadian, Italian, Belgian and American allies. Such a capability is rooted in experience that goes back generations, through the protracted war in South Vietnam to at least the Second World War and the Kokoda campaign.[2] It has resulted in an approach that a civilian writing to the newspapers during the 1999 East Timor campaign called 'pussy cats with guts'. She wrote of how

> parts of Timor will never forget our army not only because it swept in with strong weaponry and scared away evil but because of the manner in which it subsequently behaved. And that's because our soldiers were generally honest, didn't let each other down, and treated others in a reasonable and respectful way. The same men who stood their ground in the dangerous ridges and valleys along the western border defending unfamiliar territory, a week later, could be seen putting up water tanks in orphanages and having their photos taken with children.[3]

Tellingly, whatever the institution's feelings about the unremarkable nature of this aspect of professional behaviour, it is nevertheless regarded as a topic for organisational learning and improvement. Lynda Liddy cites 5/7 Royal Australian Regiment's experiences in East Timor in 1999.[4] The unit's mission included security of the population, protection of vital assets and management

---

2   David Schmidtchen (2006), *The rise of the strategic private: technology, control and change in a network-enabled military* (Canberra: Land Warfare Studies Centre); Adrian Threlfall (2014), *Jungle warriors: from Tobruk to Kokoda and beyond. How the Australian Army became the world's most deadly jungle fighting force* (Sydney: Allen & Unwin).
3   Judith Brooks, in a letter to *The Australian*, 12 February 2001, 12.
4   Lynda Liddy, 'The strategic corporal: some requirements in training and education', *Australian Army Journal* 2, 2 (2005), 139–148.

of relations with the Indonesian armed forces, with soldiers routinely involved in humanitarian assistance and supervision of internally displaced people. As the Brooks letter above attests, much of the battalion's success was attributed to the actions of its platoon and section commanders, who were often called on to mediate or negotiate with a variety of groups, ranging from Indonesian forces, civilian police, non-government and humanitarian agencies to groups of civilians. Post-operational examination showed that training for such tasks had been largely ad hoc, and confirmed the need for more emphasis on the development of soft skills such as cross-cultural sensitivity, language training and mediation and negotiation skills, as part of preparation for future operations.

Similar recommendations were reached by Stringer in his analysis of the 'three block war' activities of American soldiers in Afghanistan. He argues that, given 'the self-inflicted damage' caused by its propensity to fail to understand the enemy of the day, the US Army was coming from even further behind its allies.[5] Stringer called for a major rethink on the skills and values required at all levels, including—very importantly—those at junior non-commissioned officer (NCO) level. And so enthusiastically have such ideas been embraced across the Pacific that the US Army invested a considerable effort in a 'Campaign for the Professional Ethic', aimed in part at finding ways to get better leverage from the junior NCO leader asset: an asset that had demonstrated a surprising but essential level of facility in the Middle East sphere of operations.[6]

Virtually all writing in the now considerable military professional literature on the strategic corporal phenomenon approaches the topic in its literal sense, ie as applying largely to the most junior levels of command. But while a snappy label has obvious utility as a focus for cultural change, there is a danger that excessive attention will be focused on the most junior levels of command at the expense of more general issues in leadership.

This chapter argues for the utility of thinking more broadly about military leadership and leadership culture. A leadership culture characterised by a distinct approach to shared leadership gives rise to at least as many implica-

---

5   Kevin D Stringer, 'Educating the strategic corporal: a paradigm shift', *Military Review* 89, 5 (September–October 2009), 90.
6   Center for the Army Profession and Ethic (CAPE), 2011. I was invited to participate in a number of the phases and can attest to its technical and professional rigour.

tions for officers as it does for NCOs. A broader perspective is needed, with the strategic corporal concept seen as a metaphor for all activities associated with junior leadership up to and including the sub-unit level.

The chapter begins by examining the strategic corporal metaphor in the context of a growing literature on shared leadership, and concludes with a brief discussion of the ramifications for the philosophy and practice of officership.

## Shared leadership and team performance

Shared leadership is a process whereby all team members, no matter what their rank or status, play a part in the leadership processes of sense-making, adjusting, responding and learning. This creates 'a dynamic, interactive process amongst individuals and groups'[7] that contributes to the achievement of group organisational goals. Much of the small, but rapidly expanding, literature on the topic draws on cases and contexts associated with action teams, both military and civilian emergency services and medical operating teams.[8]

---

7  Craig L Pearce and Jay A Conger (2003), 'All those years ago: the historical underpinnings of shared leadership', in CL Pearce and JA Conger (eds), *Shared leadership: reframing the hows and whys of leadership* (Thousand Oaks, CA: Sage), 1.

8  For example: Nadine Bienefeld and Grote Gudela, 'Teamwork in an emergency: how distributed leadership improves decision-making', *Proceedings of the Human Factors and Ergonomics Society Annual Meeting* 55 (2011), 110–114; Gregory Bigley and Karlene Roberts, 'The incident command system: high-reliability organizing for complex and volatile task environments', *Academy of Management Journal* 44, 6 (2001), 1281–1299; Arjen Boin and Paul 't Hart, 'Organising for effective emergency management: lessons from research', *The Australian Journal of Public Administration* 69 (2010), 357–371; David J Bryant, 'Rethinking OODA: toward a modern cognitive framework of command decision making', *Military Psychology* 18, 3 (2006), 183–206; D Scott DeRue, 'Adaptive leadership theory: leading and following as a complex adaptive process', *Research in Organisational Behavior* 31 (2011), 125–150; Sean T Hannah, John T Eggers and Peter L Jennings, 'Complex adaptive leadership: defining what constitutes effective leadership for complex organizational contexts', in George B Graen and Joni A Graen, *The Knowledge-driven corporation: complex creative destruction* (Charlotte, NC: Information Age Publishing, 2008), 79–124; Peter AJ Hayes and Mary M Omodei, 'Managing emergencies: key competencies for incident management teams', *Australian and New Zealand Journal of Organisational Psychology* 4 (April 2011), 1–10; Katherine J Klein, Jonathan C Ziegert, Andrew P Knight and Yan Xiao, 'Dynamic delegation: shared, hierarchical, and deindividualized leadership in extreme action teams', *Administrative Science Quarterly* 51, 4 (2006), 590–621; Alex J Ramthun and

The utility of shared leadership reflects a truth confirmed by both research evidence and common sense: that in the increasing complexity of professional life, 'no single leader [is likely to] have all the answers or even be able to make sense of the more significant challenges'.[9] Lindsay et al discuss the opportunities for the leadership activities of sense-making, adjusting, responding and learning in military organisations, and the considerable benefits that accrue when a team acts according to a shared process. They argue that teams best equipped to handle complexity are those where sense-making and influence can be located anywhere and in any member, can be directed anywhere (up, down or sideways) and shift according to the dynamics of the situation as much as by the management of the situation by the formal/appointed leader. They conclude that shared leadership can become more than a 'pipe dream' for the military, but only if the process is leadership-centric rather than leader-centric, ie is conceptualised and practised as a *process* rather than simply as an *activity* performed by a designated senior member.

A number of factors shape the extent to which the leadership process can be leadership-centric rather than leader-centric.[10] Leadership-centric teams possess collective and individual expertise, established by a mixture of training, experience and formal career development. They benefit from members who have sufficient experience with each other to form a working understanding of the nature and whereabouts of such expertise. Members need to have confidence in themselves and in others. Techniques—both routine and adaptive—must be well established by experience or at least practice under realistic conditions. Designated leaders themselves need particular values in addition to professional expertise. (Both factors are discussed below.) In such teams, leadership responsibility tends to shift dynamically according to the urgency, complexity and novelty of the task, ie designated leaders should be more directly involved when the requirement is urgent, the issue is relatively simple, or the context or problem is novel.

---

Gina S Matkin, 'Leading dangerously: a case study of military teams and shared leadership in dangerous environments', *Journal of Leadership & Organisational Studies* 21, 3 (2014).

9  Douglas R Lindsay, David V Day and Stanley Halpin, 'Shared leadership in the military: reality, possibility, or pipe dream?', *Military Psychology* 23, 5 (2011), 529.

10 Benjamin Baran and Cliff Scott, 'Organizing ambiguity: a grounded theory of leadership and sense-making within dangerous contexts', *Military Psychology* 22, Suppl 1 (2010), S42–S62; Hannah, Eggers and Jennings, 'Complex adaptive leadership', 2008; Lindsay et al, 'Shared leadership in the military', 2011.

Shared leadership is different from democratic leadership. In democratic leadership, all members get a say in the group's response to most issues; in contrast, shared leadership is often based on the practices associated with a more traditional approach to leadership, ie with a designated leader and designated followers, and hierarchy as the default organisational form. The distinctive thing about leadership-centric shared leadership is that designated leaders deliberately manage the process so that the direction and nature of influence can shift dynamically as the situation requires.[11] Among other benefits, this frees them up to focus on and manage external opportunities and threats, helps them both make sense of what is happening and accurately report to higher authorities, broadens the leadership repertoire within the team, facilitates team development, enhances engagement and commitment, and—very much not least—creates a reserve of leadership capability for situations when the designated leader is unavailable or incapacitated.

Such benefits are particularly relevant to the military situation. Military teams are often geographically dispersed across an operational area, which means that, among other challenges, they cannot rely so strongly on the influence associated with personal charisma. However, the disadvantage of physical separation can be mitigated when the designated leader leads in ways that allow them to establish a level of 'credit' or 'capital' in advance of the stresses and distractions of dispersed operational activities.[12] This includes presenting one's self as someone who is worthy of being followed, particularly in terms of the attributes valued by that particular team or collective; establishing a clear ethical climate; building strong relationships of trust and mutual respect with team members; and demonstrating that one is capable of managing a team effectively and engaging members in the process, whatever the situation.[13]

For example, an analysis of the leadership practices in US Air Force teams before and after deployment[14] showed that the best-performing teams

---

11   Klein et al, 'Dynamic delegation', 2006.
12   Bruce J Avolio, Fred O Walumbwa and Todd J Weber, 'Leadership: current theories, research, and future directions', *Annual Review of Psychology* 60 (2009), 421–449.
13   For a comprehensive summary, see Nicholas Jans (2014), *New values, old basics: how leadership shapes support for inclusion*, Centre for Defence and Strategic Studies, Australian Defence College, September 2014.
14   Martin Pitt and Michael Bunamo, 'Excellence in leadership: lessons learned from top-performing units', *Air & Space Power Journal* 22 (Spring 2008), 44–48.

were those in which designated leaders had used opportunities during pre-deployment activities to establish themselves as somebody worth following. Such leaders had given their followers a vision based on the priorities and requirements of the bigger picture but also reflecting internal goals developed collaboratively; and they had established a sense of inclusiveness in advance of the stress of operations by making every effort to work through others and to establish clear performance expectations for individuals and groups.

Physical separation also makes the tasks of sense-making and communication more difficult. However, leaders can overcome problems of geographic separation by measures such as providing a command intent, presenting a narrative to assist members at all levels to make sense of what is going on, and taking a constructive approach to helping both subordinate leaders and themselves to make sense of evolving situations.[15] Taking a constructive approach means being continually open to information, even that which challenges conventional wisdom, and avoiding dogmatism and an attitude of 'I am your leader so do what I say'.

Much of this is confirmed by a meta-analysis of the performance effects of different leadership styles.[16] This shows that, while a directive-authoritative approach will often deliver satisfactory performance, it is much less likely to contribute to team and organisational learning. In contrast, a supportive–collaborative approach is not only somewhat more likely to contribute to performance outcomes, but considerably more likely to result in organisational learning.

Shared leadership is also a key factor in organisational reliability.[17] 'High reliability organisations' are those that, despite often being complex in terms of organisational structures, are able to consistently perform to high levels of safety and effectiveness (typical case studies that have been used in the litera-

---

15   Stacey Connaughton, Marissa Shuffler and Gerald F Goodwin, 'Leading distributed teams: the communicative constitution of leadership', *Military Psychology* 23, 5 (2011), 502–527.

16   C Shawn Burke, Kevin C Stagl, Cameron Klein, Gerald F Goodwin, Eduardo Salas and Stanley M Halpin, 'What type of leadership behaviors are functional in teams? A meta-analysis', *The Leadership Quarterly* 17, 3 (2006), 288–307.

17   Karl E Weick and Kathleen M Sutcliffe (2001), *Managing the unexpected* (San Francisco: Jossey-Bass).

ture include airline systems, aircraft carriers, nuclear power stations and the like). One of the key success factors in their doing so is what the literature calls 'mindfulness': being aware of not just what is happening right now but also of what might happen as a consequence of the evolving situation. This requires each member, however low their organisational status, to be continually alert to what is going on and the implications for the bigger picture, and to be committed to playing their part in maintaining the collective standard. This is difficult to make happen unless people at all levels of the organisation are led in ways that gives them a strong sense of 'we' as opposed to 'me'.[18]

## Distinctive issues for military institutions

Military cultures often contain a number of factors that can impede a shared leadership process. These include:
- overreliance on rank as a source of authority
- reluctance on the part of leaders to act in ways that might divert the credit for success from themselves
- a propensity for officers to maintain close control over activities and resources in the barracks environment
- shortfalls in the professional capacities of combat team leaders themselves.

The fear that shared/distributed leadership poses a threat to the traditional sources of hierarchical authority often results in an overreliance on rank as a source of power.[19] Such an approach obviously limits the extent to which teams can prepare for and form effectively when faced with the challenges discussed above. In reality, this poses less of a problem than most people might believe. To begin with, the better military leaders—and there are many such in the contemporary Australian military institution—lead in ways that help them to establish inherent authority while preparing for missions. (See

---

18  Avolio et al, 'Leadership', 2009; Burke et al, 'What type of leadership behaviors are functional in teams?', 2006; Francis J Yammarino, Eduardo Salas, Andra Serban, Kristie Shirrifs and Marissa Shuffler, 'Collectivistic leadership approaches: putting the "we" in leadership science and practice', *Industrial and Organizational Psychology* 5, 4 (2012), 382–402.
19  Lindsay et al, 'Shared leadership in the military', 2011.

the discussion above.) And, during operations, the Australian Defence Force (ADF) practises the devolved approach to command and control known as 'mission command', 'directive control' or 'commander's intent'. Notwithstanding the way in which the mission command reality frequently falls short of the ideal,[20] such an approach serves as the institutional solution to any conflict between formal and devolved command authority. Moreover, as the work of Breen and McCauley[21] indicates, devolution of authority to the lowest levels is a long-standing practice within the Australian military, based as it is on national norms of egalitarianism and resourcefulness.

The second barrier to shared leadership within the military is more subtle and thus potentially more challenging. Military culture is strongly meritocratic and professional success is generally earned not just by performing well, but also by being seen to be doing so. Lindsay et al[22] argue that this provides strong incentives for overuse of 'leading from the front' styles and for designated leaders to grab most of the credit for collective success. But while this can pay off for the career-minded individual (at least in the short term), it tends to be damaging for longer-term member motivation and collaborative practice.[23]

Again, however, this is perhaps more a problem for institutions like the US Army, which is both large and has an 'up or out' career development policy. With the Australian situation differing in both senses—with its comparatively small various professional cohorts, together with the tendency for evaluating officers to seek a range of information sources when assessing subordinate performance—the problems that Lindsay et al identify are less likely to occur.

Nevertheless, the risk of ego-separation should not be dismissed too lightly. One strategy for countering its adverse effects is for the evaluation system to give greater weight to the practice of 'stewardship' or 'officership' within the

---

20  Eitan Shamir (2011), *Transforming command: the pursuit of mission command in the US, British, and Israeli armies* (Stanford, CA: Stanford Security Studies).
21  Breen and McCauley, *The world looking over their shoulders*, 2008.
22  Lindsay et al, 'Shared leadership in the military', 2011.
23  Hannah, Eggers and Jennings, 'Complex adaptive leadership', 2008, call this the problem of 'ego-separation'.

suite of leadership behaviours expected of officers (see below).[24] As a formal concept, this is a comparatively novel notion within the Australian military institution. However, the principle that an officer's responsibilities include institutional continuity and maintenance of values and standards, including morale and member well-being, is inherently accepted. In reality, therefore, it would take little to lift the salience of stewardship as a concept, particularly if more weight was given to it during both formal career development and performance management.

A third barrier to the practice of shared leadership in the military is the strong propensity of military institutions to use different modes of leadership according to whether the team is either on operations or in barracks. While shared leadership in the form of mission command is common on deployment, not least because its practice is imperative in getting things done, this is much less likely to be the case back in barracks. In the home environment, officers frequently complain about their lack of autonomy and the stifling nature of what they call 'corporate governance'.[25] (Stringer[26] draws attention to a similar phenomenon in the US military.) There are a number of reasons why more senior commanders want closer control in the non-operational environment, including resource scarcity, the inexperience of subordinate commanders, and health and safety requirements. Whatever the reasons and their rationale, however, close control in unit activities does limit the extent to which teams can practise as teams, become familiar with members' styles and idiosyncrasies, and hone their collective abilities for shared leadership across a range of situations before they face the much greater challenges of deployment.

The final barrier to the effective practice of shared leadership relates to the professional capacities of team leaders, ie those designated leaders with-

---

24   Nicholas Jans, with Stephen Mugford, Jamie Cullens and Judy Frazer-Jans (2013), *The Chiefs: a study of strategic leadership* (Canberra: Australian Defence College). Available at www.defence.gov.au/ADC/Publications/Chiefs/TheChiefs.pdf, accessed on 11 April 2017.

25   Nicholas Jans (2009), 'Careers in conflict 21C: the dynamics of the contemporary military career experience', paper presented at the Biannual Conference of the Inter-University Seminar for Armed Forces & Society, Chicago, October 2009.

26   Stringer, 'Educating the strategic corporal', 2009.

in the military hierarchy. Hannah et al[27] argue that the practice of 'complex adaptive leadership' requires a professional identity reorientation, in terms of not only developing distinctive skill-sets, but also of the way that officers conceptualise or orient themselves to their roles.

In terms of *skill-set*, they propose that the adaptive leader must be competent in four main areas: maintaining situational awareness (knowing and understanding what is going on and the implications therein), recognising when and what changes are needed, making those changes and learning from the experience. In terms of the distinctive *orientation* needed by the adaptive leader, two features in particular are important.[28] First, leaders need to see themselves as catalysts rather than as controllers. Such a perspective should govern their whole approach to the development, organisation and management of their teams. Above all else, besides understanding and sense-making, this requires leaders to let go of the delusion that they can control most activities most of the time. This suggests that would-be adaptive leaders should act according to a 'servant leadership' mode, seeing themselves as a resource to enable the performance and commitment of team members at every level. (One of the implications has already been noted: the need for ego-separation, so that team members, rather than the leaders themselves, can take credit when it is warranted.) A leader's success in doing this depends on their ability to understand themselves as well as their subordinates. This not only requires abilities such as emotional intelligence, but also a quality called 'meta-cognition', the capacity to dispassionately observe oneself while one is engaged in thinking and acting. This enables the leader to adapt their interpersonal and professional responses to any particular issue, so as to consistently perform in a constructive and reliable fashion.

The ultimate expression of this approach is a form of 'stewardship' or 'officership'.[29] Officership is a broader expression of the servant leadership ethos described above. Its ethos is built around the competency and moral responsibility needed for effective and responsible performance in leadership

---

27   Hannah, Eggers and Jennings, 'Complex adaptive leadership', 2008.
28   Ibid.
29   Patrick Mileham (2008), 'Officership: some first principles', in Stephen Deakin (ed), *'Take me to your officer': officership in the army* (London: The Strategic and Combat Studies Institute), 2–13.

roles in the profession of arms. An ethos of officership is a more explicit and direct expression of leadership responsibilities, with appropriate weight given to duty to the institution, duty to the task and duty to those subordinates for whom one is responsible. A more explicit articulation of officership may well contribute to a greater sense of comfort—at both the individual and the collective levels—with the practice of shared leadership as a response to complexity and risk.

Stewardship was seen as a distinct form of leadership behaviour in the strategic leadership framework used in a recent analysis of senior leadership behaviour in the ADF.[30] This framework conceived of leadership in terms of four main groups of activities: directing, exploring, managing and stewardship. *Directing* (eg command) is the function appropriate to situations in which a critical problem emerges that must be dealt with immediately. *Exploring* is appropriate to situations in which the problem and its potential solution are ambiguous, and in which the leader must engage others, intellectually and emotionally, in identifying the nature of the problem and how it needs to be tackled. *Managing* is the mode of leadership that a leader follows when an issue is structured and the approach is fairly unambiguous. However, while these modes of behaviour are given close attention in professional doctrine and development, stewardship tends to be an implied function, albeit one that many middle-level and senior officers take seriously. *Stewardship* involves the activities needed to preserve or reinvigorate the professional and moral character of the institution. At the unit and sub-unit levels, this includes leading in ways that enhance the professional identities of subordinates. Such an approach includes the imperative of ego-separation, as already discussed. A greater emphasis on stewardship at all stages of officer career development would go some way to encouraging the servant leadership practices that contribute to ego-separation and its attendant benefits.

## Conclusion

The Australian Army's experience and skill in practising the 'strategic corporal' approach to operations is one of its greatest strengths. This is a personification of Clausewitz's dictum of using natural assets wisely in order to create inherent

---

30   Jans et al, *The Chiefs*, 2013.

advantage.[31] The current spotlight on the concept is bound to lead to further refinements and improvements. However, those who are tackling these would do well to understand that improving the professional capabilities of junior NCOs themselves is only a part of the solution. Appropriate focus on officer-related factors—how officers approach their roles as leaders, how they are prepared for such roles, and how they are evaluated—will result in benefits that are at least as great. Attention to such matters could well be one of the best investments that the Australian Army is likely to experience in the twenty-first century.

This chapter has shown that the 'strategic corporal' metaphor embraces much more than simply the behaviour of the corporal. The strategic corporal might be the spearhead, but the quality and effect of that spear relies very much on its being delivered from a strong foundation of competence and ethical and moral standards. Leaders at all levels are responsible for the development, effective and ethical use, and preservation/adaption of this foundation. The most 'strategic' aspect of the 'strategic corporal' concept is that it represents a form of professional behaviour that is well suited to a range of complex, longer-term contingencies.

---

31  Barak A Salmoni and Paula Holmes-Eber (2011), *Operational culture for the warfighter: principles and applications* (Quantico, VA: Marine Corps University Press), 5.

# 3

# The Strategic Corporal: Suffocated by Bureaucracy

## Richard Adams

FOLLOWING THE END OF THE COLD WAR, global disorder has been inflamed by the rise of organised terrorism, rogue regimes, extremist ideologies and the proliferation of weapons of mass destruction. Long-held ideas about security and the use of military power have been discarded or rewritten, as Western militaries are confronted by irregular conflicts and crises. These are circumstances that call for reconsideration of the strategic corporal.

Coined in 1999, 10 years after the Berlin Wall came down, by the then-Commandant of the US Marine Corps, General Charles C Krulak,[1] the strategic corporal idea remains static and theoretically undeveloped, a descriptive term that does not rise to the level of a scholarly model. As an illustrative turn of phrase, the 'strategic corporal' reverberates with the myth of military machismo. However, as a theory, the idea lacks sufficient rationalisation.

As a slogan, the strategic corporal drew heavily for its rationalisation upon the mission command idea, in German *Auftragstaktik*.[2] Conceived during the

---

1   The son of Lieutenant General Victor (Brute) Krulak.
2   Bruce Condell and David Zabecki (eds) (2011), Introduction to *On the German art of war: Truppenführung—the German Army manual for unit command in World War II*, (Mechanicsburg, PA: Stackpole Books), 3–4. Condell and Zabecki write: 'One of the most important concepts in the post-World War I German military system was that of *Auftragstaktik*. The term can be translated loosely as "mission-type orders," but there is no real English equivalent that adequately conveys the full meaning. *Auftragstaktik* is based on the principle that a commander should tell his subordinates what to do and when to do it by, but not necessarily tell them how to do it. In accomplishing their mis-

Napoleonic Wars, the *Auftragstaktik* is a thought-through and settled concept, which scotches outré claims of strategic corporals as extravagantly competent super-soldiers. The *Auftragstaktik* takes tactical nous as the bread and butter of any competent military, presuming maladroit soldiers are discharged from the army.

On the account given in this chapter, independent tactical nous and strategic prescience are not fostered by the prevailing military culture. Where autonomous, purposeful and astute soldiers emerge—Krulak would call them 'strategic corporals'—they emerge in spite of the presently dominant culture and not because of it.

## The strategic corporal: a descriptive phrase, not a concept

Coining the 'strategic corporal' as a phrase, General Krulak described the impact and the worth of junior leaders on the battlefield:

> *In many cases, the individual Marine will be the most conspicuous symbol of American foreign policy and will potentially influence not only the important tactical situation, but the operational and strategic levels as well. His actions, therefore, will directly impact the outcome of the larger operation and he will become ... the Strategic Corporal.*[3]

Krulak's Marines were technically proficient, and tactically autonomous. They were young soldiers, giving breath to the *Auftragstaktik* idea, and bearing responsibility beyond their years. As Tom Ricks put it:

> *The kid whom we wouldn't trust to run the copier is the squad or platoon leader addressing questions that could alter national policy ... And he is doing it under the glare of real-time global television broadcasts.*[4]

---

    sion, subordinate commanders are given a wide degree of latitude and are expected to exercise great initiative.' This system is described as an advance on the similar, but more restricted, First War doctrine.

3    Charles C Krulak, 'The strategic corporal: leadership in the three block war', *Marine Corps Gazette* 83, 1 (January 1999), 21. This article, which coined the term 'strategic corporal', was reprinted in *Leatherneck* 82, 1 (January 1999), 14–17, and in *Marines Magazine* (January 1999), 1–7.

4    Thomas E Ricks (1997), *Making the Corps* (New York: Scribner & Sons), 24–25. Cited by Captain James B Reid, USMC, 'Educating the strategic corporal: restructure the course for better mental preparation', *Marine Corps Gazette* 93, 3 (March 2009), 43.

But years after Krulak coined his catchy phrase, the strategic corporal remains theoretically undeveloped, trotted out as a stock response to 'complexity', but disarticulated from theoretical substance. Full of metastasising assumption that the whole value of soldiers is in tactical skill at arms, the phrase presumes much and appreciates little. Taking the weapon for an analogue, the strategic corporal concept supposes the soldier will always act unhesitatingly, according to doctrine. But such an impassive pawn, says Du Picq famously, is an abstract creature born of the library and not a real soldier.[5] Failing to appreciate the soldier's humanity, the strategic corporal idea fails as well to contemplate the larger context. The phrase throws a wet blanket on illuminative scrutiny of the institution, and the liability of those responsible for securing critical background conditions.

Trotting out the fish story of corporals as 'strategic' and ever so competent, the military props up familiar vanities. Among these is the idea that soldiers are unaffected by the dumb tricks of institutional farce. However, the bureaucratic memes that mark the dysfunctions of military governance have a significant and adverse effect upon the development of autonomous and effectual soldiers.

This chapter argues that the military institution needs to evolve, to become less bureaucratic, and to intentionally foster conscientious, independently-minded and responsible soldiers.

## The mission command idea

To understand the strategic corporal, it is constructive to reflect upon the *Auftragstaktik*, the doctrine of mission command. Perceived and realised during the Napoleonic Wars, the doctrine has its most immediate and fabled provenance in the German armies of the First and Second World Wars,[6] finding forceful and famous expression in the 1933 *Truppenführung*, the German Army manual for troop command. Articulating the mission command idea, the *Truppenführung* underlines the strategic value of individual

---

5   Colonel Charles Ardant du Picq (2006), *Battle studies: ancient and modern*, translated by JN Greely and RC Cotton (Milton Keynes: Bibliobazaar), 53.
6   Jim Storr, 'A command philosophy for the information age: the continuing relevance of mission command', *Defence Studies* 3, 3 (Autumn 2003), 119, 121, 122.

soldiers amid the confusion of conflict, arguing: 'the emptiness of the battlefield requires soldiers who can think and act independently, who can make calculated decisions and daring use of every situation'.[7] Articulating the *Auftragstaktik*, the *Truppenführung* sets down views that 'would still be considered radical in many of the world's armies today'.[8]

Written largely by Generals Beck, Von Fritsch and Von Stülpnagel, the *Truppenführung* expected individual soldiers would have a clear understanding of circumstances so they could act on their own initiative in accordance with the larger strategic intent. Giving doctrinal weight to ideas known later by the colloquialism of the 'strategic corporal', the *Truppenführung* recalls Von Seeckt, who argued: 'the principal thing is to increase the responsibilities of the individual man, particularly his independence of action, and thereby to increase the efficiency of the entire army …'.[9]

But, while ideas of initiative and enterprise have an unimpeachable provenance, and even as they resonate with military myth, they have become essentially rhetorical, since militaries have grown to be more centralised, less adaptable, more prescriptive and more bureaucratic. On the account of this chapter, the institution needs to evolve, to become more intuitive, more responsible, less hesitant, managerial and pettifogging.

Describing the civil-political-military conglomerate, 'bureaucracy' is a term of art that covers not merely the combination of institutions, but encloses as well the customs, mores and assumptions that define the praxis and judgement of people in organisations. Honeycombed by avoidance behaviour, inconclusive language and the irrational presumption of prowess,[10] bureaucracy

---

7 Condell and Zabecki (eds), *On the German art of war*, 18.
8 Condell and Zabecki, op cit, 4.
9 Ibid.
10 Gary A Rumble, Melanie McKean and Dennis Pearce (2011), *The report of the review of allegations of sexual and other abuse in Defence: facing the problems of the past* (DLA Piper Report), (Canberra: Commonwealth of Australia), 16. Available at www.defence.gov.au/pathwaytochange/docs/DLAPiper/Volume1.pdf, accessed on 24 April 2017. Citing the Inspector General of the Australian Defence Force—a retired senior naval officer—this report offers an example of the irrational presumption of competence and the inability to face facts that plagues the ADF. In the face of established claims of reprehensible abuse by members of the ADF, the Inspector General asserted that the ADF 'is world's best practice'. His seeming failure to comprehend the possibility of shortcoming is symptomatic of the semblant bureaucratic culture.

cultivates acquiescence, dependence and excuse. Bureaucracy suffocates personal responsibility, which should distinguish leaders and the independently responsible voice—hallmarks of the strategic corporal. In bureaucracy, cliquish rackets provide sanctuary for those too senior to fall. The chronic scapegoating is captured by Colonel Paul Yingling, who writes tartly: 'the soldier who loses a rifle faces a more severe punishment than the general who loses a war.'[11]

Bound and gagged by red tape and exposed to the unfeasibly high cost of even petty error, the chance that soldiers will be in the habit of acting decisively and independently is slim. This chapter identifies those who bear institutional responsibility, and underlines the failing by reference to official reports. At their most memorable, these reports are plain-spoken and powerful. At their best, the official reports offer explicit and undistorted insight. More usually, however, the official reports are faint-hearted and unimpressive.

By and large the official reports are oblique, nervous and not noteworthy. In this chapter, their importance lies in the habituated phraseology of people unaccustomed to taking a stand. Shy of moral language, scared of ideals, over-eager to seek the asylum of formulaic morally meaningless language, the official report allows bureaucracy to cavil for itself.

## Centralised and bureaucratic

The Australian Defence Leadership Framework exemplifies the bureaucratisation of the military. Embedded within doctrine, this framework defines service in terms of hierarchy and precedence disconnected from individual merit and moral responsibility.[12] The model asserts, 'Defence espouses a philosophy of

---

11   Paul Yingling, 'A failure in generalship', *Armed Forces Journal*, 1 May 2007. Available at armedforcesjournal.com/a-failure-in-generalship/, accessed on 11 April 2017.

12   Australian Defence Force (2007), *Leadership in the Australian Defence Force*, Australian Defence Doctrine Publication 00.6, 22 March 2007 (Canberra: Australian Defence Headquarters), paragraph 3.26–3.27: 'The Defence Leadership Framework (DLF) provides a structured listing of the skills, capabilities and knowledge for Defence personnel to perform at eleven identified levels … The DLF is constructed around five capability areas which are further broken down into proficiencies for each classification. Against each of these proficiencies are a number of behaviours.' In the Executive Summary to Chapter 6, we read that 'the ADF trains toward the Defence Leadership Framework which outlines the behaviours expected of leaders and managers …'.

values-based behaviour'[13] while prescribing 'the core leadership proficiencies and capabilities that people are expected to demonstrate' in order to meet 'opportunities' for 'development and assessment' and 'to allow skilling.'[14] Detailing more than 400 performance criteria over umpteen unvarying pages, this model catalogues the trivialities of managerial habit, supposing that this 'provides guidance to supervisors and employees in relation to staff management and performance.'[15]

The Defence Leadership Framework is an anti-individualistic inventory of minutiae, which reflects a bureaucratic culture of rules and blame. The purpose of the framework is not to develop and encourage morally responsive and principled service, but to preserve established hierarchies and to protect officialdom. Criteria, so numerous and detailed that they are like rules, do not outline service ideals. Rather, these measures serve the bureaucratic purpose of what Professor Andrew Hopkins called 'butt protection'.[16] The framework reflects the sort of 'puffery'[17] that should have no place in the military.

Richard Gabriel explains why bureaucratic thinking is antithetic to the military ideal, arguing that it is 'nonsense when ... institutions attempt to substitute bureaucratic procedures for ethical judgment and responsibility. [The end result is] a reliance upon bureaucratic rules and mechanisms of control, while undercutting the soldier's opportunities to exercise ethical judgement.'[18]

Arguing against the suffusive influence of bureaucratic transaction thinking, Gabriel points to what Foucault called the 'subtle, calculated technology of subjugation ... the separation, coordination and supervision of tasks (which) constitutes an operational schema of power'.[19] This is bureaucratic 'panopticism',

---

13  Australian Government, Department of Defence (no date), *The Defence leadership framework: growing leaders at all levels* (Canberra: Australian Government, Department of Defence, Defence Personnel Executive), 2.
14  Australian Government, op cit, 5.
15  Ibid.
16  Andrew Hopkins (2005), *Safety culture and risk: the organisational causes of disasters* (Sydney: CCH Australia), 37.
17  James Toner (2009), *Morals under the gun: the cardinal virtues, military ethics and American society* (Lexington, KY: The University Press of Kentucky), 17.
18  Richard Gabriel (1982), *To serve with honour: a treatise on military ethics and the way of the soldier* (Westport, CT: Greenwood Press), 13.
19  Michel Foucault (1995), *Discipline and punish: the birth of the prison* (New York: Vintage), 221.

designed 'to ensure the prompt obedience of the people and the most absolute authority of the magistrates',[20] which MacIntyre understood to depend for its success upon disguise and concealment.[21] Applied through an insidious ensemble of technical interventions, bureaucratic influence commodifies people and dissolves moral autonomy. In bureaucracy, people are valued when their character is inclined toward rule-following. And, bureaucracy is valued for its calculable data for seeming impartiality and for the centralisation of its control.

The bureaucracy's oppressive attention to marginal detail is in parallel with the technical evolution of communications networks. In the vernacular, 'comms' have made it possible and appealing for headquarters to exercise unconstructive, meddlesome control to a previously unimagined degree. Bureaucratic centralisation means that information from the seat of events is passed upward to headquarters, which issues direction. This dissolves the autonomy of the individual soldier and, as Storr observes, is fundamentally unconstructive, since

> [t]he amount of information passed between a group of people increases roughly with the square of the number involved (a consequence of many-to-many information strategies), while the ability to deal with it increases only linearly.[22]

## Procedure and routine

Inherently centralising and controlling, the bureaucratic monolith depends upon the cold accretion of regulation and official procedure. This red tape routine has an overwhelming effect: inhibiting human initiative and responsibility. It is a routine, which derives from and epitomises a body of belief. There is a Kuhnian cultural gestalt or paradigm.[23] Samuel Huntington describes a 'professional mind'[24] that structures distinctive and persistent habits of

---

20   Foucault, op cit, 195, 196, 197.
21   Alasdair MacIntyre (1984), *After virtue*, 2nd edition (Notre Dame, IN: University of Notre Dame Press), 109.
22   Storr, 'A Command philosophy for the information age', 126.
23   Thomas Kuhn (1970), *The structure of scientific revolutions* (Chicago: University of Chicago Press), 114, 150, 151.
24   Samuel P Huntington (1981), *The soldier and the state: the theory and politics of civil-military relations* (Cambridge, MA: the Belknap Press of Harvard University), 61.

thought and action—framing a worldview from within which behaviour is rationalised. Embedded in the military context, individual choice is not entirely personal. Dovetailed with prevailing and complex institutional process, human decision adheres to conventions and accepted etiquette. The effect of military bureaucracy upon soldiers is significant and substantial.

Pervasive, suppressive and frequently undue, military bureaucracy induces habits of wooden compliance. Soldiers are duped by a culture of compulsory consensus into thinking character equals rule-following. Strategic corporals must think differently, independently and conscientiously. But the military system fails them. Soldiers, who ought to think for themselves and act decisively, are disabled by the military proclivity for bureaucratic hesitancy. Bearing a fiduciary duty to exercise the state's lethal force thoughtfully, with a singular sense of individual responsibility, soldiers are deceived and compromised by the cordial hypocrisy that hallmarks military life. The Final Report of the 2012 Australian Senate Foreign Affairs Defence and Trade References Committee into Defence Procurement offers an illustration. The report noted that the Department of Defence was an organisation

> [w]here people get 'bogged down' with too much paper work ... and miss the important things going on. (There are) confused or blurred lines of responsibility, accountability ... is too diffuse to be effective (and) the organization is unable or unwilling to hold people to account. (As well, people have) little understanding or appreciation of the importance of contestability and (the prevailing) mindset simply cannot or refuses to comprehend the meaning of 'independent advice'.[25]

This report spells out the swither that dissolves individual decision. The report makes clear that, inoculated by bureaucracy, soldiers are immunised against self-reliance; their sense of responsibility is numbed by rituals of evasion and double talk.

Yet, responsible independence is critical, since for soldiers to be properly effective it is not enough that they are obedient, that they follow conventions,

---

25  Australian Senate, Foreign Affairs Defence and Trade References Committee (2012), *Procurement procedures for Defence capital projects: final report*, August 2012 (Canberra: Commonwealth of Australia, Senate Printing Unit), xxi.

abide by rules and 'play the game'. Soldiers must be clear-thinking, conscientious and decisive. They must answer the call to individual action and responsibility, which is constricted—if not asphyxiated—in the bureaucratic system.

Regarded by Jonathan Shay as 'the most fundamental incompetence in the Vietnam War',[26] the misapplication of bureaucratic and industrial process thinking is an institutional failing, and the death knell for autonomous and strategically effectual soldiers.

## The obligation to act responsibly

Military enlistment confers, not an excuse to be obedient at all costs, but an obligation to act deliberately for justice. Underlining this idea, the philosopher Jeff McMahan asks rhetorically how the establishment by certain people of political or bureaucratic relations among themselves may confer on them a right to behave in ways which are impermissible in the absence of those relations:

> How could it be (he asks) that merely acting collectively for political (or bureaucratic) goals, people can shed the moral constraints that bind them when they act merely as individuals ...[27]

McMahan illuminates the moral obligation people bear as individuals. And he illuminates the moral obligation that should inform the strategic corporal: the soldier who acts of their own initiative to take the moral high ground, to do what's right, to advance justice. On McMahan's account, the capitulation of individuals to bureaucratic rote and the unquestioning pliability, which articulates policy into action, is the neglect of a duty.

HR McMaster makes this thought plain in his book, *Dereliction of Duty*. Considering the Joint Chiefs of Staff during Lyndon Johnson's presidency, McMaster describes 'five silent men'.[28] He describes how the Joint Chiefs,

---

26   Jonathan Shay (2003), *Achilles in Vietnam: combat trauma and the undoing of character* (New York: Scribner), 17.
27   Jeff McMahan, 'Collectivist defenses of the moral equality of combatants', *Journal of Military Ethics* 6, 1 (2007), 53.
28   HR McMaster (1998), *Dereliction of duty: Lyndon Johnson, Robert McNamara, the Joint Chiefs of Staff and the lies that led to Vietnam* (New York: HarperPerennial), 330.

trapped by an alleged military code in routines of bureaucratic deference, were acquiescent and persuadable. These men were silent when they should have spoken, malleable when they ought to have been conscientious and uncompromising.

Analysing the political calamity of Vietnam, McMaster describes a uniquely human failing. Among the many and reinforcing frailties he identifies, the biggest was the craving by the Joint Chiefs for approval, their need to appear loyal, to fit in and to do the accepted thing. Playing along with bureaucratic convention, the Joint Chiefs abdicated their responsibility to speak up, to articulate a professional vision and to exert constructive influence over the policy they were entrusted to enact. The generals failed to act with the purpose and individual resolution expected of the corporal.

Conforming reflexively to familiar punctilios, the generals perpetuated the dependencies of bureaucratic custom. These habits, which relegate the strategic corporal to a rhetorical part, must be reformed. They are the habits of rococo politesse and inadvertent conformance, which embellish military failure.

History speaks of the failure by soldiers to measure up, and of the collapse of the military institution. In her book, *Eichmann in Jerusalem*, Hannah Arendt offers former SS Lieutenant Colonel Adolf Eichmann as a poignant and paradigm case.

Seduced by the bureaucracy of the Third Reich, Eichmann was 'not Iago and not Macbeth, and nothing would have been further from his mind than to determine with Richard III "to prove a villain"'.[29] Habituated to bureaucratic conformance, Eichmann's evil was monstrous. But more significantly it was, in Arendt's famous term, 'banal'. He '*merely*, to put the matter colloquially, merely never realized what he was doing'.[30] When on trial, Eichmann was described predictably by his defence as 'only a "tiny cog" in the machinery of the Final Solution (and) in its judgment the court naturally conceded that such a crime could be committed only by a giant bureaucracy.'[31]

Though this is to underplay the moral collapse of Eichmann as a man, the decisive point is that Eichmann acted in accordance with established rules

---

29 Hannah Arendt (2006), *Eichmann in Jerusalem: a report on the banality of evil* (New York: Penguin), 287.
30 Arendt, op cit, 287 (emphasis in the original).
31 Arendt, op cit, 289.

and legal orders. He never felt a need to rely upon his conscience, since—as Arendt says—his autonomous judgement was suffocated by bureaucratic orthodoxy and habit.[32] In *Criminal Case 40/61: The trial of Adolf Eichmann*, Harry Mulisch coined the term 'psycho-technology',[33] which speaks to the quintessentially bureaucratic engrossment with obedience, to the culpable torpor that sustains bureaucratic habit. Mulisch explained how 'a dull group of godforsaken civil servants doing their godforsaken duty'[34] turned the bureaucracy into a weapon—and an excuse. The polymath CP Snow underlines the evil that follows from unthinking conformance:

> *When you think of the long and gloomy history of man, you will find more hideous crimes have been committed in the name of obedience than have ever been committed in the name of rebellion. If you doubt that, read William Shirer's Rise and Fall of the Third Reich. The German Officer Corps were brought up in the most rigorous code of obedience ... in the name of obedience they were party to and assisted in the most wicked large-scale actions in the history of the world.*[35]

Snow captures the magnitude of the idea: soldiers will be most strategically effective when they are taught and accustomed to think independently. Conditioned by bureaucracy to obey, soldiers may commit crimes of obedience, acts 'performed in response to orders from authority that [are] considered illegal or immoral by the larger community'.[36] Eichmann's perverse *reductio* demonstrates the appalling human competence for evil. However, on the account of this chapter, the example also demonstrates the banality of bureaucracy, the officialism and procedure that suffocates the strategic corporal and facilitates the human failure to measure up.

---

32   Arendt, op cit, 293.
33   Harry Mulisch (2005), *Criminal case 40/61: the trial of Adolf Eichmann*, translated by Robert Naborn (Philadelphia: University of Philadelphia Press), 113.
34   Mulisch, op cit, 141.
35   CP Snow (1961), cited by Stanley Milgram, 'Behavioural study of obedience', *Journal of Abnormal and Social Psychology* 67, 4 (1963), 371.
36   Herbert C Kelman and V Lee Hamilton (1989), *Crimes of obedience* (New Haven, CT: Yale University Press), 46.

Bureaucracy's failure is the failure to establish circumstances in which independently responsible, dutiful soldiers might flourish. Military pencil-pushers have allowed themselves to be hoodwinked by the myth that routine observance equals rightness, while deviation from standard procedure is the opposite.

But military people have allowed themselves to be duped against the weight of evidence. There is no failure to understand. The strategic implication of unthinking compliance at the tactical level is well known. As an illustrative phrase, the 'strategic corporal' derives its rhetorical power from appreciation of the large-scale significance of tactical autonomy. Still, as a theory, the idea is out of step with the military bureaucracy.

Focused on formalities and official rules, the bureaucracy fails to secure background conditions critical to the strategic corporal. Bound by red tape and conditioned to seek endless permissions, people are unfitted to act responsibly and independently on their initiative. More generally, people become shy of moral language, scared of ideals, in a hurry to find safe haven in artful phrases, reluctant to speak up and unwilling to hold people accountable. The shortcomings of bureaucracy are revealed by the official reports.

Commissioned, hoarded and ignored, the reports and reviews exemplify ubiquitous failing. Though they are mandated and explained as the penetrating instruments of inquisition and reform, they are mostly palaverous and largely neglected. Their significance lies, not in their intendment, but in their milquetoast prose.

## Official reports

The report of the Australian National Audit Office into the Super Seasprite helicopter project[37] offers an example. Super Seasprite helicopters were acquired for the purpose of enhancing the capability of the Navy's eight ANZAC-class ships. The project was approved in February 1996, with a budget of A$746 million. Provisionally accepted aircraft were operated by the Navy between late 2003 and early 2006, when flying was suspended. The project was cancelled in 2008. All in all, expenditure exceeded A$1.4 billion.

---

37  Australian Government, National Audit Office (2009), *The Super Seasprite: the Australian Auditor General Audit Report No. 41 2008–09* (Canberra: Australian National Audit Office, Commonwealth of Australia, Attorney General's Department).

Notwithstanding disingenuous terms of reference, the Seasprite Report reveals a bureaucracy riddled with the habits of avoidance and evading. Yet, despite evident waste and obvious failure—since no Seasprite helicopter capability exists, or ever existed—the Seasprite Report manages to avoid moral language and moral ideas. The word 'wrong', for example, occurs three times in the report. On pages 260 and 319, the word 'wrong' appears in the phrase 'wrong side of the aircraft'. On page 334, we read of a 'wrong impression'. Despite the non-event that was the Seasprite helicopter, no person is seen to have been wrong. No person is seen to have made a mistake.

Yet, recalling Robert Kempner's interrogation of the truculent Wannsee participants after the Second World War, there were people who 'knew the things you had to know',[38] and who made the decisions significant people make. Such people accept large salaries, from the public purse, to remunerate the heavy burdens of responsibility. Incredibly, no person was considered responsible. No person was found to bear any blame.

The word 'blame' appears once in the report, on page 333, where we read that the Seasprite Report 'summarize(s) the apportionment of blame against the audit objective to identify those factors that contributed to the on-going poor performance of the project'. So, factors are responsible, but not people. And, the word 'responsible' appears in the report, as a descriptive word in reference to legal or bureaucratic responsibility. The word 'responsible' is never used in a normative or moral sense.

Materially unrevealing and inscrutable, this report was accepted by the bureaucracy as an explanation. But the report is not enlightening, not a proper account of reasons why the Seasprite project failed. Gnomic phrasing, such as 'the failure of the project to provide the required capability',[39] skirts around the fact that the project was an unequivocal catastrophe. The project is described as cancelled, but not failed.[40]

---

38   Robert Kempner (1980), *Das Dritte Reich im Kreuzvehör: Aus den unveröffentlichten Vernehmungsprotokollen des Anklägers* (Konigstein/Taunus: Athenaum/Droste Taschenbucher), 189 (Kempner was interrogating Erich Neumann), cited in Mark Roseman (2012), *The Wannsee Conference and the Final Solution: a reconsideration* (London: Folio), 61.
39   Australian Government, National Audit Office, *The Super Seasprite*, paragraph 9, 15. The phrase is repeated at paragraph 1.26 on 66.
40   Australian Government, op cit, paragraph 10.60, 278. The idea of 'project failure' occurs once, in a sub-heading where the discussion concerns the cost of cancellation.

Oblique and mealy-mouthed, the Seasprite Report is assumed to palliate and disguise unsound performance. This reasoning is underlined by remark that lessons gleaned from the Seasprite Project have become the responsibility of a new bureaucratic division, known as the Helicopter Systems Division.[41] The Seasprite Report claims:

> By having the Head (of the) Helicopter Systems Division assisting Mr Mortimer with his Review, the lessons learnt from the Seasprite were included in the Mortimer Review.[42]

However, lessons learned from the Seasprite fiasco are invisible in the Mortimer Review—officially the Defence Procurement and Sustainment Review, chaired by Mr David Mortimer AO between May and September 2008. The Mortimer Review does mention the name 'Seasprite'—but only once—and then in a table, to illustrate a 'developmental' project.[43] The Mortimer Review identified five principal areas of concern,[44] including a shortfall of bureaucratic resources, but not including the imperceivable erosion of individual responsibility by arbitrary routine.

Evading moral ideas by euphemism and periphrasis, these reports demonstrate a broad underlying failure and a need for institutional reform. The reports reveal the politic voice of a bureaucracy preserving its *modus operandi* and senior cadre. Lacking any sense of right and wrong, these reports reveal institutional insolvency: a failure to interpret critical ideas, and a failure to inspire the culture of moral responsibility critical to the strategic corporal.

The Australian National Audit Office performance audit of the air warfare destroyer programme is a further case in point. Though the project is years

---

41  Australian Government, op cit, paragraph 1.23, 65.
42  Ibid.
43  Commonwealth of Australia (2008), *Going to the next level: the report of the Defence Procurement and Sustainment Review*, chaired by Mr David Mortimer AO (Canberra: Commonwealth of Australia: Defence Materiel Organisation), 18.
44  Commonwealth of Australia, op cit, xi. The report describes these concerns as 'ranging from inadequate project management resources in the Capability Development Group, the inefficiency of the process leading to government approvals for new projects, shortages in Defence Materiel Organisation personnel, to delays due to inadequate industry capacity and difficulties in the introduction of equipment into full service'.

behind schedule and hundreds of millions over budget, no person is named as responsible. In this report, personal accountability is obscured by the use of collective nouns. Underperforming people evade personal responsibility behind terms such as 'Defence' or 'industry' or 'industry partners' or 'committee,' 'sub-committee' or 'standing committee'.[45] The underpinning reasons are unlikable.

## The underpinning reasons

The underpinning reasons involve scapegoating, excuse-making and complacency. Time and again, those in senior positions have failed to bear the responsibilities of their appointment; they have failed to secure background conditions within which soldiers might rise to the challenge of individual responsibility.

In the words of the Moffitt Review, concerning Australian submarine sustainability, there is a 'crisis of leadership'[46] and a feckless 'benign acceptance of the status quo [among] more senior rank groups'.[47] Describing the 'poor leadership' of people 'in positions of power',[48] Admiral Moffitt takes a refreshing hard line. In this, he resembles the tone and accent of Lord Levene's 2011 review of the UK Ministry of Defence. Investigating the senescence of British military bureaucracy, Lord Levene makes the official

---

45  Australian Government, National Audit Office (2014), *The Air Warfare Destroyer Program: the Australian Auditor General Audit Report No 22 2013–14* (Canberra: Australian National Audit Office, Commonwealth of Australia, Attorney General's Department). Investigating the undertaking to build three Hobart-class guided-missile destroyers, the performance audit notes a project budgeted at A$8.455 billion and estimated conservatively to be A$300 million over budget and approximately two years behind schedule (paragraphs 23 and 24, p 22).

46  Royal Australian Navy (2008), *Report of the review of submarine workforce sustainability, 31 October 2008, undertaken by Rear Admiral RC Moffitt AO, RAN*, paragraph 7.3, 64, 65. Available at www.defence.gov.au/publications/SubmarineWorkforceSustainability.pdf, accessed on 11 April 2017.

47  Royal Australian Navy, op cit, paragraph 3.2.3, 13. The Moffitt review is quoted in Nicholas Jans (2010), 'Respite and predictability guidelines review (phase 4) the way ahead', Sigma Consultancy, Marysville Victoria, 9 April 2010, 15.

48  Royal Australian Navy, op cit, paragraph 12.4.2, 99.

shortcomings explicit. In categorical style, he criticised a 'culture of consensual, committee-based decision-making',[49] and an institutionalised failure to hold people to account.[50] He identified an over-inflated senior cadre,[51] a pervasive 'inability to take tough, timely decisions, (and an insidious) conspiracy of optimism.'[52]

Lord Levene describes an etiolated culture fostered by shopworn leadership. His themes find close resonance in the dismaying narrative of the DLA Piper Report.[53]

The *Report of the Review of Allegations of Sexual and Other Abuse in Defence*, subtitled 'Facing the problems of the Past,' and undertaken by the legal firm DLA Piper, paints a picture of the sort of difference that resolute and morally courageous leadership might make, since it is a counterfactual inventory of consequences that follow when leadership is absent. Beside the narrative of persistent and recurrent abusive behaviour,[54] the report suggests an entrenched habit. And it is not a habit of abuse. Observing the 'substantial inadequacy'[55] and 'lack of seriousness'[56] that has characterised the institutional response to allegations of abuse, the DLA Piper Report lifts the lid on

---

49  UK Government, Ministry of Defence (2011), *Defence reform: an independent report into the structure and management of the Ministry of Defence, chaired by Lord Levene of Portsoken KBE* (Levene Report) (London: The Stationery Office), paragraph 4.6, 21.

50  UK Government, op cit, paragraph 4.7, 21; also at paragraph 8.20 at 41. At paragraph 13.6, 59, Lord Levene argues that senior people, whose performance falls short, should be managed more 'robustly'.

51  UK Government, op cit, recommendation 11, 71.

52  UK Government, op cit, paragraph 2.3, 13.

53  Rumble et al, DLA Piper Report. The background to this report is set down in paragraph 1.1 at 1: In April 2011, the Minister of Defence asked the Secretary of the Department of Defence to identify a suitable team to review and report on hundreds of communications about abuse within Defence that had come into the Minister's office in the two weeks following the so-called Skype incident at the Australian Defence Force Academy. The department identified Dr Gary Rumble, at the time a partner with law firm DLA Phillips Fox (later DLA Piper), as a suitable person to lead that review. At Dr Rumble's suggestion, Professor Pearce AO (DLA Phillips Fox Special Counsel) and Ms Melanie McKean (DLA Phillips Fox Partner) were proposed as joint leaders of the Review.

54  Rumble et al, DLA Piper Report, 48.

55  Rumble et al, op cit, 50.

56  Rumble et al, op cit, 54.

familiar bad habits of whitewash and circumvention. The root cause is—and was—the failure of those who bear institutional responsibility. Blind eyes are turned. Prefabricated chatter is passed off as argument.[57]

These failings are so deep-seated, they are not seen for what they are. An example is in a Department of Defence media release, published as the DLA Piper Report was being finalised, and cited by that report:

> A female Australian soldier ... was allegedly sexually assaulted at a military base in Tarin Kot, Uruzgan Province, last month while on deployment in Afghanistan.
>
> The soldier reported the alleged assault to superiors on Wednesday (5 October, 2011) and the matter is now the subject of an investigation.
>
> Defence does not condone inappropriate behaviour and treats such allegations seriously.[58]

The failure to express intense remonstrance by description of sexual assault as merely 'inappropriate', diminishes the gravity of events, and suggests a critical need for scruples. The weak language suggests a dearth of *thumos*—appropriate self-assertion, the self-respect and right-minded desire to be acknowledged as standing for something valuable.[59]

Confronted by an adversary motivated by the most repellent ideology to commit acts of abhorrent viciousness, the habitual failure of Western society to acknowledge and articulate high ideals reveals a deeply concerning philis-

---

57  The *Report on abuse in Defence*, prepared by the Hon Justice Roberts-Smith RFD, QC (Canberra: Commonwealth of Australia, Attorney General's Department, Commonwealth Administrative Law Branch, 2014), observes (7) that 'many complainants expressed a strong belief that members of senior rank and Defence more generally ... knowingly took no action to address or prevent (abuse)'. This report acknowledges the weak institutional response of Defence to reports of abuse, but does not recommend a Royal Commission since such an expensive and demanding undertaking is unlikely to shed much more light on events than the many and recent reviews and inquiries which have pointed to the deliquesce of leadership.

58  Rumble et al, DLA Piper Report, 150.

59  Francis Fukuyama (2006), *The end of history and the last man* (New York: Free Press), 162–163.

tinism. In the second edition of *Justice in Tribunals*, JRS Forbes captures the indecisive ring of bureaucracy's reflex moral sciolism:

> *'Inappropriate' is a contemporary 'weasel word' denoting anything from grave criminality to conduct merely in bad taste, contrary to the prevailing sense of fashion, like wearing brown shoes with a navy suit or drinking red wine with fish.*[60]

Forbes illuminates set-piece verbalism as the sallow language of people who coin justifications and pretexts. But the deeper significance of the lame phrasing is in the intention, which was not to deliberately minify an assault. Powerless and hesitant language is merely the habituated phraseology of people unaccustomed to taking a stand and not given to articulating high ideals.

Speaking to these ideas, Norman Dixon observed in his seminal work, *On the Psychology of Military Incompetence*, how military officers regularly slough off all sense of moral awareness. Dixon's concern was that officers convinced of their own superiority lose all feeling for the moral basis upon which they exercise command.[61] Similarly, on the account of this chapter, military leaders habituated to bureaucratic inanity lose touch with the language and ideals that will inspire soldiers to act decisively with a mind to translating high ideals into practice. That is significant, since it is as personally responsible and high-minded individuals that soldiers find profound effect.

## The institution and the strategic corporal

Writing in the *Marine Corps Gazette*, Captain James Reid states that 'NCOs must maintain the high moral ground',[62] an acknowledgement that soldiers must be individually principled and responsible. Reid echoes the claim of US Army and Marine Corps counterinsurgency doctrine: 'lose moral

---

60 John RS Forbes (2006), *Justice in tribunals*, 2nd edition (Annandale, NSW: The Federation Press), 71: quoting J Spender in *The Australian*, 30 August 1995.
61 Norman Dixon (1994), *On the psychology of military incompetence* (London: Pimlico), 48. Dixon cites S Raven (1959), 'Perish by the sword', in *Encounter* (May 1959), 37–49.
62 Captain James B Reid, USMC, 'Educating the strategic corporal: restructure the course for better mental preparation', *Marine Corps Gazette* 93, 3 (March 2009), 45.

legitimacy, lose the war."[63] Acknowledging the functional relevance of military honour,[64] the doctrine repeats lawyer and academic Mark Osiel, who observes the duty of soldiers to behave honourably, consistent with the ideals of people constitutively committed to the rule of law.[65]

Yet, notwithstanding consistency with the evolving character of war—where national interests are entwined with national values—and despite acknowledgment in military doctrine, moral sensitivity is inconsistent with habits cultivated by bureaucracy. In bureaucracy, individual merit and moral responsibility are suffocated by acquiescence, dependence and excuse.

This matters because no soldier acting in the pursuit of justice can commit to action they consider evil. This may, of course, mean nothing more than that soldiers obey lawful orders, and conscientiously refuse manifestly illegal orders. However, American doctrine seems to suggest more than this, holding that soldiers are 'expected to act ethically' and in accordance with shared national values and Constitutional principles, which are reflected in the law and military oaths of service'.[66]

Making explicit mention of 'shared national values' and 'principles', the doctrine separates ideas of ethics from ideas of the law. Doctrine argues that ethical standards are reflected in law, not defined by law. These expressions are significant, since they suppose autonomous choice. Soldiers are expected—if they are not instructed—to act in accord with ideals which are implied but not explicit. At a deeper level, the doctrine gestures toward a cosmopolitan

---

63   US Army/USMC (2007), *The US Army and Marine Corps counterinsurgency field manual* (US Army Field Manual No 3-24, Marine Corps Warfighting Publication No 3-33.5), foreword by General David H Petraeus and Lt General James F Amos, USMC (Chicago: University of Chicago Press), paragraph 7.44, 252. The example of the French counterinsurgency in Algeria is provided as an example. In this campaign, the French condoned the use of torture against insurgents. This was seen to undermine the moral legitimacy of the French campaign, and to empower the insurgent campaign, which became associated with ideas of just cause and seen as a defensive action against oppression.

64   US Army/USMC, op cit, paragraph 7.11, 240.

65   Cited in Dale Stephens (2011), 'The age of lawfare', in Raul 'Pete' Pedrozo and Daria P Wollschlaeger (eds), *International law and the changing character of war. U.S. Naval War College International Law Studies Series* 87 (Newport, RI: United States Naval War College), 348.

66   US Army/USMC, *The US Army and Marine Corps counterinsurgency field manual*, paragraph 7.1, 237–238.

argument for justice,[67] seeming to accept that political realism is not the catholicon, which conventional bureaucracy might have it to be. Yet, despite the weight of doctrinal and scholarly argument, the military bureaucracy is unlikely to cultivate the requisite self-reliance and autonomous judgement.

Characterised by disproportionate emphasis on conformance, and by a weaseling patois, the bureaucracy suffers from the gratuitous reporting of minutiae[68] and the entrenched avoidance of responsibility. The zeal and the sense of independent duty that characterise the strategic corporal are smothered by an engrossment with superintendence and avoidance. In his January 2011 *Review of the Defence Accountability Framework*, Professor Rufus Black was plain. Black described an institution where 'too many committees … create diffused and confused accountability'.[69] In his report, Black noted ambiguous organisational requirements, and indefinite personal accountabilities undermined the organisation. His criticisms, the subject of untold preceding reports, were unwelcome in a culture described as insular, inward-looking, excessively rules-based and driven by process not by outcomes.[70]

The strategic corporal is at odds with the actuality of military life. Institutional customs and usages, which reflect and structure a body of belief, must be interrogated and understood. Their significance must be recognised and their influence appreciated. The corporal exists in a context, and cannot be properly understood in isolation. The significance of this claim is in its radius and reference. The claim illuminates the strategic corporal beyond the bounds of their tactical skill. Asserting the power and influence of the organisational

---

67    For example: Geoffrey Robertson (2006), *Crimes against humanity: the struggle for global justice* (London: Penguin), xxxiii. Robertson observes: 'at the beginning of the 21st century, the dominant motive in world affairs is the quest—almost the thirst—for justice. [This thirst is] replacing even the objective of regional security as the trigger for international action.'

68    Commonwealth of Australia (2009), *Report on the strategic review of naval engineering*, 12 November 2009 (Canberra: Commonwealth of Australia), recommendation 3.5, x. The report argues: 'The administrative and reporting burden in ships and air squadrons should be reviewed with the express purpose of reducing it to the essential items only.'

69    Australian Government, Department of Defence (2011), *Review of the Defence Accountability Framework, carried out by Professor Rufus Black*, January 2011 (Canberra: Australian Government, Department of Defence), 9.

70    Australian Government, op cit, 99.

context, this chapter opens the door to significant new inquiry. Beyond the ubiquitous ten-day corporals' course and the token sessions on Pashtun and cultural alertness, this chapter suggests that to cultivate and nurture the strategic corporal, we must first interrogate and then reform the military establishment. This is change that must be at the top, and driven from the top of the organisational structure. And it must be genuine and constructive change, not the calculating and Pickwickian reform that Aldous Huxley describes in *Brave New World Revisited*.[71]

## Genuine and constructive change

Describing genuine and constructive organisational change, Theo Farrell draws a distinction between the complementary processes of adaption and innovation. Developing a theory of military adaptation, illuminated by an analysis of the British campaign in Helmand, Farrell describes the changes to tactics, techniques and technologies which improve operational performance. Such innovation is a ground-level response, which may in time be captured in doctrine and reflected in an evolved organisational structure.[72]

Farrell explains how, in even the most rule-driven militaries, strategic corporals will emerge to find success. However, autonomous and innovative soldiers will emerge despite formal systems, not because of them. For enduring organisational change, evolution must be driven from the top down, sustained over generations, captured in doctrine, and supported by receptive and malleable regulative structures. This means organisational networks, doctrine and thinking must evolve. The military must wean itself from the

---

[71] 'Brave New World Revisited', in Aldous Huxley (2004), *Brave New World and Brave New World Revisited* (New York: HarperCollins), 333–334. Describing the erosion of democracy, Huxley writes: '[By means of] increasing over-organisation, and by means of ever more effective mind-manipulation, the democracies will change their nature; the quaint old forms—elections, parliaments, Supreme Courts and all the rest will remain. The underlying substance will be a new kind of non-violent totalitarianism. All the hallowed slogans will remain exactly where they were in the good old days. Democracy and freedom will be the theme of every broadcast and editorial—but democracy and freedom in a strictly Pickwickian sense. Meanwhile the ruling oligarchy and its highly trained elite of soldiers, policemen, thought-manufacturers and mind-manipulators will quietly run the show as they see fit.'

[72] Theo Farrell, 'Improving in war: military adaptation and the British in Helmand Province, Afghanistan, 2006–2009', *The Journal of Strategic Studies* 33, 4 (August 2010), 569.

heroin of unchanging official procedures and formula language. Reports must be frank and fearless, not phobic and weak-kneed. Official writing should be judged by its clarity and power, not by margins and tabulations.

In an organisation that would encourage the strategic corporal, military leaders must lead by example; they must give expression to the truth that, as soldiers, ideas of duty are most richly informed and most exquisitely defined by ideas of individual merit and moral responsibility. The metaphors of practice that compel and emphasise unconstructive subordination must be reformed. Some obligations will—and indeed ought—to be prescribed. But in setting out rules, people must not lose sight of inexpressible standards, and indefinable ideals. Medal of Honor winner Vice Admiral James Stockdale illustrates this idea powerfully.

## Conclusion

As President of the US Naval War College, Stockdale argued against the over-prominence of legalistic and bureaucratic thinking. Arguing against 'officers' ticket punching [focusing on] organisational efficiency at the expense of honour', Stockdale observed:

> *Today's ranks are filled with officers who have been weaned on slogans and fads of the sort preached in the better business schools of the country. That is to say, that rational managerial concepts will cure all evils. We must regain our (ethical) bearings.*
>
> *It is certainly convenient to adopt the mores of the bureaucracy. However, if anything has power to sustain an individual in peace or war, regardless of occupation, it is one's conviction and commitment to (high) standards of right and wrong.*
>
> *Regardless of the fairness of our (bureaucratic or) judicial system it must not be allowed to take the place of moral obligation to ourselves, to our Service, to our country. Each (person) must bring (themselves) to some stage of ethical resolution.*
>
> *In the Naval Service we have no place for amoral gnomes lost in narrow orbits; we need to keep our gaze fixed on the high-minded principles standing above the law.*[73]

---

73  James Bond Stockdale, 'Taking stock', *United States Naval War College Review* 31, 2 (1978), 2: order of paragraphs changed.

Beyond the parabolic complexity of the battlefield, the importance of these ideas derives from the evolution of international affairs. The military profession can no longer hide behind the unrealistically realist excuse that action was 'in the national interest'. Soldiers must think for themselves, they must be individually responsible, and they must hold others accountable. In a world inspired by ideals of justice, soldiers must exert—or at least seek to exert—a constructive moral influence over the policies they enact. They must be more than tactically adept.

Writing in the *Military Law Review*, Jack Goldsmith, a Harvard academic and former senior government lawyer, offers a compelling conclusion. Remember, he says, when it's all over

> *[y]ou will be judged in a quiet, dignified, well-lit room, where your judgments will be viewed with the perfect and brutally unfair vision of hindsight, where it is impossible to capture even a piece of the urgency and exigency felt during crisis.*[74]

When judgment comes, the soldier will wish to have acted rightly. Confronted by judgment, the soldier will regret passive obedience. And faced with judgment the soldier will regret remaining silent when, by speaking up, a difference might have been made.

For these reasons the institution must seek to give soldiers their voice, to empower them to act deliberately and responsibly, and not merely obediently and with technical finesse.

---

74  Jack Goldsmith, 'The Third Annual Solf-Warren Lecture on International and Operational Law', *Military Law Review*, 205 (2010), 201.

# 4

# The Strategic Contractor

## *Deane-Peter Baker and David Pfotenhauer*

THE SLAYING AND SUBSEQUENT MUTILATION of Scott Helvenston, Jerry Zovko, Wes Batalona and Mike Teague on 31 March 2004 in Fallujah in Iraq has been described by Jeremy Scahill as 'the Mogadishu moment of the Iraq War'.[1] The four men, while travelling through Fallujah, were ambushed and killed when their convoy came under intense small-arms fire from multiple directions. Their vehicles were then set on fire, their bodies pulled from the burning wrecks, mutilated, set alight and hung up from a bridge. The brutal scene was screened by television stations around the globe against the backdrop of a euphoric chanting mob. It was without question a key moment in the Iraq war, but Scahill's analogy with the so-called Black Hawk Down incident misses the fundamental differences between what happened in Fallujah and the disastrous 1993 operation in Somalia. The four slain men were not members of the US military but were instead private contractors belonging to the booming Private Military and Security Company (PMSC) Blackwater USA. And their killing did not prompt a US military withdrawal; instead, the ambush was a critical stimulus for launching Operation Vigilant Resolve, the first Battle of Fallujah. The operation was launched despite serious misgivings from the US military hierarchy regarding the tactical and strategic outcomes the operation could be expected to produce. Former Assistant Secretary of Defense Bing West maintained in an interview that the military offensive in Fallujah launched on the back of the contractor killings was 'a decision by our top leadership against the advice of the Marines. They were

---

1    Jeremy Scahill (2007), *Blackwater: the rise of the world's most powerful mercenary army* (New York: Avalon Publishing), 103.

not going to change their entire strategy because of a tactical error. They were overruled'.² The battle that ensued went on for almost a month, before US forces were withdrawn in the face of growing criticism over mounting civilian casualties. The operation did very little to pacify or quell insurgent activity and resulted in reported civilian deaths of up to 600, many of them women and children, as well as seven Marines killed and 100 wounded.³

As a tactical event with far-reaching strategic consequences, the brutal killing of the four contractors has been described as 'irrevocably alter[ing] the course of the war'.⁴ The key role played by the contractor deaths in Fallujah is evident when considered in the context of an ambush of a US Marine convoy just a few days before, which resulted in the death of one and the wounding of two others.⁵ Indeed, in the eleven days prior to the contractor ambush, nine Marines had been killed in various contacts throughout the city.⁶ In spite of these casualties, it was the contractors' deaths that played the central role in pushing the US military to reassert its presence in Fallujah, even though the operational tempo had in fact been significantly decreased as a result of the previous military deaths. The speed with which the Bush administration responded militarily to these contractor deaths underscores the defining strategic role their deaths had in escalating military operations in Fallujah.

It was arguably the death of Scott Helvenston and his colleagues in Fallujah that first raised significant global awareness of the extent to which contractors were being employed in the counterinsurgency war in Iraq. But this is by no means the only occasion in recent history in which contractors have been responsible for, or contributed to, events that have had strategic effects (in the broad sense of that term employed in this volume). The now-defunct private military company Blackwater had featured prominently, most notably in their involvement in the shootings in Baghdad's Nisour Square, which left 17 Iraqi civilians dead, and significantly strained relations between the US and Iraqi governments. Employees of another firm, CACI, were involved, according

---

2   Molly Dunigan (2011), *Victory for hire: private security companies' impact on military effectiveness* (Stanford: Stanford University Press), 69.
3   Ibid.
4   Ibid.
5   Scahill, *Blackwater*, 100.
6   Ibid.

to a US Department of the Army report, in 36 per cent of the incidents of abuse and torture that led to the Abu Ghraib scandal,[7] which arguably tarnished the image of US involvement in Iraq more than any other single incident during the almost nine years of major US operations there. Less well known, however, are the ways in which contractors have contributed to positive strategic outcomes. In the 1990s, for example, the South African private military company Executive Outcomes (EO) was contracted first by the government of Angola and then by the government of Sierra Leone, and in both cases was directly responsible for high-tempo military operations that forced the governments' military opponents (UNITA in Angola, and the RUF in Sierra Leone) to the negotiating table. In both cases, however, these strategic gains were lost shortly thereafter when international pressure forced the governments concerned to terminate their contracts with these 'mercenaries'.

In this chapter, we explore, employing the conceptual framework of the strategic corporal first articulated by US Marine Corps General Charles Krulak in 1999, the potential strategic impacts, both positive and negative, of the employment of contractors in the zones of armed conflict of tomorrow.

## The strategic corporal and the three block war

In 'The strategic corporal: leadership in the three block war', General Krulak begins by describing a fictional scenario in which a platoon of Marines, led by a Second Lieutenant Franklin, is deployed to provide security for a food distribution point in the war-torn central African city of Tugala, the capital of the nation of Orange, which is described as 'wracked by civil unrest and famine'. Lieutenant Franklin's Marines are part of a Marine Expeditionary Unit (Special Operations Capable) that has been deployed on a stabilisation mission designed to allow international humanitarian assistance organisations to deliver food to those affected by the famine. US involvement in the theatre has become necessary as a result of the failure of a previously deployed Regional Multi-National Force (RMNF) to adequately implement security for the famine relief efforts.

The 2nd Platoon's unglamorous mission seems, a month into the deployment, to be reaping rewards: as a result of the security the platoon is providing, relief aid is reaching those who need it and '[t]he grim daily death tolls ha[ve]

---

7   Peter W Singer, 'Outsourcing war', *Foreign Affairs* (March/April 2005), 125.

slowly begun to decrease and the city ha[s] begun to recover some sense of normalcy'.[8] However, a threat arises as members of a hostile militia, 'led by the renegade warlord Nedeed, [is] observed congregating near the river that [divides] the capital in half and [marks] the boundary separating the turf of [Nedeed's militia] from that of its principal rival',[9] a faction led by the warlord Mubasa. Though no attacks have yet been committed against the Marines in-theatre, threats have been made by Nedeed and his cronies, and there have been frequent attacks on members of the RMNF. To meet this looming threat, 1st Squad, under the command of Corporal Hernandez (the 'strategic corporal' of Krulak's title), are deployed to form a roadblock at Checkpoint Charlie. As the day unfolds, Corporal Hernandez finds himself faced with what Krulak calls a 'three block war', that is, an environment that is fluid, complex and requires multi-layered responses to different and simultaneous challenges.

The first challenge that Hernandez faces is the requirement to provide security to the usual crowd of locals, mostly women and children, who have begun queuing at Checkpoint Charlie in order to collect the relief supplies that had rolled in on the morning's convoy. Today, however, the crowd has been swelled by a significant number of hostile young males, who begin chanting and hurling rocks and Molotov cocktails at Hernandez's Marines. Another threat also looms: two groups of armed and vehicle-mounted militia, one from each of the competing factions led by Nedeed and Mubasa, are converging on Hernandez's position, seemingly intent on engaging one another and any Marines who come between them. Mubasa's group is, furthermore, accompanied by a network news crew. Then, just when it looks as though things couldn't get any more challenging, they do. A helicopter operated by one of the international relief organisations engaged in the famine relief effort is shot down by ground fire and has crashed nearby. The survivors are unarmed and in serious need of medical assistance, and a group of Nedeed's militia are rapidly closing in on the crash site. While help, in the form of reinforcements, is on the way, Hernandez must make quick decisions

---

8    Gen Charles C Krulak, 'The strategic corporal: leadership in the three block war', *Marines Magazine* 28, 1 (January 1999), 26–33. Available at www.au.af.mil/au/awc/awcgate/usmc/strategic_corporal.htm, accessed on 11 April 2017.

9    Ibid.

about what to do, decisions that could potentially have a strategic-level impact on the overall mission.

Hernandez's predicament is, of course, designed to illustrate the leadership qualities that Krulak believes junior Marine Corps leaders require if the Corps is to successfully execute missions in circumstances of complex and irregular armed conflict. For the purpose of this chapter, however, it is useful to set aside Krulak's original purpose and instead to isolate the central elements of the complex environment he describes in order then to draw out the potential implications of employing contractors in such circumstances.

## The strategic contractor

The operational environment that Krulak describes to give context to his 'three block war' has four key themes that we need to consider in order to tease out the potential strategic implications of employing contractors in conflict zones. In no particular order of importance, they are as follows:

- The tactical environment will be prone to a rapid escalation of hostilities from multiple and diverse threats. The threat environment will be fluid and complex, and requires flexibility in response from the 'boots on the ground'. The operational spectrum will cover a wide range, from non-kinetic humanitarian assistance to low-intensity combat and urban operations.
- Decisions made under extreme pressure in the face of a rapid escalation in hostilities from multiple and often simultaneous points of contact will require junior leaders to recognise the link between potential tactical errors and strategic setbacks.
- To be successful, junior leaders will need to have a previously unthinkable degree of autonomy in their tactical decision-making.
- The media will be omnipresent.

The key question this chapter asks is this: how might we expect contractors to function in this environment and could their involvement, in the place of or alongside uniformed military forces, elicit different strategic outcomes? To address this question, the four key elements mentioned above will be examined using recent examples of military contractors employed in conflict zones.

## Theme 1: The fluidity and complexity of the tactical environment

One of the major concerns regularly raised regarding contractors undertaking conflict-zone tasks traditionally performed by uniformed military personnel is the worry that this introduces a lack of flexibility that is particularly problematic in the kinds of fluid, complex and cross-spectrum operations to which Krulak's 'three block war' notion draws our attention, and which seem to be becoming the norm rather than the exception. Imagine, for example, that instead of Krulak's scenario focusing on Corporal Hernandez's platoon of Marines, a team of armed private security contractors are in approximately the situation that Krulak describes. They might, for example, have been contracted by an aid organisation to provide security for the food distribution point, or be doing the same thing under contract to the US or another government. If that were the case, could we expect 'Team Leader Jones' and his contractors to respond to the rapidly changing environment as effectively as Corporal Hernandez and his Marines did?

A central problem here is the comparatively narrow scope of the contract under which the contractors will most likely be operating, compared to the so-called unlimited liability contract under which the Marines are operating. While there is no question that the Marines can reasonably be expected to respond to the fluid environment by taking on tasks not originally in their orders—such as conducting a rescue mission for the survivors of the downed helicopter, or interposing themselves between the rival militia groups—the same cannot easily be said for the contractors. For them to undertake, for example, the downed-helicopter rescue mission would be supererogatory, not a matter of duty. And for them to do so would potentially raise significant problems that simply would not arise for the Marines. For example, would the contractors' insurance still cover them if they undertook a dangerous rescue mission of this kind, beyond the terms of their employment contract? Might they even face financial penalties, or loss of employment, for neglecting their contracted task of protecting the food aid in order to carry out the rescue operation?

There are also potential legal and ethical considerations here. While it might, on the face of it, be laudable if the contractors did launch a rescue mission, what would their legal and ethical position be if, say, one or more innocent bystanders were killed in the process? While in this scenario the contractors can be assumed to have a legal and moral right to use force in self-defence, and while defence of others is a legitimate extension of the right to self-defence, there is at least a question mark over whether launching a rescue operation that could reasonably be expected to result in an intense firefight would be considered to fall legitimately under the extended case of self-defence.

Then there's the question of capability. While some armed security contractors are highly trained former members of Western military forces, many are not; the quality of the contractors in any particular situation will depend largely on market forces. And even if we assume that all the members of Team Leader Jones' security team are individually well trained, the effectiveness of a military unit is more than simply the sum of the individual capabilities of its members. A team of security guards may simply not be able to succeed in circumstances where the tactical environment shifts rapidly 'up' the operational spectrum.

It's clear, then, that there would be significant disincentives for contractors to conduct a rescue operation in this case that go beyond the challenges the Marines would face in like circumstances. That's not to say we should assume that contractors wouldn't choose to conduct the rescue; there have been examples of contractors doing similar things in the recent wars in Iraq and Afghanistan. A recent example is the case of the four ex-Gurkha contractors who were awarded the Queen's Gallantry Medal in 2014 for actions taken to save the lives of members of the British Council in Kabul in 2011.[10] But what about the job of interposing themselves between rival militia groups? There seems little reason to think the contractors would take it upon themselves to undertake *that* task. Ensuring the strategic success of the overall operation is literally not their business.

This is clearly a significant limitation, and, under the wrong circumstances, one with potentially significant strategic consequences. In part, though, it arises because we've described the contractors in the scenario in a certain way: as a small team with a limited contractual mandate. But many of the problems described here would fall away if our fictional contractors were part of a much larger team engaged on a much broader contract. Consider, for example, the case of EO in Angola and Sierra Leone. For them strategic success *was* their business, and they designed their force element to have the capability to

---

10  See Clare Sambrook, 'G4S private army of Gurkhas wins medals for gallantry in Kabul', 3 September 2014, OpenDemocracyUK. Available at www.opendemocracy.net/ourkingdom/clare-sambrook/g4s-private-army-of-gurkhas-wins-medals-for-gallantry-in-kabul, accessed on 23 May 2017.

address all the threats they could foreseeably face in-theatre. Furthermore, they had, as one of us has argued elsewhere,[11] the moral right to engage in these conflicts, and arguably the legal right as well.

Admittedly, though, high-end contractor-led operations like those conducted by EO are likely to be very rare indeed, so in most cases of contractors engaged in zones of armed conflict we will need to accept that their ability to respond with agility to the fluid and complex operational environments that General Krulak warns us about will be limited by contractual, legal and ethical, and capabilities constraints. It is worth pointing out, though, that these sorts of limitations are not unique to contractors. As recent coalition operations in Afghanistan and elsewhere have highlighted, coalition allied forces often come with caveats of varying severity, which limit their ability to be employed in, or respond effectively to, fluid and complex operational environments. These caveats are a frustration for operational planners, but are a fact of life, and do not (usually) nullify the value of the allied forces concerned. Likewise, it is important for force planners to understand the limitations associated with the contracted personnel under their purview, and then to work around those limitations to make best use of the capabilities that the contractors can provide.

## Theme 2: Strategic success will sometimes hinge on tactical decisions taken at the lowest level

A defining feature of Krulak's thesis in the 'three block war' is the role played by the tactical environment in shaping strategic outcomes. Krulak stresses the role that tactical commanders will play by underlining the independent and, at times, entirely autonomous decision-making that junior commanders will be expected to employ under conditions of extreme duress. The crucible of Krulak's vision of future junior leaders in the Marine Corps is the implementation, cultivation and constant revision of an institutional culture that reflects the current and future threat environment in which these junior leaders will be deployed. The hallmarks of this institutional culture are, from Krulak's (1999) perspective:

- Building junior leaders with the mental agility and toughness to effectively navigate moral challenges and quandaries in the operational theatre

---

11   Deane-Peter Baker (2010), *Just Warriors Inc.: the ethics of privatized force* (London: Continuum).

- A deep commitment to professionalism
- The mantra of 'freedom to fail' as opposed to a 'zero-defects mentality', which encourages junior leaders to make, rather than avoid, key decisions
- Balancing strict accountability to the chain of command with an avoidance of micro-managing junior leaders in conflict zones.

What Krulak is emphasising here is the merging of mission orders with the commander's intent. Not only must junior leaders have set mission parameters and objectives, but they must also be aware of the broader aims to which their specific mission profile will be contributing. In effect, synergy in the command structure will form the axis around which the validity and impact of tactical decisions will be determined.

The question to ask, then, is whether contractors are able to replicate this highly synergistic institutional command culture. Past experiences in Sierra Leone, Iraq and Afghanistan could arguably be said to deliver a resounding 'No!' in response to this question. But is this a result of the essential nature of contractors and their contractual obligations vis-à-vis strategic outcomes, or is it a matter of contingent associated elements such as coordination, interoperability and structural alignment of all role players to achieve unity of effort? In Sierra Leone, EO achieved a noteworthy degree of tactical success against RUF rebels by employing tactics that emphasised coordination, communication and unity of effort. Underlying this example is the fact that EO operated independently without having to align their objectives with other 'blue forces' in the operational theatre. In Iraq, contractors and the military had a dislocated relationship, with very little coordination between tactical and strategic objectives. The friction caused by this lack of interoperability and command and control has tarnished the role contractors play in the tactical environment and contributed to the perception that contractors have generally been considered a liability to the strategic goal in volatile environments.

Whether or not contractors can display the kind of low-level initiative that Krulak is seeking will depend largely on the background of the individual contractors concerned. Certainly, the looser command structure inherent in a commercial organisation gives scope for this flexibility, where the human resources are up to the task. Companies such as MPRI, DynCorp, Aegis, Triple Canopy and Olive Group are known to employ a large workforce of former special operations personnel, all of whom have varying degrees of operational experience. These personnel have been trained and nurtured within military organisations that reflect the kind of command culture that Krulak was lobbying for. There is no particular reason to think that these 'habits of a lifetime' simply evaporate when the individual concerned takes off their uniform and takes up a commercial contract.

Krulak's notion of allowing junior leaders the 'freedom to fail' in order to foster the space to succeed does, however, pose a significant problem when applied to contractors. What is perceived as tactical agility for uniformed personnel is likely to be viewed as 'cowboy' behaviour when exhibited by contractors. Contractually, a failure to perform and meet the obligations and expectations of the contractual agreement has, at its core, financial and market implications for PMSCs. Punitive claims for non-performance and a damaged market profile resulting in less confidence in the company are just some of the effects 'freedom to fail' may have on a PMSC. Legally, the line of accountability may create further implications, particularly since the notion of accountability is one of the core arguments against the employment of PMSC personnel in conflict zones. In the US Marine Corps, the Uniform Code of Military Justice legislates and referees the actions of all service personnel and illuminates a clear line of command accountability when failures to perform duty occur. With PMSCs, no unifying legislative tool exists at present despite recent international attempts to clearly demarcate lines of command accountability.[12]

The minimisation of micro-management in Krulak's appraisal of the strategic corporal may also present further challenges to the use of contractors in scenarios similar to Krulak's fictional operation, particularly given the current levels of concern about a perceived lack of accountability for contractors, which seems to lean towards greater, rather than less, direct oversight of contractor operations. This liability, however, should not necessarily be couched as an inherent challenge posed by PMSCs. Rather, it is a challenge that could be overcome with a concerted drive to accommodate PMSC activities and objectives within the broader scope of an operation. Given the reliance on their services, especially from the US, their presence in the operational theatre is an expectation and should thus form part, arguably an integral

---

12   The Montreux Doctrine is an example of the recent international attempts to align PMSCs with a transparent and functional set of legislative principles and rules of use.

part, of the commander's appreciation of the threat environment, the disposition of forces and the projected mission profiles that the commander will likely have to plan for. In Krulak's scenario, contractors would then have the ability to make decisions under the mantle of the commander's intent and the mission-specific objectives. Their situational understanding would be enhanced and they possibly would not, as was the case in Iraq, operate in a tactical vacuum.

## Theme 3: Operations will be conducted far from the flagpole

General Krulak's fictional scenario is one in which available forces are, of necessity, deployed in small and widely distributed units across the theatre of operations. Such distributed operations unavoidably loosen the control and direct oversight that senior leaders have over their subordinate forces, thereby not only shifting the centre of gravity for operational decision-making down the chain of command, but also pushing greater responsibility for ensuring the appropriate behaviour of deployed troops down to junior leaders. The traditional disciplinary and mentoring role played by, for example, the unit's command sergeant major or regimental sergeant major, is significantly eroded during distributed operations.

At the same time, distributed operations also complicate the ability of different units to reinforce or support one another. While this can be mitigated to some degree by airmobile or ground-based rapid response forces, as the Black Hawk Down battle in Mogadishu in 1993 illustrates, airmobile forces can be particularly vulnerable in urban and peri-urban environments, and ground-based response forces will often face difficulty in responding rapidly in such operations. Similarly, the potential of close air support and artillery support is significantly undermined by the environment, particularly because of the considerable danger of causing non-combatant casualties.

These factors mean that where small units find themselves operating far from the flagpole, these units will need to be both highly disciplined and have the inherent capability to effectively face a wide range of opponents and circumstances for sufficient time to allow support to arrive. While there is an aspect of the latter requirement that is dependent on weaponry and other technical capabilities, the strongest implication, and the one that Krulak emphasises, is that the calibre and training of the men and women deployed in these environments—particularly, but not only, junior leaders—is of paramount importance.

What are the potential implications of having contractors operating in distributed operations of this kind? One of the major concerns that has been expressed about the employment of contractors in conflict environments is that of control and accountability; what is to stop contractors, for example, taking advantage of the vulnerable state of the non-combatants that they will encounter in these environments? Much of the literature in this regard has focused on problems with the legal frameworks that apply to contractors, which, it is argued, make it far more difficult to ensure that contractors are accountable for their behaviour in these lawless environs. One of us has argued elsewhere that while this is true (and was a particularly acute problem during the US-led war in Iraq), legal regimes are beginning to catch up, and there is no intrinsic reason why contractors should not be legally accountable for their behaviour in conflict zones in similar ways to uniformed personnel.[13] Certainly, it is critical that contractors only be allowed in conflict zones where their legal rights and responsibilities are clear and enforceable, both for their own protection and the protection of those around them.

More challenging, though, is the hard-to-define, but clearly important, issue of unit discipline. This is not simply reducible to members of a unit knowing that they will be held legally accountable for their behaviour, but instead goes well beyond that to being a matter of unit culture. In a unit such as Corporal Hernandez's platoon of Marines, each member of the platoon will have become accustomed to following orders in accordance with the practice and culture of the US Marine Corps, and Corporal Hernandez's authority will be undisputed. In a team of contractors, however, these factors are far less certain. While the contractors under Team Leader Jones may well have significant military experience, they will likely have come from different units with different military cultures, and more importantly there is far less likely to be an institutional culture within the company to which they have been contracted that is anything like as powerful as that of the Marine Corps. Likewise, the authority that Team Leader Jones has is likely to carry significantly less weight than the stripes on Corporal Hernandez's arm.

The issue of contractors behaving appropriately in distributed environments is, then, clearly a serious one, and one with potential strategic consequences. That said, we should not fall into the trap of thinking that this is a challenge

---

13   Baker, *Just Warriors Inc.*

that is unique to contractors. Unit discipline and even legal accountability in practice differs also between different military forces around the world. We can imagine that some of the units deployed as part of the RMNF in Krulak's scenario might present the same sort of challenge in this regard, should the US choose to operate in coalition with the RMNF. In fact, it may turn out that contractors are easier to keep accountable than wayward or ill-disciplined units of coalition armed forces, given that contractors have little to no weight at the level of international politics.

Something similar is true of the capability challenge. While a similar-sized team of contractors will likely not be as capable as, say, US Marines, they may well be as capable as or even more capable than coalition or local allies. There have been cases where contractors have been able to respond more quickly and effectively than the US military. In April 2004, for example, a group of eight Blackwater contractors, together with four US Army military police and a Marine gunner, fought off an attack by hundreds of Iraqi militia on the US government's headquarters in Najaf, Iraq. As their ammunition supplies reached critical levels, and with a badly wounded Marine in their midst, it was a Blackwater helicopter that provided ammunition resupply and evacuated the wounded Marine, well before US military forces were in a position to offer support.

The nature of the distributed operations that form the backdrop to Krulak's 'three block war' notion clearly presents both an accountability challenge and a capability challenge that must be considered when the decision is made to employ (or allow) contractors in such operations. Whether or not the strategic risk is worthwhile must be evaluated in the context of the specifics of the operation and the contractors concerned. The risk cannot be overlooked, but nor does it necessarily mean that under the right circumstances contractors cannot be a viable and valuable force-multiplier.

## Theme 4: **The omnipresent media**

The challenge of the 'mercenary moniker' in this theme underscores the major obstacle when replacing Corporal Hernandez with contractors. It is clear that in most media coverage military forces benefit from an assumption of legitimacy while contractors are usually viewed through a suspicious and even hostile lens. It is a truism that media reporting impacts, to a substantial degree, on the manner in which society digests events, and the selectivity of issues on which the public chooses to focus is often derived from media attention on a specific event or process. In the case of the Blackwater ambush in Fallujah, the media focused its analysis on questioning the role of the contractors and what authority or legitimacy these civilians had in a conflict zone. The Nisour Square incident, which involved Blackwater personnel again, was framed by the media as an event that underscored the lack of accountability and transparency these entities had. The core message derived from media attention on the role of contractors in Iraq was that of unaccountable and wayward actors that impeded strategic outcomes and destabilised an already volatile operational climate.

Given that Krulak's fictional scenario takes place in Africa, it's worth considering the specific challenge of strategic communication for missions involving contractors in this area of operations. The bleak history of mercenaries in Africa is a constant hindrance to characterising current contractor operations on the continent, even where on any objective basis it is clear that the contractors are playing a legitimate role. It is fair to suggest that any journalistic report on contractors involved in an operation like Operation Absolute Agility would be prefaced by an account of mercenary involvement in the Congo (1960s), the Biafra War (1967–1970), the abortive coup in the Seychelles (1978), Angola (1993–1995), Sierra Leone (1995), and Equatorial Guinea (2004). In a humanitarian context, such as the one described in Krulak's fictional operation, contractors could well be portrayed negatively by the media since their presence may not be clearly articulated, their role not defined and their objective obscure. This need not be the case, however, and depends in significant part on how media relations are handled. For example, the role of MPRI,[14] contracted by the US Department of State to provide training to Ugandan military forces operating in Somalia has been well documented since 2007. MPRI contractors have support from Marine Corps personnel to assist in training and therefore could arguably derive legitimacy of presence through this relationship. Yet, the *Washington Post* reported in 2012 that, although some journalists were allowed access to US and Ugandan military personnel, no interaction with the MPRI contractors was sanctioned.[15]

---

14  Military Professional Resources Incorporated is a subsidiary company of L-3 Communications.
15  Craig Whitlock, 'US trains African soldiers for Somalia mission', *The Washington Post*, 13 May 2012.

Whether this interaction between contractors and the media may have compromised contractual obligations has yet to be determined; however, it is reasonable to assume that if the media is not given access to contractors, there will be little motivation for them to amend their generally negative account of the sector.

The relationship between military contractors and the media in Africa has yet to be fully articulated through in-depth research. What is relevant to this particular theme is the challenge of the 'mercenary moniker' as an overarching characterisation of contractors in Africa. While this is a contingent fact, and one that may change over time, it represents a significant strategic risk factor that must be taken into consideration when decision-makers weigh up whether or not to employ contractors in operations on African soil. More generally, while there may be less historical baggage involved in contractor operations elsewhere on the globe, the fact remains that the media maintains a generally jaundiced view of contractors that must be considered to be of potentially strategic importance.

## The contractor as strategic enabler

Thus far we have focused on the potential strategic challenges of employing armed contractors in circumstances similar to those faced by the Marines in General Krulak's fictional scenario. But to stop there would be to overlook the most strategically significant possible use of contractors in that scenario. In Operation Absolute Agility, the deployment of the Marine Expeditionary Unit is linked, directly, to the inefficiency of the RMNF. Not only had the RMNF been unable to decrease hostilities and protect humanitarian relief columns, but they had also been targets of numerous ambushes and sniper fire. It was this failure that led to the deployment of the Marines; but what if that had not been necessary? Clearly, if the RMNF had been able to address the situation themselves, it would have been a strategically optimal outcome. As implied in Krulak's account, the failure of the RMNF to adequately fulfil its operational mandate resulted from a lack of capability. With this in mind, we conclude this chapter by briefly examining what roles contractors could undertake as strategic enablers to less-capable military forces.

The use of contractors to augment, support, train and advise military forces is not a new phenomenon, though it was used on a far wider scale than ever before in the wars in Iraq and Afghanistan. Lately, and particularly since the formation of AFRICOM in 2007, Africa has emerged as a large market for this type of contractor utilisation. Liberia, Benin, Nigeria, Ethiopia, Ghana, Kenya, Senegal, Somalia and Uganda are recent customers of this relatively new type of commercialised defence relationship. Prior to being outsourced to the private sector, US 'train and equip' programmes staffed by either the US Department of Defence (DoD) or the US State Department were criticised for their use of generic blueprints relating to tactics, procedures, doctrine and equipment in situations that often demand a tailored force structure/design solution. Contractors, it is argued, are able to avoid this pitfall because they are not bound to bureaucratic structures, and are therefore allowed the freedom of innovative thought.[16] Innovation in this setting enables contractors to operate outside rigid bureaucratic guidelines by tailoring solutions to reflect the specific requirements of a client. This was the case in Liberia, with MPRI designing a military structure that mirrored the contextual limitations of manpower, capability, doctrine and equipment.

An additional area emphasised by proponents of contractors as proxy capability providers is that of logistics. Degraded, and in some instances nonexistent, functional logistics support is a common capability limitation of African forces. The maintenance and sustainment of in-house logistic capabilities for militaries, particularly in developing countries, is prohibitively expensive. Consequently, many humanitarian and peacekeeping operations suffer from inadequate logistics to support security operations. Contractors argue that their flexibility and responsiveness to market needs enable them to respond swiftly to urgent requirements for operational support. For example, in 2006, all 18 United Nations (UN) peacekeeping missions under way made use of contractors for logistics.[17] The immediate impact of this outsourcing reduced the need for countries such as the US, the UK and France to provide manpower to operations that had no direct causal link to national interests. As Peter Gantz of Refugees International has opined, 'If nations with first-class militaries refuse to put their troops in harm's way in remote locations, and if the UN is saddled with troops from developing nations that are not

---

16   Sean McFate, 'Outsourcing the making of militaries: DynCorp International as a sovereign agent', *Review of African Political Economy* 35, 118 (2008), 645–654.
17   Eric George (2011), 'The market for peace', in Sabelo Gumedze (ed), *From market for force to market for peace: private military and security companies in peacekeeping operations*, ISS Monograph 183, 21.

up to the task, then perhaps the UN should hire the private sector to save the day'.[18] Contractors can fill a critical capability vacuum. They present a workable alternative, from a strategic view, to enabling local and regional forces to address African conflicts, thus avoiding the significant strategic danger involved in putting Western boots on the ground. Furthermore, contractors in this role can have the strategic effect of expanding overall capability, an important consideration given the overall reduction in the size of Western military forces. As Theresa Whelan, former US Deputy Assistant Secretary of Defense for African Affairs, explained:

> [W]e wanted to support operations in Africa, however we realized that our forces were tied down elsewhere around the globe and they might not be available for [the] long-term deployments ... Consequently, contractors began to play a larger and larger role particularly in the logistical support of subregional peace operations.[19]

It must be said that the potential value of contractors as strategic enablers is not without potential challenges. Some analysts have expressed concerns that an increased reliance on these entities may generate a broader market for force in conflict environments that could attract unscrupulous and unaccountable PMSCs. In Liberia, MPRI operated in tandem with the US Department of State and thus possessed institutional legitimacy as a lawful agent of the state. However, the involvement of third parties, such as NGOs hiring contractors for protection and even training services, may overload the operational space of the conflict and exacerbate coordination between all parties working towards the end or cessation of hostilities.

Ultimately, however, the capabilities offered by contractors offer a viable alternative means of building capacity in developing militaries, thereby potentially decreasing the necessity of countries such as the US deploying troops to messy and potentially hostile conflict zones such as the one described by Krulak.

---

18  Deborah Avant (2005), *The market for force: the consequences of privatizing security* (Cambridge: Cambridge University Press), 238.
19  George, 'The Market for Peace', 23.

## Conclusion

The hypothetical exercise of imagining contractors engaged in circumstances similar to those described by General Krulak in his influential article on the 'strategic corporal' has been a useful, albeit necessarily incomplete one. It has highlighted a range of potential strategic risks in employing contractors in such environments, though none of them, it seems to us, so severe that they would undermine totally the potential value added by contractors in such circumstances. What is clear, though, is that planners must be aware of these risks, and work to hedge against them. What has also emerged is the very significant strategic potential of contractors employed as force enablers for local and regional forces in Africa and elsewhere. The simple fact is that contractors are a reality of today's conflicts, and the better we understand the potential implications of that fact for strategic success or failure, the better we will be able to plan for optimal outcomes.

# 5

# The Strategic Civilian: Challenges for Non-Combatants in 21st-century Warfare[1]

## *Alan Ryan*[2]

THE NOTION OF THE 'strategic corporal' in conflict is a necessary but not sufficient concept. This idea recognises what we have long known. Effective operational outcomes rely on having good leaders at every level who know what they are doing. Military leadership, whether it is of an army or an infantry section, is something that we recognise easily. However, we must recognise and make better preparations for the fact that we are already deploying civilians into conditions of modern warfare. These complex operations range from counterinsurgency, stabilisation and reconstruction to peacebuilding, where even relatively junior officials and non-government organisation representatives are making decisions with long-term strategic ramifications.

Even short of conflict, overseas deployments will involve military and civilians working together in humanitarian relief and disaster response. Natural disasters are often as politicised as warfare, the main distinction being that while the military will lead in combat operations, in virtually every other circumstance the military only supports the civil lead. Yet while our analysis of military leadership requirements is highly developed, our appreciation of

---

1   This chapter was previously published as a paper in *Small Wars Journal*. The editors would like to thank *Small Wars Journal* for permission to republish the paper.
2   Disclaimer: the views expressed are the author's and not necessarily those of the Department of Defence. The Commonwealth of Australia will not be legally responsible in contract, tort or otherwise for any statement made in this publication.

the civilian leadership requirements for complex operations hardly exists. We need to develop a concept of the 'strategic civilian'.

The strategic civilian is the natural corollary to the strategic corporal. Military forces may provide some life-saving humanitarian assistance, but they are not aid agencies. They may be called on to mediate at the local level to prevent conflict, but they cannot broker lasting agreements. They will fight, and only the military can legitimately deliver military force. However, only civilians can deliver civilian capabilities. And only civilian police can conduct civilian policing.

Military solutions, even those employing the most enlightened of directive command styles, still draw on a hierarchy based on military command structures. Yet when you admit the need for civilians, you are drawn to alternative mission approaches. The model of mission leadership in highly diverse, politicised United Nations (UN) operations provides better guidance as to the role of civilians in future operations than current conventional military operations do. Civilians are untidy, messy characters. Often the most useful of them will possess little formal authority.

So, increasingly, we are going to have to accept the 'integrated mission' approach, which is based more on creating a shared vision as to the strategic objectives of all actors at the country level. They are based on the creation of a unified leadership, containing a mix of civil, military and police capabilities. The structure of the mission will be determined more by function than bureaucratic logic. Communication and shared information becomes the common language as multiple actors perform their different roles and mandates in a spirit of teamwork rather than tight control. All this requires a different language of civilian leadership.[3]

Modern warfare requires more adaptive and flexible approaches to leadership than were possible or realistic in industrial-age wars. Often leaders have to proceed armed with little formal authority, and consequently decision-making and key points of influence are often not tied to senior positions within organisations. In contemporary warfare that is fought 'among the people', military force is only one of the tools of the contending parties. As

---

3    International Forum for the Challenges of Peace Operations (2010), *Considerations for mission leadership in United Nations peacekeeping operations* (Stockholm: Challenges Forum Partnership/Folke Bernadotte Academy), 19.

the current US Joint Doctrine on counterinsurgency operations (COIN) states:

> *It is always preferable for civilians to lead the overall COIN effort, in addition to performing traditionally civilian tasks. Even where civilians' capability and capacity do not match their expertise, they should lead in the areas of governance, economics, rule of law, etc. as policy guides and decision makers who define the role the military should and will play to support the effort.*[4]

Contemporary armed conflict involves a far greater range of participants than just combatants. The leadership of junior military leaders in conditions of complex operations can only achieve so much. No military leader, however accomplished, will have all the skill-sets required to do all the tasks required of them. Civilian leaders at every level have roles to play in managing confrontation, mitigating the effects of violence and shaping the ultimate outcomes.[5] It is sufficient that strategic corporals make as good decisions as they can when they are put on the spot. But they do not do this in a civilian-free environment. In contemporary warfare among the people, the strategic corporal will deal with, and defer to, a wide range of civilian counterparts.

President Obama made this clear in his speech to the Commencement Ceremony at West Point in May 2014 when he told America's future junior military leaders that they were 'part of a team that extends beyond your units or even our Armed Forces, for in the course of your service you will work as a team with diplomats and development experts. You'll get to know allies and train partners.'[6] He famously stated that 'military action cannot be the only—or even primary—component of our leadership in every instance.

---

4   Joint Chiefs of Staff (2013), *Counterinsurgency*, Joint Publication 3-24, 22 November 2013, A-13 (my emphasis).
5   Rupert Smith (2005), *The utility of force: the art of war in the modern world* (London: Allen Lane).
6   Office of the White House Press Secretary (2015), 'Remarks by the President at the Academy Commencement Ceremony', US Military Academy-West Point, West Point, New York, 28 May 2015. Available at obamawhitehouse.archives.gov/the-press-office/2014/05/28/remarks-president-united-states-military-academy-commencement-ceremony, accessed on 28 April 2017.

Just because we have the best hammer does not mean that every problem is a nail.' In the operations that we mount today, the military do not and cannot perform all the tasks necessary to achieve strategic objectives, much less assure lasting peace. They are the hammer; civilians and police provide a full range of other tools. We need to better understand the role of those other tools of state policy and prepare them better for the roles that they are already being given.

## Strategic corporal and strategic civilian: who are these young people?

General Charles Krulak's short article 'The strategic corporal: leadership in the three block war', in the January 1999 edition of the *Marine Corps Gazette*, posed a vision that has shaped the way we think about our military over the past fifteen years.[7] It is not, perhaps, as new an idea as we might think. My well-thumbed copy of Robert A Heinlein's 1959 science fiction classic *Starship Troopers* was bought at the Marine Corps Bookshop in Quantico, where it has long been a best-seller. Its description of the modern soldier easily anticipates Krulak's vision:

> 'Got any idea what it takes to make a soldier?' 'No', I admitted. 'Most people think that all it takes is two hands and two feet and a stupid mind. Maybe so, for cannon fodder. Possibly that was all that Julius Caesar required. But a private soldier today is a specialist so highly skilled that he would rate "master" in any other trade ...'[8]

The point is unarguable; in the circumstances of contemporary complex operations we expect that modern soldiers may be required to engage in direct-fire battle, be ready to negotiate and mediate with warring parties, and be able to offer humanitarian assistance simultaneously. What we expect and what is realistic is perhaps not the same thing. While the idea of the strategic corporal has done good service, it is worth critically examining why

---

7   Charles C Krulak, 'The strategic corporal: leadership in the three block war', *Marine Corps Gazette* 83, 1 (January 1999), 18–23. Available at www.au.af.mil/au/awc/awcgate/usmc/strategic_corporal.htm, accessed on 11 April 2017.
8   Robert A Heinlein (1987 [1959]), *Starship troopers* (New York: Ace Books), 27.

the Commandant of the US Marine Corps felt the need to make this case. It is also time perhaps to roll back our expectations of our deployed military and ask when civilians should properly be expected to undertake civilian tasks.

It is no reflection on the notion of the 'strategic corporal' to identify an element of special pleading in Krulak's formulation. In the never-ending struggle to survive as a distinct service, the Marines have always sought to define what makes them 'special'. This is not unhealthy, nor does it detract from Krulak's point. Marines are the '911' force of the US. Their soldiers are very likely to find themselves positioned at the critical point in any evolving crisis. Other forces from developed states, including Australia's, quickly latched on to the point. We have high expectations of our military and see them as much more than warfighters. They have become the 'master tradesmen' of modern conflict and we expect them to be able to adapt to operations ranging from peacekeeping to humanitarian assistance and disaster relief—often all at the same time.

Krulak's justification of the strategic corporal was founded on his appreciation of the demands of leadership in the 'three block war'. In circumstances short of major interstate war (which is to say almost every conflict), those who find themselves in the field must deal with confused circumstances and competing demands. They must have the skills, training and intellectual tools to be able to 'read' a situation and to react appropriately. Krulak's article was a plea for an 'institutional commitment to lifetime professional development' to 'prepare Marines for the complex, high stakes asymmetrical battlefield'.[9]

The notion of the 'strategic corporal' is founded on the expectation that young leaders (often very young: section or squad leaders are generally in their early twenties) will make decisions and take actions that may have strategic ramifications. It implies that leadership training at junior levels needs to be high. This requirement means that we need to invest in them to give them the skills, knowledge and virtual experience so that when they are put on the spot they do the right thing. It is not perhaps for every military, but militaries that place small specialist units at the decisive point of action require that they exercise precision, discretion and discrimination. They are not deployed just to fight, but to play a part in creating circumstances where fighting is no longer required. This is where the corporal's civilian counterpart becomes important.

---

9   Krulak, 'The strategic corporal', 4/5.

If the truth be told, we have always had need of junior leaders, both military and civilian, with a strategic perspective. A young decurion occupying Judea two millennia ago would face critical operational decisions, or a twenty-something-year-old member of the British Imperial Indian Civil Service in India could have authority over vast populations and responsibility for decisions that rebounded down the generations.[10] It is just that now, with 24/7 news cycles, the ubiquity of social media and the omnipresent impact of a global commentariat (some of whose members are ill-informed and often malicious), junior decision-makers will literally feel the weight of the world on their shoulders.

Australia's operational experience has borne out these observations. Writing about his experience of the tense early days of the International Force for East Timor (INTERFET) in 1999, General Peter Cosgrove wrote:

> *In my day as a junior leader, my decisions had an immediate impact on my troops and on the enemy. In today's military operations the decisions of junior leaders still have those immediate impacts, but modern telecommunications can also magnify every incident, put every incident under a media microscope, and send descriptions and images of every incident instantly around the world for scores of experts and commentators to interpret for millions of viewers and listeners.*
>
> *Thus the decisions of junior leaders and the actions of their small teams can influence the course of international affairs.*[11]

The concept of the 'strategic corporal' is thus a potent metaphor that can be used to justify investment in education, training, and the whole notion of military expeditionary capability as a tool of national power. It has played a positive function in shaping both military and civil awareness of the indis-

---

10   Philip Mason (1954), *The guardians*, Volume 2 of *The men who ruled India* (New York: St Martin's Press). This magisterial book describes how young university graduates exercised civilian control over enormous provinces with few resources. Whether in the imperial context or in contemporary overseas crisis response and development, older people tend to stay at home. It is the young and ambitious who take on the rigours of overseas operations—with all the responsibilities that they entail.

11   Peter Cosgrove, 'The night our boys stared down the barrel', *The Age*, 21 June 2000, 15.

pensable role played by modern armed forces and in ensuring that we train and equip these forces to carry out their missions.

However, the concept has its limits. We should not let it caricature itself like the picklehaube-clad Colonel Von Holstein in the classic 1965 film *Those Magnificent Men in their Flying Machines* who expostulated that 'There is nothing a German officer cannot do!' In a thoughtful essay in the *Canadian Military Journal*, Walter Dorn and Michael Varey warn: 'It is doubtful that it is even possible to carry out peacekeeping and play a humanitarian role while, at the same time, fighting a war against a determined enemy who can readily threaten or sabotage such efforts'.[12] They conclude:

> *Personnel* cannot *and* should not *be expected to serve as humanitarian workers, peacekeepers, and warfighters all at the same time, and within a small area. Combat should be separated as much as possible from other functions, which should, preferably be done by distinct organizations, including UN agencies, police, and peacekeepers.*[13]

There is a very real danger that, by focusing on the much-needed attributes of the strategic corporal, we follow this with an unrealistic expectation of what our junior military leaders *can* and *should* do. It is in a very real sense a trope, a rhetorical device that counterpoises 'strategic' and 'corporal' to effect. We should not take it to mean that these highly trained warriors should supplant their civilian counterparts, but rather that at times their functions may complement or supplement civilian roles.

Current US counterinsurgency joint doctrine captures the fact that the military may be called upon to complement civilian skill-sets without supplanting them. Yet at the same time the doctrine fails to capture the implications of the mismatch between the availability of military resources and the shortfall in civilian capability. A virtue of military forces is their self-sufficiency and robustness. A military organisation can sustain itself within a violent conflict, providing a degree of protection to its members while still continuing to provide services to support its members and conduct its mission. No civilian

---

12   A Walter Dorn and Michael Varey, 'The rise and demise of the "three block war"', *Canadian Military Journal* 10, 1 (2009), 42.
13   Dorn and Varey, op cit, 44.

agency can do that. Civilian agencies may be supremely efficient at doing their civil job, but in warfare they generally depend upon the military for protection. These observations suggest that we need to re-examine the division of labor in conflict and admit a greater role for civilian and police participants. As the US joint doctrine concludes:

> *Long-term security cannot be imposed by military force alone; it requires an integrated, balanced application of effort by all participants with the goal of supporting the local populace and achieving legitimacy for the HN (Host Nation) government. Military forces can perform civilian tasks but often not as well as civilian agencies with people trained in those skills. Further, military forces performing civilian tasks are not performing military tasks. Diversion from those tasks should be temporary and only taken to address urgent circumstances ... Military forces should be aware that putting a military face on economics, politics, rule of law, etc, may do more harm than good in certain situations.*[14]

What has made the notion of the 'strategic corporal' so popular is how recognisable it is. We can all envision the young military leader on the frontline confronted with a range of invidious choices, most of which well exceed their pay grade. Many of us might empathise, having been in similar positions ourselves. However, unless you have actually been present during a conflict as a civilian, and a junior one at that, it is perhaps less easy to imagine what civilians do, and what in modern conflict they are increasingly being called upon to do.

## Civilian actors: government, international and non-government

The focus of this chapter is on government employees, but it is shortsighted to ignore the role played by non-government actors. When we envision the junior leader whose decisions have strategic consequences, we tend to think of representatives of the state. Equally decisive roles in modern conflict are being

---

14  Joint Chiefs of Staff, *Counterinsurgency*, A-14.

performed by junior UN officials, employees of international organisations and humanitarian actors from non-government organisations. Far too many texts on modern warfare merely pay lip service to the existence of non-state civilian actors. They are strategic actors in their own right and are often the key to the resolution of the conflict.

However, for a government official, considering how to deal with 'other people's civilians' is a topic in itself. Before they can be effective in promoting integrated missions, government agencies need to develop a more rigorous conception of the challenges involved in preparing and deploying their own civilians. They (and I really mean we) must build more robust frameworks to ensure that the employment of civilians on operations is effective.

At the same time, many civilian organisations will reject the notion that they are even employed on 'operations'. It is a fair point. They are certainly not deployed on 'military operations', but very often they find themselves as civilians accompanying the military, often embedded for security, transport and logistics. Yet they still need to maintain some distance from the military so that they can perform their civilian functions separate from combat operations.

International organisations like the International Committee of the Red Cross (ICRC) have long been present in warfare, their only protection being their independence, impartiality and neutrality. For those military personnel who argue that it is not possible to be neutral in a war, they should remember that it is the ICRC who often alone is able to provide humanitarian assistance to combatants and non-combatants when states are unable to do so. Voluntary non-government organisations and humanitarian relief organisations are present in civil communities before, during and after conflict. They are there because they meet the needs of the situation. They provide leadership and subject-matter expertise. Host nations will have functioning governments, local governments or even just tribal authorities operating during different phases of a conflict. These too are comprised of civilians. We might not be responsible for deploying them, but our personnel will need to be prepared to work with them.

Which civilians governments deploy on operations will vary according to the operation. States will deploy civilian staff into theatres of operations to conduct a range of activities. Diplomats have always had a role in negotiating with coalition partners, host nation governments and sometimes belligerents. In modern warfare, aid and development officials have a role to play because peacebuilding is often reliant on establishing the economic conditions that favour stability and build a constituency of support for a peace dividend.[15] While conflict is still ongoing, civilians from other government agencies can be involved in providing support to governance, security sector reform, constitutional and legal drafting, and the development of functioning systems of government finance.

Increasingly, states are developing specific capability to deploy civilians into crisis contingencies on an emergency, as-required, basis. The demands of contemporary conflict have called for the creation of a surge capability similar to the military reserves. The British were among the first to do so with the Stabilisation Unit, which is a part of the Foreign and Commonwealth Office.[16] The US Department of State maintains a deployable capability within the Bureau of Conflict and Stabilization Operations known as the Civilian Response Corps.[17] Canada maintains the Peace and Stabilization Operations Program (PSOPs) in the Department of Foreign Affairs, Trade and Development to promote a 'whole-of-government effort, using the full range of Canada's military and police as well as other capabilities in integrated responses'.[18]

Australia's counterpart organisation is the Australian Civilian Corps (ACC).[19] The mandate of the ACC is to 'provide Australian specialists, pri-

---

15   Australian Government, Australian Civil-Military Centre (2012), *Partnering for peace: Australia's peacekeeping and peacebuilding experiences in the Autonomous Region of Bougainville in Papua New Guinea, and in Solomon Islands and Timor Leste* (Queanbeyan, NSW: Department of Defence,), 58–60.
16   Stabilisation Unit, Foreign and Commonwealth Office website. Available at www.stabilisationunit.gov.uk/how-to-get-involved/civilian-stabilisation-group.html, accessed on 11 April 2017.
17   Bureau of Conflict and Stabilization Operations, State Department website. Available at www.state.gov/j/cso/, accessed on 11 April 2017.
18   'The Peace and Stabilization Operations Program', Government of Canada. Available at http://international.gc.ca/world-monde/world_issues-enjeux-mondiaux/psop.aspx?, accessed on 29 May 2017; Global Affairs Canada, 'Canada to support Peace Operations', Press release 26 August 2016. Available at http://news.gc.ca/web/article-en.do?nid=1117209, accessed on 29 May 2017.
19   Australian Civilian Corps, Department of Foreign Affairs and Trade website. Available at dfat.gov.au/aid/topics/investment-priorities/building-resilience/acc/Pages/australian-civilian-corps.aspx, accessed on 11 April 2017.

marily to help our neighbours in the Indo-Pacific region, to prevent, prepare for, stabilize and recover from disasters and conflict'. The ACC (and its international counterparts) does not supplant other civilian capability, but bridges the gap between emergency response and long-term disaster-recovery programmes. The ACC maintains a register of civilians who possess expertise in aid coordination, risk reduction, elections support, health administration, gender issues, engineering and law and justice. The ACC, and its international counterparts, are a good start and will merit close study as they bed themselves in. However, they represent a surge capacity. There is an undoubted demand for a reserve of civilian skill-sets that can be rapidly deployed to deal with the 'hump' of operations when there is never enough of anything. However, contemporary operations can last for years and this requires that governments 'normalise' their deployable civilian capability.

## Comprehensive operations

The military are often accused of 'preparing to fight the last war', but, to be fair, the notion of the 'strategic corporal' demonstrates how the military favours adaptability to meet new circumstances. At the same time, the idea of the 'strategic corporal' reflects a very military 'can do' approach. What contemporary operations require is less a focus on what military forces can do, and more a focus on what they should do. Operational planners and military and civilian leaders require a sharper appreciation of the implications of the comprehensive approach if they are to use the right people in the right jobs.

A recurring characteristic of modern complex warfare is that the military struggles to keep the peace, because there is no peace to keep. Intractable conflicts continue because the conditions that favour peace and stability do not exist. Advocating the dramatic expansion of civilian response capacity for complex operations, Terry Pudas and Catherine Theohary noted that, in the absence of adequate civilian response capacity from other agencies, the Department of Defense was 'mobilizing its own civilians'.[20] Yet what was really required were capabilities that could help to rebuild

---

20 Terry J Pudas and Catherine Theohary (2009), 'Reconsidering the Defense Department mission', in Hans Binnendijk and Patrick M Cronin (eds), *Civilian surge: key to complex operations* (Washington, DC: National Defense University Press), 89.

> indigenous institutions, including various types of security forces, correctional facilities, and judicial systems necessary to secure and stabilize the environment; reviving or building the private sector, including encouraging citizen-driven, bottom-up economic activity and constructing necessary infrastructure; and developing representative governmental institutions.[21]

Clearly these tasks are beyond the strategic corporal, and, if we are honest, most generals. They also focus on the reality that long-term peace and stability, not to say prosperity, are dependent on promoting indigenous capability. Civilians drafted in from outside are not going to be able to create conditions within another society. What they can do is to provide the seed stock of civil society at times when it is in short supply. Properly prepared, they will only do so much as to establish the conditions for successful transition to host nation governance. They need to provide restrained, servant leadership, and for this reason it is better that the bulk of civilian post-conflict advisers be junior enough to provide a wealth of assistance without it being seen as an imposed solution. To do these tasks, missions need to apply the comprehensive approach rather than attempt to impose an externally sourced solution.

The notion of a 'comprehensive approach' receives a great deal of lip service in consideration of contemporary operations, but its implications are little understood. Australian defence doctrine defines the comprehensive approach as 'a multinational approach that responds effectively to complex crises by orchestrating, coordinating and de-conflicting military and non-military activities'.[22] It is a broad statement of a desirable objective that remains, as yet, unsupported by much practical advice on how we can do so. In any case, it assumes a division between 'military and non-military activities' that is often difficult to discern.

While it is beyond the scope of this chapter, it is clear that there is a lot more work to be done in clarifying civil–military relations within operations. For example, governments ideally seek to achieve integrated operations where all government agencies achieve unity of effort through strong collaboration.

---

21  Pudas and Theohory, op cit, 71.
22  Australian Defence Force (2012), *Campaigns and operations*, edition 2, Australian Defence Doctrine Publication (ADDP) 3.0, edition 2, 12 July 2012, 2.64.

However, in complex operations that involve a multiplicity of state and non-state actors, this is never going to be easy. Accordingly, the notion of 'comprehensive operations' is about achieving, as a minimum, unity of understanding and an undertaking that, where possible, all operational actors will seek common cause, or at least take steps not to frustrate the efforts of others. In turn, achieving unity of understanding requires a degree of unified political direction.

Within NATO the comprehensive approach has assumed a much larger status, with the Heads of State and Government declaration at the November 2010 Lisbon Summit stating:

> *Our operational experience has taught us that military means, although essential, are not enough on their own to meet the many complex challenges to our security. Both within and outside the Euro-Atlantic area, NATO must work with other actors to contribute to a comprehensive approach that effectively combines political, civilian and military crisis management instruments. Its effective implementation requires all actors to contribute in a concerted effort, based on a shared sense of responsibility, openness and determination, and taking into account their respective strengths, mandates and roles, as well as their decision-making autonomy ... As a general rule, elements of stabilisation and reconstruction are best undertaken by those actors and organisations that have the relevant expertise, mandate, and competence.*[23]

No government does this particularly well, the historical legacy of stove-piped departmental responses have long frustrated concerted efforts across government, much less with other actors. Operational realities now are leading states to the recognition that if they want to be effective then they are going to need to learn more about the comprehensive approach and embed it in their operational responses. This means that we have to move from a concept of warfare founded on military actions to one that sees the military as only one of a comprehensive suite of tools to be used.

---

23  North Atlantic Treaty Organization (2010), *Lisbon Summit Declaration, issued by the Heads of State and Government participating in the meeting of the North Atlantic Council in Lisbon*, 20 November 2010. Available at www.nato.int/cps/en/natolive/official_texts_68828.htm, accessed on 11 April 2017.

## Time-critical aspects of civilian leadership during conflict

If there is one characteristic of modern operations that all field staff—military and civilian—will agree on, it is that in the rapid-reaction cycle of information-age operations, it is no longer possible to learn 'on the job'. Speed of response, a high level of situational awareness and the mental and physical robustness to 'hit the ground running' are essential attributes of civilian staff deployed into conflict zones. As the UN Secretary-General put it in his report *Political Missions* to the General Assembly:

> *The fast-paced environment of peacemaking and peacekeeping initiatives demands that special political missions be agile in responding to changes on the ground. In a peace process, even minor delays could mean missing a unique window of opportunity for a settlement. In post-conflict settings, the window of opportunity closes quickly. Special political missions should be able to deliver promptly in order to make long-term gains in peace consolidation.*[24]

One senior official summarised this reality at a recent conference: 'As an operational success factor, leadership is number one.'[25] So if we are to deploy strategic civilians we need to provide them at least the same level of preparation that we do our soldiers. At present our approach to this is ad hoc, inchoate and muddled.

To prepare our civilians for roles in conflict, we need to match our appreciation of what civilians do with our much better awareness of what soldiers have always done. In a contemporary take on Krulak's vision of war, Emile Simpson, a young former Gurkha officer with three tours of Afghanistan, describes how in contemporary conflict the strategic and tactical have become conflated. Civilians find themselves working on the same issues as their military colleagues:

---

24   United Nations Political Missions (2013), *Report of the Secretary General of the United Nations, 2013*. Available at www.unis.unvienna.org/pdf/0_Regular_Updates/Political_Missions_Report.pdf, accessed on 11 April 2017.

25   The conference was held under the Chatham House Rule.

> *The composition of forces at the tactical level, where civilian diplomats and development advisers, among others, often pursue the same local political goals as their military counterparts, reflects this fusion of the violent and the non-violent.*[26]

Simpson concludes that for military and civilian alike:

> *In contemporary conflicts, however, the tendency is an expansion of the strategic domain. This domain includes, but also goes far beyond, those who have strategic authority ... Relatively junior commanders find themselves making decisions which although nowhere near as significant in scale as 'strategic' decisions made by those with strategic authority, nonetheless have a directly political quality, however insignificant those actions in themselves may be, and so are also, in an alternative sense 'strategic'.*[27]

Simpson's argument is based on the perspective of Afghanistan, and it is a good place to examine the future of warfare. While most government officials sincerely hope that we won't see another operation such as Afghanistan in our future, they probably hope in vain. All the characteristics of contemporary complex operations were present in Afghanistan, and after the 2009 'surge', the sheer diversity of civilian representation put an entirely new character on operations.

In his account of his time as British Ambassador to Kabul, *Cables from Kabul*, Sherard Cowper-Coles paints an amusing picture of the range of institutional cultures represented in his embassy alone. He also provides a warning:

> *Few of the home civil servants had ever worked in an embassy or dealt with the Diplomatic Service, let alone operated in an environment as difficult and dangerous as Afghanistan.*
>
> *Turning such a mixed bag of officers, officials and civilian experts into a real team would be a never-ending challenge, especially as the working pattern*

---

26  Emile Simpson (2012), *War from the ground up: twenty-first century combat as politics* (Oxford: Oxford University Press, Kindle ebook), Introduction.
27  Ibid.

*for most civilian staff of six weeks on, two weeks off, with six or twelve-month tours meant that the turnover was unending.*[28]

In contemporary operations, we know that we need civilians, but we have yet to fully think through the implications of this. We have yet to build operational deployments into civilian career cycles, or develop reward structures that parallel military remuneration and honours systems. We rarely provide government civilians with training for the field that equates to that provided to even the most junior soldier.

Civilians do not undergo 'force preparation' and their training for operations is varied.[29] The agencies responsible for posting them into roles in contemporary conflict must take into account issues of risk (actual and political), oversight and accountability, selection and training, and civil-military relations. In this area at least, the NGO community has taken the initiative. Organisations such as RedR provide a range of high-quality training programmes for both government staff and the NGO community.[30] These programmes are a good start, but still represent a very basic level of preparedness for operational readiness.

Another model of preparation and training is that of the Australian Federal Police (AFP) International Operations Group. AFP personnel complete a two-week training programme to prepare them for deployment overseas. The training emphasises police capacity development, cultural awareness, and teamwork. The training has a field component which covers practical skills, including operating in austere environments, four-wheel driving, navigation and first aid. Participants are exercised in a variety of mission-specific scenario activities. Police also complete UN core pre-deployment training materials and specialised training materials for UN police roles.

---

28  Sherard Cowper-Coles (2011), *Cables from Kabul* (HarperPress, Epub), Chapter 2.
29  This interpretation is contested. Many civilians, including the author, have received pre-deployment training from the military. However, even when a civilian is deployed subject to military jurisdiction, they are not part of 'the force'. Some military dismiss this distinction as hair-splitting, but as we have seen it is important to maintain the distinction between civilian and military roles.
30  RedR Australia, 'About RedR', no date. Available at www.redr.org.au/about-us/about-redr#.VQpH3hscTCw, accessed on 11 April 2017.

From the perspective of due diligence, ministers and officials who are responsible for the deployment of civilians carry a personal level of responsibility for the staff they deploy. This imperative will require that civilian government agencies devote considerable resources to preparing their staff for deployment in the future. The AFP model provides an excellent example of what that preparation might involve.

Current operations require that governments must not leave the preparation of their civilian capability to after operations have commenced. Inevitably, while retaining civilian character, we will need to pre-prepare more of our staff to be posted into crisis contingencies. This is not to suggest that civilians need to emulate military training. But government needs to think more about the security and management of the people we deploy. The preparation they receive may be more in keeping with that which UN staff and NGO staff receive than with military force preparation.

## Conclusion

It is easy to admit the problem of the strategic civilian on operations, but less simple to come up with principles for action. The following reflects some of the lessons that the Australian Civil-Military Centre has derived from broad-ranging consultation with Australian government departments and agencies, international counterparts, international organisations and non-government organisations:

- Complex operations require solutions that recognise complexity. A military response may be necessary, but it is not sufficient. Governments need to be ready and prepared to deploy the full suite of civilian capabilities from the outset of a crisis. A civilian 'surge' late in an operation will not suffice.
- Government, civilian and military personnel need to integrate within a framework that reflects the full spectrum of security, good governance, economic development and social resilience.
- Civilians are not 'second-rate citizens' on operations. If the military always represent the first option, don't be surprised if all you get are military solutions.
- Civilians are not just advisers; they provide operational leadership at every level. Ultimately, most operations are led by a civilian. Success in complex operations relies on the application of adaptive leadership

principles whereby the collective intelligence of all personnel informs the planning and execution of operational solutions.[31]
- Leadership on complex operations should not be confused with authority. Often leadership is more a matter of exerting influence, or exercising relevant expertise at a critical point. This point needs to be explicitly recognised by mission staff and factored into day-to-day operational coordination functions.
- Separation of responsibility between civilians, military and police is healthy. Contrary to some (mis)interpretations of the 'strategic corporal', operational outcomes are not best served by imposing too much responsibility at too junior a level—particularly on junior military personnel.
- Government agencies need to put more effort in assisting their staff to understand the roles and functions of international organisations, non-government organisations and host nation civilians. Civil-military is not a black and white distinction between the military and everybody else.
- Multidisciplinary education, training and exercises are required to prepare civilians, military and police alike for operational employment.

The growth of civilian capability is a good thing and represents an opportunity to do more with operational responses than just apply Band-Aid solutions. We need to appreciate that many committed young people are putting their lives at risk to do the work of the strategic civilian. The distinguished Australian journalist Graeme Dobell captured this in a lecture he gave in 2003 on the topic of Australia's leadership responsibilities in the Pacific. He concluded:

> *To be flippant for a moment, we are taking up as a burden the place everybody else in the world wants to go on holiday. The lucky country lucks out again—we get to do institution building in paradise. We may not be able to get too many of the young adults or the 'young retireds' to do extended time in much of the developing world. But what a pitch in the Pacific—we want you to help save countries only a few hours' flight away,*

---

31   Further explanation of adaptive leadership is found in Ronald Heifetz and Donald Laurie, 'The work of leadership', *Harvard Business Review* 75, 1 (January–February 1997), 124–134.

*that are ... English speaking, that know and understand us but at the same time offer extraordinary riches of history, culture, environment and community ... oh, and by the way you can leave your jumper at home and take your pick of the surfing and the diving.*[32]

The efforts taken by military forces to empower their junior leaders through identifying the role of the strategic corporal serve as a valuable exemplar to civilian agencies. They highlight what could emerge as a critical operational deficiency in the future if we expect civilians to continue to serve within complex situations overseas. Understanding civilian contributions in these circumstances and preparing our people accordingly may well be the key to future operational success.

---

32   Graeme Dobell (2003), 'The South Pacific: policy taboos, popular amnesia and political failure', The Menzies Research Centre Lecture Series: Australian Security in the 21st Century, Canberra, February 2003. Available at web.mit.edu/12.000/www/m2009/teams/students/kennyd/australia.pdf, accessed on 11 April 2017.

# 6

# Protection of Civilians: Challenges for the 'Strategic Corporal' in Peacekeeping Missions

*Siobhán Wills*

IN 1999, GENERAL CHARLES C KRULAK, in his seminal paper 'The strategic corporal: leadership in the three block war', wrote:

> *The inescapable lesson of Somalia and of other recent operations, whether humanitarian assistance, peace-keeping, or traditional warfighting, is that their outcome may hinge on decisions made by small unit leaders, and by actions taken at the lowest level ... Success or failure will rest, increasingly, with the rifleman and with his ability to make the right decision at the right time at the point of contact.*[1]

Undoubtedly the essence of Krulak's argument still holds true. However, in the years since Krulak was writing, the practice of peacekeeping in particular has transformed radically, creating new challenges and undermining some of the perceptions as to the nature of peacekeeping commonly held in the late 1990s. In some of today's missions, war, three block or otherwise, may have little or no bearing on the problems that the mission is faced with since there may be no armed conflict of any type. Moreover, even where missions were originally deployed to assist in keeping peace between parties to an armed conflict, since mission exit plans tend to be more poorly thought-through

---

1   General Charles C Krulak, 'The strategic corporal: leadership in the three block war', *Marines Magazine* (January 1999). Available at www.au.af.mil/au/awc/awcgate/usmc/strategic_corporal.htm, accessed on 11 April 2017.

than mission entrance plans, peacekeepers may find themselves still deployed in the country years, sometimes decades, after the conflict has ended. In these circumstances, the presence of the mission may become an integral part of a web of local interests and power plays, which may create new challenges with regard to missions' responsibilities. Troops may find themselves having to respond not only to fighters in armed groups and 'spoilers', but also to local businessmen, politicians and host state government officials.

Tasks such as assisting in elections, policing public protest marches, securing refugee camps, assessing security risks to civilians, monitoring and protecting against gender-based violence (all of which are commonly mandated in peacetime, post-conflict and ongoing conflict missions) entail legal and administrative responsibilities, particularly in relation to human rights protections. Corporals cannot be expected to take on complex human rights protection issues on their own; but they may still have to respond quickly to a difficult situation involving tasks that should be carried out in accordance with human rights standards. The necessity for an immediate response may be just as urgent as in General Krulak's example of riflemen having to make the right decision at the right time in a conflict context, but the nature of the soldier's obligations may be different. In such situations, it is critical that procedures are in place to ensure that any victim receives appropriate care; that the effects of any improper conduct (whether by mission personnel or someone else) are mitigated; and that effective mechanisms for enabling perpetrators to be held accountable are put in place. This is particularly important where the mission is providing assistance or support to a host state government that has a poor record on human rights protection, or where there are high levels of corruption. Therefore, to be effective, initiative on the part of the 'strategic corporal' to make the right decision at the right time must be supported by a regulatory framework running through the entire command and control structure, a framework that ensures that unexpected incidents, especially those that raise protection or human rights issues, are not dealt with in isolation but receive appropriate follow-up, even where the host state objects.

## The legal responsibilities of UN missions vis-à-vis the host state population

One of the most controversial and rapidly developing areas of potential United Nations (UN) responsibility relates to the question of the relationship between the mission and the host state population. The role of UN peacekeeping has developed within an armed conflict perspective. Although early missions were not expected to engage in hostilities, and peacekeeping rules of engagement limited use of force to self-defence only, the whole peacekeeping framework was premised on a military and armed conflict model. Peacekeeping forces were, and to a large extent still are, drawn from contributing states' defence forces and are trained in the skills that they would need to defend their country; peacekeeping skills were an 'add-on' and the quality of training for this 'add-on' task tended to be quite poor. Happily, this is improving with the recognition that peacekeeping is not only a core UN function but also a highly specialised one. However, it remains the case that most peacekeepers are trained as soldiers first and foremost. Inevitably in such circumstances the overarching prism through which mission personnel view their role is likely to be armed conflict and the laws and norms applicable in armed conflict. Short of occupation, the laws of armed conflict do not envisage extensive positive obligations on the part of foreign armed forces towards the population of the state in which they are deployed.

Today, peacekeeping missions are frequently heavily engaged in humanitarian and policing tasks. The laws applicable to armed conflict operations, whatever their nature and label (international, non-international, low intensity, counterinsurgency, etc.), are generally inadequate for these sorts of tasks, many of which would normally be undertaken by the host state government and would normally be subject to international, regional and national human rights laws, and usually also to a host of procedural rules put in place to ensure that the population is able to challenge state agents and state-regulated professionals (e g army, police, sanitary, health service and schools personnel) if they believe that they have acted negligently, with bias, or corruptly. What happens to these obligations if these tasks are in fact being undertaken by the UN at the request or with the consent of the host state, or by the UN working alongside the host state?

The extent to which international human rights law is directly applicable to the UN remains controversial, and the debate on it is an evolving one.[2]

---

2    Kjetil Larsen (2012), *The human rights treaty obligations of peacekeepers* (Cambridge: Cambridge University Press); *Mothers of Srebrenica* v *The Netherlands*, The Hague District Court C-09/295247/HA ZA 07-2973 (2014).

However, it is not necessary that this debate be resolved to determine whether UN peacekeeping operations should adopt, as policy, a human-rights-oriented framework when carrying out humanitarian and policing functions: unquestionably they must. If the UN does not put in place procedures for securing its own legitimacy in a human rights context; eventually, slowly, bitterly, incrementally, somebody else will, almost certainly through a combination of damning NGO reports, public inquiries and the courts. The extent to which this is already happening is increasing so quickly and exponentially that it would not be surprising if it were to reach a norm-shifting critical mass in a relatively short space of time, resulting in radical legal changes. A few of the many examples include: damning criticism of the UN's failure to respond to atrocities committed towards the end of the war in Sri Lanka, resulting in a UNHCHR-led inquiry and the UN's Rights Up Front plan of action in 2014;[3] criticism of the UN's active support to the governments of the Democratic Republic of Congo and, later, South Sudan, despite their appalling record on human rights violations, resulting in the adoption of the UN's Due Diligence Policy in 2013, an overhaul of the mandates of the missions deployed there, and references to the potential legal responsibilities of UN peacekeeping missions in the Commentary to the Draft Articles on the Responsibilities of International Organizations;[4] criticism of UN negligence contributing to a serious outbreak of cholera in Haiti leading to several attempts to bring charges against the UN in court,[5] an attempt to serve legal papers directly on the Secretary-General Ban Ki-moon,[6] months of popular protests against the

---

3   United Nations (2013), *Rights Up Front: a plan of action to strengthen the UN's role in protecting people in crises. Follow-up to the report of the Secretary-General's Internal Review Panel on UN Action in Sri Lanka*, 9 July 2013.

4   Identical letters dated 25 February 2013 from the Secretary-General addressed to the President of the General Assembly and to the President of the Security Council, A/67/775–S/2013/110 5 March 2013.

5   *D Georges v United Nations et al*, United States District Court, Southern District of New York (2013); *Jean-Robert et al v United Nations*, United States District Court, Southern District of New York (2014); *LaVenture et al v United Nations*, United States District Court, Eastern District of New York (2014).

6   Rick Gladstone, 'U.N. chief served papers in suit by Haitian victims, lawyers say', *The New York Times*, 20 June 2014. Available at www.nytimes.com/2014/06/21/world/americas/un-chief-served-papers-in-suit-by-haitian-cholera-victims-lawyers-say.html?_r=0, accessed on 11 April 2017.

UN Stabilization Mission in Haiti and a visit to the country by a delegation of the Security Council;[7] and an embarrassing leak to the press of the UN's failure to take action in response to allegations of sexual abuse by French peacekeepers.[8]

## The UN's Rights Up Front plan of action 2014

The UN's Rights Up Front plan of action was a response to criticism of the UN's failure to act in the face of widespread and severe human rights violations and war crimes in Sri Lanka in 2009. It aims to mainstream human rights obligations and a commitment to the protection of civilians into all UN operations, both military and civilian. Although it is 'designed primarily for settings where the UN does not have a political or peacekeeping mission … its spirit can and should also be applied to "mission" settings'.[9]

As part of the plan of action, the UN undertakes to 'renew a vision of the UN's responsibilities with respect to serious violations [of international human rights law, IHRL, and international humanitarian law, IHL], communicate it to staff, Member States and the general public' and to 'hold staff and institutions accountable'.[10] The report set out a number of actions it intends to implement to address the problems and recognises that success 'demands that we have the courage and confidence to speak truth to power, on a consistent, principled and impartial basis, and back our own staff who live up to the

---

7   United Nations Stabilization Mission in Haiti (2015), 'UN Security Council visit to Haiti', 23 June 2015. Available at reliefweb.int/report/haiti/un-security-council-visit-haiti, accessed on 11 April 2017.
8   France24, 'UN accused of covering up report into alleged sex abuse by French troops', 29 April 2015. Available at www.france24.com/en/20150429-un-accused-covering-report-french-troops-sex-abuse, accessed on 11 April 2017. Sexual abuse by peacekeepers is unfortunately common, but allegations against troops belonging to a permanent member of the Security Council makes front-page news, particularly since the official that leaked the confidential report to French authorities (because of months of failure to act by the UN) has been suspended and faces dismissal. See also www.theguardian.com/world/2015/may/08/un-human-rights-peacekeeper-abuse-claims-inquiry-delay; www.theguardian.com/world/2015/apr/29/un-aid-worker-suspended-leaking-report-child-abuse-french-troops-car, accessed on 11 April 2017.
9   United Nations, *Rights Up Front*, 5.
10  United Nations, op cit, 3.

Charter and the Universal Declaration of Human Rights'.[11] It also undertakes 'to systematically gather information on violations of international human rights and humanitarian law and to present it to Member States with full impartiality'.[12] The plan of action recognises that these commitments 'will require different ways of doing things, and reprioritisation of existing resources'.[13] More importantly, it will also necessitate 'a change in our institutional culture'.[14] A change in institutional culture cannot be effected without the active engagement of all personnel, at the highest and at the lowest ranks.

## The UN's Due Diligence Policy 2013

The Due Diligence Policy was drawn up in response to criticism of the UN Mission in the Democratic Republic of Congo (MONUC, now replaced by MONUSCO) for failing to take action against the *Forces Armées de la République Démocratique du Congo* (FARDC), which it was mandated to support, but which was notorious for its human rights violations. FARDC had known war criminals serving in its ranks,[15] including some who have been indicted by the International Criminal Court.[16] In 2009, the Under Secretary General for Legal Affairs and UN Legal Counsel, Patricia O'Brien, stated, in a note to the Under Secretary General for Peacekeeping Operations, Alain Le Roy, that the UN has 'obligations under customary international law and from the Charter to uphold, promote and encourage respect for human rights, international humanitarian law and refugee law'.[17] Moreover:

---

11   United Nations, op cit, 4.
12   United Nations, op cit, 1.
13   United Nations, op cit, 4.
14   Ibid.
15   Pursuant to a 2009 amnesty pact agreed between President Kabila of the DRC and President Kagame of Rwanda.
16   Former general of the Congrès National pour la Défense du Peuple, Bosco Ntaganda, became a commander of the armed forces of the DRC, despite his indictment by the International Criminal Court for war crimes.
17   Patricia O'Brien, Note of 12 October 2009 to Alain Le Roy, cited in Vladyslav Lanovoy (2014), 'Complicity in an internationally wrongful act', SHARES project research paper 38, 19. Available at www.sharesproject.nl/publication/complicity-in-an-internationally-wrongful-act/, accessed on 19 May 2017.

> *If MONUC has reason to believe that FARDC units involved in an operation are violating one or other of these bodies of law, and if, despite MONUC's intercession with FARDC and with the Government of the DRC, MONUC has reason to believe that such violations are being committed, then MONUC may not lawfully continue to support that operation, but must cease its operation completely ...*[18]

Later that year the UN did in fact withdraw its support from a unit of the Congolese Army, a decision that 'represents a constitutional moment for the United Nations' and confirms 'that the Secretary-General is normatively constrained under the Charter, including by the Organization's obligations, when implementing the decisions of the Security Council'.[19]

The Due Diligence Policy requires that support by UN entities to non-UN security forces must be consistent with the UN's 'obligations under international law to respect, promote and encourage respect for international humanitarian, human rights and refugee law'.[20] Before support is given, an assessment of 'the risk of the recipient entity committing grave violations of international humanitarian law, human rights law or refugee law' must be made and 'procedures for monitoring the recipient entity's compliance with international humanitarian, human rights and refugee law' must be established as part of an effective implementation framework.[21] Grave violations for the purposes of the policy include a 'pattern of repeated violations of international humanitarian, human rights or refugee law committed by a significant number of members of the unit' and the 'presence in a senior command position of the unit of one or more officers about whom there are substantial grounds to suspect' *inter alia* '[f]ailure to take effective measures to prevent, repress, investigate or prosecute other violations of international humanitarian, human rights or refugee law committed on a significant scale

---

18 Ibid.
19 Scott P Sheeran, 'A constitutional moment?: United Nations peacekeeping in the Democratic Republic of Congo', *International Organizations Law Review* 8, 55 (2011), 55.
20 Identical letters dated 25 February 2013 from the Secretary-General addressed to the President of the General Assembly and to the President of the Security Council, A/67/775–S/2013/110 5 March 2013.
21 Op cit, para 2.

by those under their command'.²² The policy requires that if the record of the recipient entity is good enough to allow the UN to provide support but, subsequently, the recipient entity does commit grave violations and does not stop despite intercession from the UN entity, 'then the United Nations entity must suspend or withdraw support from the recipient'.²³

How is the UN to comply with these obligations if it does not establish consistent and effective monitoring systems and ensuring that all ranks are aware of these obligations and are trained in how to respond? The UN's responsibility under the policy is not mitigated simply because a low-ranking member of the mission failed to report up the chain of command on human rights violations by host state agents. Nor can senior personnel turn a blind eye for the sake of maintaining the 'greater good' of a workable relationship with the host state, however essential the cooperation of the host state government might be to the success of the mission. The obligation to monitor and report cannot be set aside for pragmatic reasons (even where these seem critical to the effective functioning of the mission) because to continue to support a force or other entity that is committing IHL or IHRL violations on a significant scale may render the force culpable for failing to exercise due diligence and even complicit in the wrong done. The UN would then be in breach of its general legal responsibilities as an international organisation and in breach of its own unilateral undertakings on the matter.

## The Draft Articles on the Responsibilities of International Organizations

The Under Secretary General for Legal Affairs' 2009 statement,²⁴ that the UN has 'obligations under customary international law and from the Charter to uphold, promote and encourage respect for human rights, international humanitarian law and refugee law', and that therefore the UN 'may not lawfully continue to support a host state that is committing serious violations of these rights', is cited in the commentary to Article 14 of the Draft Articles on the Responsibilities of International Organizations (DARIO) as an example

---

22   Op cit, para 12.
23   Op cit, para 27.
24   Discussed in the text accompanying footnote 17.

of the kind of situation in which an international organisation might be held responsible for giving aid or assistance in the commission of an internationally wrongful act.[25]

Article 42 (1) of the DARIO provides that 'States and international organizations shall cooperate to bring to an end through lawful means any serious breach' of a peremptory norm. Missions are now routinely mandated to protect civilians under Chapter VII of the UN Charter,[26] and often also to monitor and support human rights standards. Protection of civilians from war crimes and crimes against humanity is often a core justification for the deployment of peacekeeping missions. Hence it could be argued that, in some instances, peacekeeping missions are a means by which states and international organisations 'cooperate to bring to an end through lawful means' serious breaches of peremptory norms and that therefore they have at the very least a moral responsibility, underpinned by the legal framework of Article 42 of the DARIO, to carry out that obligation.

Article 42 (2) of the DARIO provides that '[n]o State or international organization shall recognize as lawful a situation created by a serious breach' of a peremptory norm 'nor render aid or assistance in maintaining that situation'.[27] Article 42 (2) is particularly pertinent to peacekeeping missions that are mandated to render assistance to host state governments that may be tempted to maintain control through breaches of peremptory norms, such violations of the right to life or torture. MONUC is not the only mission to have faced this problem. The UN Operation in Côte d'Ivoire (UNOCI) is another example of a mission that has been strongly criticised for failing to respond to serious violations of human rights by the government that its forces were supporting.

UNOCI, working alongside French troops, was instrumental in assisting Alassane Ouattara's forces to oust Laurent Gbagbo, the former president, fol-

---

25  United Nations (2011), *Draft Articles on the Responsibility of International Organizations, with Commentaries, adopted by the International Law Commission at its sixty-third session, in 2011, and submitted to the General Assembly as a part of the Commission's report covering the work of that session* (A/66/10), commentary to article 14.

26  Chapter VII of the Charter gives the Security Council authority to authorise action, including enforcement action in order to maintain international peace and security.

27  Ibid.

lowing controversial elections,[28] in order to prevent a return to civil war, and with it a likely return to human rights abuses on a large scale. However, throughout 2011, after Gbagbo had been arrested and then sent to The Hague following UNOCI's assistance in his removal, 'former rebels loyal to Ouattara' were 'still committing abuses such as executions and torture' without any response from UNOCI.[29] French peacekeepers had earlier found nearly 100 bodies, their hands tied behind their backs, that had been executed by forces commanded by Martin Kouakou Fofié, who was immediately promoted by Ouattara when he became president.[30] Despite UN DPKO's first-hand knowledge of the human rights abuses being committed by Ouattara's troops, and the extension of Fofié's 'warlord-style predatory economic activities' to 'the entire Ivorian territory',[31] Amnesty International reported that that when

---

28   The Ivorian Independent Electoral Commission had declared that Ouattara had won the presidential election and therefore was the legitimate president, a declaration reiterated by the UN Secretary-General Ban Ki-moon, but the Constitutional Council of Côte d'Ivoire had confirmed Gbagbo as the winner of the presidential election, prompting controversy as to the authority of the Secretary-General to make such pronouncements on an apparently internal matter.

29   Aaron Gray-Block, 'Gbagbo, Ouattara forces engaged in war crimes: ICC', Reuters, 23 June 2011. Available at www.reuters.com/article/2011/06/23/us-ivorycoast-icc-idUSTRE-75M76620110623, accessed on 11 April 2017; Martin Kouakou Fofié, one of the commanders promoted by Ouattara after his presidential victory in 2011, had been placed on the UN Security Council sanctions list in 2006 (and is still on it), for a catalogue of serious human rights violations. Forces under his command engaged in recruitment of child soldiers, abductions, imposition of forced labor, sexual abuse of women, arbitrary arrests and extra-judicial killings: Human Rights Watch, 'Côte d'Ivoire: military promotions mock abuse victims', 5 August 2011. Available at www.hrw.org/news/2011/08/05/cote-divoire-military-promotions-mock-abuse-victims, accessed on 1 April 2017.

30   Ibid. See also www.africareview.com/News/Cote-dIvoire-warlord-commanders-plunder-cocoa-exports-UN-/-/979180/1761296/-/14ckv74z/-/index.html, accessed on 2 May 2017.

31   A 2013 report in *Africa Review* states that the UN sanctions experts' committee has found that Fofié's rise to power under Ouattara has enabled him to extend his 'warlord-style predatory economic activities' to 'the entire Ivorian territory' and that he is using his 'military-economic network' to plunder the country's exports of cocoa, cashew nuts and other resources to the tune of millions of dollars: *Africa Review*, 'Côte d'Ivoire "warlord" commanders plunder cocoa exports: UN', 29 April 2013. Available at www.africareview.com/News/Cote-dIvoire-warlord-commanders-plunder-cocoa-exports-UN-/-/979180/1761296/-/14ckv74z/-/index.html, accessed on 11 April 2017.

challenged on the mission's failure to protect civilians, as provided for in its Chapter VII mandate authorising it to 'to use all necessary means to protect civilians under imminent threat of physical violence, within its capabilities and its areas of deployment',[32] UNOCI officials responded that 'it is the duty of the state to protect civilians'.[33] That was just a few years ago. Today, in light of the UN's commitments under its Due Diligence Policy and Rights Up Front plan of action, as well as its obligations as an international organisation under the DARIO, such an approach would be not only politically and morally untenable (as it was at the time) but also contrary to the UN's own public undertakings, including its commitments 'to speak truth to power, on a consistent, principled and impartial basis'[34] and 'to systematically gather information on violations of international human rights and humanitarian law and to present it to Member States with full impartiality'.[35]

## Explicitly mandated reporting obligations

Some provisions in recent peacekeeping mandates explicitly require peacekeeping missions to monitor and report. For example, under resolution 1996 of 2011, the UN mission to South Sudan (UNMISS) is mandated to support the government of South Sudan through, *inter alia*,

> *monitoring, investigating, verifying, and reporting regularly on human rights and potential threats against the civilian population as well as actual and potential violations of international humanitarian and human rights law, working as appropriate with the Office of the High Commissioner for Human Rights, bringing these to the attention of the authorities as necessary, and immediately reporting gross violations of human rights to the UN Security Council.*[36]

---

32 S/RES/1975 (2011).
33 Amnesty International (2011), 'Côte d'Ivoire: both sides responsible for war crimes and crimes against humanity', press release, 25 May 2011. Available at www.amnesty.org/en/press-releases/2011/05/cc3b4te-de28099ivoire-both-sides-responsible-war-crimes-and-crimes-against-humanity/, accessed on 2 May 2017.
34 United Nations, *Rights Up Front*, 4.
35 United Nations, op cit, 1.
36 S/RES 1996 (2011), emphasis added.

Under resolution 2155 of May 2014, UNMISS is additionally authorised 'to use all necessary means' to, *inter alia*,

> monitor, investigate, verify and report specifically *and publicly on violations and abuses committed against children and women, including all forms of sexual and gender-based violence in armed conflict by accelerating the implementation of monitoring, analysis and reporting arrangements on conflict-related sexual violence and by strengthening the monitoring and reporting mechanism for grave violations against children.*[37]

Generally, mandates are regarded as powers-creating only, ie as creating legal authorisations to act rather than setting out tasks that the mission is obliged to carry out.[38] However, while a mandate to report could simply be interpreted as an authorisation to report, a mandate to report *regularly, immediately* or *specifically* imports something beyond authorisation. Semantically it makes no sense to interpret 'report immediately' as purely powers-creating, except in a context where, absent the authorisation, the addressee is prohibited from reporting immediately, which would be unlikely in a UN mission. The European Court of Human Rights in *Al Jedda* noted that resolution 1546, authorising the multinational operation in Afghanistan, 'appears to leave the choice of the means to achieve' the mission's objectives 'to the Member States within the Multi-National Force', and concluded that the effect of mandates drafted in this way is to authorise rather than oblige action on the part of the mission.[39] By contrast, the UNMISS mandates specify very precisely how the mission should carry out at least its reporting tasks. Arguably, the addition of qualifying factors as to the timing and nature of the mandated task (in this case reporting) in the UNMISS mandate suggests that those particular reporting obligations are at least intended to be obligatory,

---

37   S/RES 2155 (2014) emphasis added.
38   In 2014, the District Court of The Hague, in *Mothers of Srebrenica* v *The Netherlands*, held that '[w]hilst UNPROFOR's mandate is indeed regarded as a decision by an international law organisation it only has a powers-creating character and does not call to life any obligations Claimants can enforce at a court of law.' *Mothers of Srebrenica* v *The Netherlands*, The Hague District Court C-09/295247/HA ZA 07-2973, (2014), para 4.149.
39   *Al-Jedda* v *The United Kingdom*, European Court of Human Rights, Application 27021/08 (2011), para 105.

or at a very minimum politically coercive: otherwise the qualifying phrases in those paragraphs would have to be treated as redundant.[40] UNMISS takes its reporting duties seriously. The reason it does so, and the reason for the inclusion of detailed reporting requirements in UNMISS mandates since 2011, is largely because of credible allegations that the South Sudanese government has committed, and seemingly still continues to commit, very serious violations of human rights.[41] Failure by the UN to monitor and report human rights violations could leave UNMISS vulnerable to criticism that it is in breach of the UN's own policies on respect for human rights and in breach of its legal obligations as an international organisation under the DARIO.

## Respect for people, especially the poor, should become an internalised norm

On most mornings, the market in Monrovia, Liberia, fills the main street with hundreds of stallholders, children and their belongings. Both the UN Mission in Liberia (UNMIL), and the people themselves, seem to accept that the only way to clear the street for UN vehicles to pass is to swing large truncheons and beat the people out of the way. A whole generation of poor Monrovian children is growing up with the belief, born of experience, that officials have the right to beat them and their mothers every day to make way for foreigners to drive down the street. There are no significant protests about this, but is it an acceptable way for the UN to conduct its business, particularly given that the armed conflict in Liberia ended in 2003? Would this be acceptable conduct on the streets of penholder states[42] or the streets of the home states

---

40   Under Article 25 of the UN Charter 'the Members of the United Nations agree to accept and carry out the decisions of the Security Council in accordance with the present Charter'. But peacekeeping missions are generally UN-commanded and therefore if there are provisions in the mandate that are legally binding, it will normally be the UN itself that is responsible for carrying them out (see section on Accountability infra).

41   UNMISS was initially mandated to provide support to the South Sudanese government but its mandate was revised in 2014 to focus on protection because of the government's continued poor human rights record: see Human Rights Watch, 'South Sudan's new war: abuses by government and opposition forces', 7 August 2014. Available at www.hrw.org/node/126088, accessed on 11 April 2017.

42   The states with primary responsibility for drafting peacekeeping mandates, usually the US, France or the UK.

of the military personnel travelling in those UN vehicles? If not, why is it acceptable for women and children to be treated with less respect than they would be afforded in the penholder states and many of the contributing states?

In exceptional circumstances where speed might be an urgent priority, for example in dealing with certain aspects of a health crisis, such as an Ebola epidemic, such conduct might be tolerated, even in New York, Paris or London, but is it acceptable as a daily response to facilitating the ordinary transport needs of the UN? Surely, as a general practice, it violates basic principles of human rights and dignity and perpetuates on a daily basis a 'norm' that regards entire classes of people, mostly poor, as subordinate to others, mostly elites and foreigners. Forceful control of poorer classes of society is a feature of many missions and it is too often accompanied by (additional) abuse and exploitation. Often this additional exploitation is sexual, for example seeking sexual favours in return for food or small gifts; but other forms of abuse are also common, for example the use of disproportionate, even lethal, force to apprehend people running away who have committed very minor offences such as theft, even of ordinary goods or food, or simply negligence, as in the case of poor waste management by the mission in Haiti, which seems very likely to have been the primary cause of a serious outbreak of cholera.[43]

In one particular instance in Liberia, UNMIL was unwittingly exploited in order to facilitate corruption by local agents. In March 2005, the Quick Reaction Force (QRF), consisting of Swedish and Irish troops, received an order (pursuant to a request from local officials) to move into the rubber plantation of the Liberia Agriculture Company (LAC), near Buchanan, in order to arrest a group of armed terrorists who were about destabilise the region. The QRF dispatched its strongest military unit and arrived with armoured vehicles and heavy weapons. However, when they got there the commander of the QRF observed that a peacekeeping force from another troop-contributing state was also present and by its presence lending its authority to repressive actions that were taking place. It quickly became clear that the 'terrorists' were in fact the leaders of the plantation workers who were lobbying for an increase in their $2.60 weekly wage. The plantation

---

43  United Nations (2011), *Final report of the independent panel of experts on the cholera outbreak in Haiti*, 4 May 2011. Available at www.un.org/News/dh/infocus/haiti/UN-cholera-report-final.pdf, accessed on 11 April 2017.

management had offered an increase of 0.16 cents per person per week but the workers had rejected this and were holding out for something better. Under cover of the show of force displayed by the two UN units present, the managers of the plantation rounded up the strike leaders and had them beaten and taken away by their henchmen. These events were reported fully to the UNMIL civilian and military leadership, who were made aware of what had transpired. However, there is no record of any corrective action having been taken, or of any investigation having been initiated, or of any official at any level in Liberian society being personally called to account.[44]

## The strategic corporal

In each of these examples of potential responsibility for relations between the mission and local population (whether it is monitoring of serious human rights abuses such as genocide and crimes against humanity by host state agents or armed groups; or standing by while local elites abuse employees who reject poor working conditions; or tolerating sexual abuse and exploitation; or failing to respect the local community, for example through a negligent approach to the building of latrines and other facilities; or simply through rudeness, expecting civilians to routinely obey uncivil commands as if the mission were an occupying force) non-commissioned officers have responsibilities. As Krulak observed, '[s]uccess or failure' rests increasingly 'with the rifleman and with his ability to make the *right* decision at the *right* time at the point of contact', but in a peacekeeping mission the non-commissioned officer may be called upon to deal with a very different range of issues than would be the case for a soldier in a traditional armed conflict, especially where the mission is working closely with the host state. If UN peacekeepers stand by whilst host state forces, or local elites, abuse members of the local community, respect for the UN will be diminished, which ultimately will undermine the

---

[44] Author's interview with Swedish/Irish Quick Reaction Force. Goal Number 5 of UNMIL's Integrated Mandate Implementation Plan, adopted in 2006, is the establishment of safeguards for human rights. This goal demanded among other things: ratification of international human rights conventions, monitoring human rights violations; strengthening national human rights capacity, establishing an independent national human rights commission, establishing a truth and reconciliation commission and promoting the rule of law.

success of the mission and the status of the UN internationally. If the presence of a peacekeeping mission actually facilitates abuse, the UN may be in breach of its legal obligations. The UN's immunity from suit will not protect it from international criticism. The greater the criticism the more likely that the UN's sphere of immunity will be significantly eroded under pressure from NGOs, and from other sections of the UN's administration, such as its human rights rapporteurs, monitoring committees and the periodic review process.

In any large group of people, especially a disciplined group such as a military unit that is trained to work together, the group will probably view its own role primarily from its own perspective and from that of getting done the tasks it is mandated to do. It is therefore important that, at mission leadership level, attention is paid to trying to view the role of the mission from the perspective of the local community so as to minimise misunderstandings and mistrust. For example, in the situation described above, where UN leadership was informed that UN forces had stood by, creating an air of authority while striking plantation workers were beaten up and taken away; mission leadership should have considered how that scene would have been viewed by the rest of the LAC workers and their families. As far as the children of the plantation workers who might have been watching the incident are concerned, UN soldiers beat up and took away their fathers. Children looking at UN soldiers standing by in their uniforms, with their impressive-looking armoured vehicles and array of weapons, are unlikely to think, 'Oh, it's not the UN soldiers' fault, they didn't mean it, they were duped'. A junior officer may not be able to prevent every abuse happening, but what about the follow-up?

If workers are beaten and taken away under false pretenses in the presence of UN troops, does the UN have any responsibility to find out what has happened to them and to take steps to ensure that they are released and returned alive and unharmed? If the UN does not follow up and find out what happened to workers taken under their watch, UN troops will, at least in the eyes of local witnesses, be tainted with the same brush of abuse and exploitation as the local henchmen who initiated it. If troops are present, they create an expectation. This means that it is imperative not only that the local officer report the incident up the chain of command (which in the LAC rubber plantation example he did), but also that higher command take action, and, for example, find out what happened to the workers and put pressure on the government to ensure their safe return, so that those children get their fathers back unharmed: if the UN does not do this, the legitimacy of the UN in the eyes of that community is irreparably harmed. Thus, the 'strategic corporals' must react as best they can and make the right decision at the right time, but to do this consistently requires a supportive system. The junior officer must know that if they make a report indicating abuse on their watch, it will be taken seriously by higher command and a response will follow. If the likelihood of a response from higher command is hit-and-miss, the officer is likely to feel insecure and uncertain how to react, not quite sure what their responsibilities are. Not only should there be a follow-up response to the immediate incident, there should also be a mission-wide report, in case similar problems arise elsewhere, and a plan drawn up for dealing with future incidents, so that if another officer is faced with a similar problem they will be prepared.

In order to ensure consistency and reliability in reporting incidents up the chain of command, every contact between UN forces and local communities should be recorded. One of the best ways to do this would be to require all peacekeeping personnel to wear body cameras when in contact with local communities. The film of each day's activities should be filed and kept on record in case of any future inquiry. Troops may be reluctant to have all of their public activities recorded, but since all troublesome incidents, everywhere in the world, are likely to be filmed on mobile phones[45] and therefore any untoward incident involving UN peacekeepers will eventually emerge on film at some point, it would be better if the mission took responsibility for filming itself, as many police forces now do. The existence of a record of events provides some degree of protection against false accusations of abuse, and arguably it may aid in maintaining high standards of conduct, since, as Thomas Jefferson is alleged to have observed, we are more likely to do something well if whenever we do it we 'act as if all the world were watching'.

## Conclusion

UN peacekeeping has many successes, but unfortunately outside of the organisation itself the UN is better known for its many failures, notably the inadequate response to the genocides in Rwanda, and at Srebrenica; the

---

45  Even in the poorest of communities someone has a mobile phone because these days it is impossible to conduct business without one: even very junior employees need to be contactable and hence businessmen will give them a phone, so in any workplace or living community people will have access to mobile phones.

inadequate response, initially, to human rights abuses by Congolese state armed forces; the inadequate response to human rights abuses by government forces in Côte d'Ivoire and, initially, in South Sudan. UN civilian missions have also been heavily criticised, most notably for the UN's withdrawal and failure to respond to war crimes against the Tamils in Sri Lanka in 2009. UN personnel have also been criticised for their own mistreatment of host state residents, notably for sexual exploitation and abuse, most recently by French forces in the Central African Republic,[46] and for other crimes such as trafficking and exploitation of resources and labour.

In addition to the UN's commitments in its Rights Up Front plan of action, adopted in 2014, and its Due Diligence Policy, adopted in 2013, most multidimensional peace operations have a human rights team, including the missions to the Democratic Republic of Congo, Darfur, South Sudan, Liberia, Côte d'Ivoire, Haiti and Afghanistan. The goals of the human rights teams are:

- to contribute to the protection and promotion of human rights through both immediate and long-term action
- to empower the population to assert and claim their human rights
- to enable state and other national institutions to implement their human rights obligations and uphold the rule of law.[47]

The UN's policy document 'Gender Equality in UN Peacekeeping Operations' states that it 'is critical for peacekeeping missions to strive to enhance accountability for the violation of women's rights' and 'establish all the necessary mechanisms for the prevention of sexual and gender based violence'.[48] The missions to the Democratic Republic of Congo, Darfur, South Sudan, Liberia, Côte d'Ivoire, Lebanon and Mali all have Gender Advisors appointed to them, and the missions to Kosovo, Western Sahara, Cyprus, the Golan Heights and the Abyei Area in Sudan all have Gender Focal Points to support the mission leadership in promoting gender equality.

---

46   France24, 'UN accused of covering up report into alleged sex abuse by French troops'.
47   United Nations Peacekeeping (no date), 'Human rights'. Available at www.un.org/en/peacekeeping/issues/humanrights.shtml, accessed on 11 April 2017.
48   United Nations, Department of Peacekeeping Operations (2010), 'Gender equality in UN peacekeeping operations', policy document, 26 July 2010, paragraph C.8. Available at www.un.org/en/peacekeeping/documents/gender_directive_2010.pdf, accessed on 11 April 2017.

All of these initiatives depend on junior as well as senior personnel for their success. Human rights and gender protection issues are matters that need to be addressed day to day and all the time. Officers (of all ranks) may need to respond promptly where they witness or become aware of abuse. In order to be able to do this, all personnel need training in human rights protection. In addition, the mission must have in place a coordinated and coherent support mechanism for ensuring that human rights norms are integrated into the fabric of peacekeeping at all levels. The policy initiatives adopted in recent years will only be effective if they are translated into action on the ground. Body cameras for all personnel is one way of assisting this since if all public interactions of the mission are filmed, not only will the mission's own conduct be monitored but a great deal of the conduct of other parties will also end up being filmed, and filed, and therefore potentially open to review.

Specific, detailed and immediate reporting of the mission's day-to-day activities is also important, not only where it is explicitly mandated but in all missions. The UN is committed to upholding the rule of law, and the rule of law requires that people affected by the acts and omissions of state agents, and of agents acting on behalf or in coordination with the state, be able to access a report of how those agents carried out their duties. If the UN is carrying out law enforcement tasks, it should carry out those tasks to the standard expected of law enforcement officers. This requires a radical rethink of the role and management of UN peacekeeping missions and of the training of peacekeepers. Today, keeping the peace between warring parties is only one part of the function of UN peacekeeping. Where UN missions are carrying out broader functions they must do so in accordance with human rights and rule of law standards. That requires the active engagement of all personnel, at all ranks.

# 7

# The Strategic Corporal and the Challenge of Cyber Warfare

## Russell Buchan

IN ORDER TO PROTECT CIVILIANS from the horrors of war, international humanitarian law posits as one of its 'cardinal principles' and 'intransgressible' rules the requirement that, during international and non-international armed conflict, civilians not be made the object of attack.[1] A combatant who directly targets civilians commits a violation of international humanitarian law and responsibility attaches to the party to the armed conflict to which that combatant belongs. Moreover, a combatant who directly targets civilians incurs individual criminal responsibility for war crimes under international criminal law.[2]

Whether it be during an international or non-international armed conflict, where civilians take a direct part in hostilities the legal protection afforded by international humanitarian law is forfeited and they become liable to direct targeting.[3]

---

1   International Court of Justice (1996), *Legality of the threat or use of nuclear weapons, advisory opinion*, 8 July 1996, *ICJ Reports*, 226, para 78.
2   In the context of an international armed conflict, see Article 8(2)(b)(i) of the Rome Statute Establishing the International Criminal Court 1998. In relation to a non-international armed conflict, see Article 8(2)(c) of the Rome Statute.
3   International Committee of the Red Cross (2017), *Geneva Conventions*, Additional Protocol I (1977), Article 51(3); Additional Protocol II (1977), Article 13(3). Available at www.icrc.org/en/war-and-law/treaties-customary-law/geneva-conventions, accessed on 11 May 2017. Customary international law applicable to international and non-international armed conflicts also permits the direct targeting of civilians where they directly participate in hostilities; see *The Public Committee Against Torture in Israel et al v The Government of Israel et al*, Supreme Court of Israel Sitting as the High Court of Justice, Judgment, 11 December 2006, HCJ 769/02.

It therefore goes without saying that it is extremely important that international humanitarian law provides combatants with clear guidelines as to when civilians can be regarded as directly participating in hostilities. Significantly, however, international humanitarian law fails to provide a concrete definition of the concept of 'direct participation in hostilities' (DPH), and international lawyers have long disagreed over what conduct amounts to DPH.[4] The concept of DPH was originally coined to determine whether civilians could be directly targeted where they used conventional kinetic weapons against a party to an armed conflict. The extent to which there is disagreement over how this concept applies to the physical battlefield is only intensified when it comes to applying it to new means and methods of warfare, most notably the use of cyber weapons on the virtual battlefield.

Disagreement as to what conduct amounts to DPH in the cyber context is particularly problematic given the potential for civilians to use cyberspace for malicious purposes.[5] In fact, civilians are now increasingly exploiting cyberspace to cause harm to parties to an armed conflict. There are several reasons for this development. First, because states are now so heavily dependent upon cyberspace, a cyber-attack against cyber infrastructure can cause considerable disruption and damage, equivalent to or perhaps even greater than the disruption and damage that can be caused by a conventional kinetic attack. Second, when compared to conventional weapons, the use of cyber weapons significantly reduces the chances of being identified and can thus be employed relatively risk free: for example, cyber-attacks can be committed without physically attending the battlefield, and the potential for identity spoofing in cyberspace makes it extremely unlikely that cyber-attacks will be reliably attributed to their author(s).

The potential for civilians to commit cyber-attacks imposes additional pressures and challenges upon the strategic corporal. In the modern era, the

---

[4] See for example 'Forum: direct participation in hostilities: direct participation in hostilities: perspectives on the ICRC Interpretive Guidance', *NYU Journal of International Law and Politics* 42, 3 (Spring 2010), 637.

[5] As Schmitt notes, 'cyber operations have become embedded in modern warfare'; see Michael N Schmitt, 'Cyber operations and the *jus in bello*: key issues', *International Law Studies* 87 (2011), 89, 90.

strategic corporal will be increasingly required to determine whether cyber-attacks committed by civilians constitute DPH. Given the current confusion within international humanitarian law as to how the concept of DPH applies to cyber-attacks, the objective of this chapter is to clarify this area of law and provide the strategic corporal with guidance as to when malicious cyber conduct meets the threshold for DPH and thus under what circumstances direct targeting is permissible.

This chapter is structured as follows. To set the legal landscape, the section that follows briefly clarifies the definition of combatancy and civilian status under international humanitarian law. To provide context, the next section identifies the 2008 Georgian conflict as an example where civilians committed cyber-attacks against a party to an armed conflict. Then the concept of DPH is unpacked and how this legal framework applies to civilians that commit malicious cyber conduct is examined.

## Combatancy and civilian status under international humanitarian law

International humanitarian law requires the application of different legal frameworks depending upon whether an international or non-international armed conflict is under way. An international armed conflict is defined as 'recourse to armed force between states'[6] whereas a non-international armed conflict describes 'protracted armed violence between governmental authorities and organised armed groups or between such groups within a State'.[7]

The question of who is a civilian for the purpose of the law of targeting is relatively clear in relation to an international armed conflict but less clear in the context of a non-international armed conflict. The reason for this is because Additional Protocol (AP) I to the Geneva Conventions provides a definition of a civilian in an international armed conflict but AP II, which is applicable to non-international armed conflicts, fails to provide an express definition.

In the context of an international armed conflict, Article 50(1) AP I defines the concept of 'civilian' in negative terms: 'all persons who are neither

---

6   International Criminal Tribunal for the former Yugoslavia, *Prosecutor* v *Tadić*, Jurisdiction Appeal, IT-94-1-AR72 2 (October 1995), para 70.
7   Ibid.

members of the armed forces of a party to the conflict nor participants in a *levée en masse* are civilians'. Members of the armed forces are those card-carrying military personnel who are incorporated into the armed forces by way of domestic law. Importantly, under Article 43(1) AP I, members of organised armed groups that belong to a party to the armed conflict are also regarded as *de facto* members of the armed forces.[8] However, whereas members of the armed forces can be targeted anytime, anywhere on the basis of their formal status, members of an organised armed group can only be directly targeted where they assume a 'continuous combat function'.[9] This is a functional test that means a member of the armed group can only be targeted where they directly participate in hostilities. But where this DPH is engaged in 'repeatedly', the individual can be targeted during intervals in DPH on the basis that their repeated participation renders their participation continuous.[10] It is important to underscore that the organised armed group must 'belong to a party to the conflict' in order for its members to be regarded as combatants,[11] which means that the group must conduct 'hostilities on behalf of and with the agreement of that party'.[12] This relationship can be either declared or 'expressed through tacit agreement or conclusive behaviour that makes it clear for which party the group is fighting'.[13] Such a relationship is certainly established where the acts of the armed group are attributable to a party to the armed conflict under the law of state responsibility.[14]

Article 50(1) AP I excludes from civilian status members of a *levée en masse*, which refers to 'inhabitants of a non-occupied territory who, on

---

8   International Committee of the Red Cross (ICRC) (2009), *Interpretive Guidance on the notion of direct participation in hostilities under international humanitarian law* (Geneva: International Committee of the Red Cross), 31.
9   ICRC, op cit, 33.
10  ICRC, op cit, 35.
11  ICRC, op cit, 23.
12  Ibid.
13  Ibid.
14  Ibid. The circumstances under which the acts of an organised armed group can be legally attributed to a state for the purpose of state responsibility are generally considered codified in the International Law Commission's (ILC) Articles on State Responsibility (2001), notably Articles 8 and 11.

approach of the enemy, spontaneously take up arms to resist invading forces without having had time to form themselves into regular armed units, provided they carry their arms openly and respect the laws and customs of war'.[15]

As explained previously, unlike AP I, AP II does not expressly define the concept of 'civilian' in a non-international armed conflict, notwithstanding the fact that the agreement uses the term 'civilian' on numerous occasions. However, the phraseology of AP II means that civilians necessarily fall into a residual category of anyone who is not: a) a member of the armed forces of a state (which extends to members of organised armed groups belonging to the state); or b) a member of an organised armed group. Note that, as with international armed conflicts, it is only those individuals that assume a continuous combat function that are to be regarded as members of an organised armed group: ie those members that assume a continuous function to directly participate in hostilities.

## Civilians and cyber conflict

The non-international armed conflict between the state of Georgia and an organised armed group in the breakaway region of South Ossetia escalated considerably when, on 7 August 2008, Georgian military forces launched a coordinated attack against South Ossetia in order to re-establish Georgia's authority in the region and prevent South Ossetia's secession. Given the close historical ties between Russia and South Ossetia, the Russian response to Georgian military operations was to deploy its armed forces into South Ossetia in order to protect Russian peacekeepers that were lawfully stationed there and also the ethnic Russians resident in the region. Violent clashes occurred between the Georgian and Russian military forces and a state of war was declared.[16] Georgia and Russia became parties to an international armed conflict.

Significantly, and for the first time in the history of armed conflict, hostilities exhibited an overt cyber dimension in the sense that, alongside the

---

15  ICRC, *Interpretive Guidance*, 25.
16  Peter Walker, 'Georgia declares "state of war" over South Ossetia', *The Guardian*, 9 August 2008. Available at www.theguardian.com/world/2008/aug/09/georgia.russia2, accessed on 11 April 2017.

use of conventional kinetic weapons, Georgia claimed that it was the victim of numerous cyber-attacks.[17] In particular, Georgia reported that important websites belonging to the President, the Parliament and the Foreign Affairs and Defence and Education ministries were either defaced or subject to Distributed Denial of Service (DDoS) attacks. For example, the website of the Ministry of Foreign Affairs and Defence was defaced and a collage of photos of Adolf Hitler appeared when users accessed the site. The DDoS attacks against the websites of the President and Parliament meant that Georgia's capacity to broadcast and communicate information to its citizens and to other states and international organisations was seriously impeded. Furthermore, important websites belonging to private companies were attacked and forced offline, including domestic and foreign media associations, banks, private internet services and blogs. Although the cyber-attacks did not manifest real-world physical damage, according to the Georgian government the impact of these cyber-attacks upon both state organs and private actors was considerable and proved extremely damaging.

Georgia alleged that Russia was responsible for the cyber-attacks.[18] Evidence, however, proved inconclusive and Russia denied responsibility. Instead, Russia maintained that the cyber-attacks were launched by patriotic hackers resident in Russia or Georgia who were concerned at Georgia's treatment of Russian soldiers and ethnic Russians resident in South Ossetia. On the basis that definitive attribution was never established, and for the purpose of analysis, it is reasonable to assume that the cyber-attacks were carried out by individuals who were not part of the armed forces of Russia or an organised armed group belonging to Russia. Put differently, I assume that the cyber-attacks were carried out by civilians as defined by international humanitarian law for the purpose of an international armed conflict. In light of this, the important question becomes whether their cyber conduct amounted to DPH.

---

17  For an overview of the cyber-attacks against Georgia, see Duncan Hollis, 'Cyberwar case study: Georgia 2008', *Small Wars Journal* 7, 1 (2011).

18  Linton Chiswick, 'Cyber attack casts new light on Georgia invasion', *The Week* (UK), 15 August 2008.

## Direct participation in hostilities in cyberspace

Treaty law does not provide any guidance as to the meaning of the notion of DPH, and there has been little consideration of what this concept means by states through their military manuals. In recent years, a number of courts have sought to grapple with the content and scope of the notion of DPH—notably the Israeli Supreme Court[19] and the International Criminal Tribunal for the former Yugoslavia[20]—but such definitions remain vague and even exhibit diversity.[21] As a result, the International Committee of the Red Cross's (ICRC) Customary International Humanitarian Law Study explains that 'a precise definition of the term "direct participation in hostilities" does not exist'.[22]

Concerned at the ambiguity surrounding this important international humanitarian law concept, the ICRC conducted a six-year process of informal research and expert consultation with the aim of clarifying the circumstances in which a civilian can be regarded as directly participating in hostilities. Importantly, the ICRC's Interpretive Guidance 'does not purport to change the law, but provides an interpretation of the notion of DPH within existing parameters'.[23] This notwithstanding, upon publication the Guidance was heavily criticised, with many arguing that it adopted an 'overly narrow interpretation'[24] of the concept of DPH and 'fail[ed] to pay sufficient regard to military realities'.[25] Moreover, scholars claimed

---

19  The Israeli Supreme Court considered that 'all those persons [who] are performing the function of combatants' would be civilians that are taking 'direct part in hostilities'; see *The Public Committee Against Torture*, para 35.

20  'To take a "direct" part in the hostilities means acts of war which by their nature or purpose are likely to cause actual harm to the personnel or materiel of the enemy armed forces'; see International Criminal Tribunal for the former Yugoslavia, *Prosecutor v Stanislav Galić*, Judgment, Case No IT-98-29-T (5 December 2003), para 48.

21  Emily Crawford and Alison Pert (2015), *International humanitarian law* (Cambridge: Cambridge University Press), 109–113.

22  Jean-Marie Henckaerts and Louise Doswald-Beck (2005), *Customary international humanitarian law*, Volume 1 (Cambridge: Cambridge University Press), 22.

23  ICRC, *Interpretive Guidance*, 6.

24  Michael N Schmitt, 'Deconstructing direct participation in hostilities: the constitutive elements', *NYU Journal of International Law and Politics* 42 (2010), 679, 720.

25  Shane Darcy (2016), 'Direct participation in hostilities', *Oxford Bibliographies*. Available at oxfordbibliographies.com/view/document/obo-9780199796953/obo-9780199796953-0137.xml?rskey=3jCnSY&result=50, accessed on 11 April 2017.

that the Guidance deviated sharply from state practice on the topic of DPH.[26]

Nonetheless, in the years subsequent to its publication the ICRC's Interpretive Guidance has gained traction[27] among states and is thus 'becoming the authoritative guidance on defining and interpreting DPH for the international community'.[28] As such, the ICRC's Interpretive Guidance will be employed in this chapter as an authoritative statement on the meaning of the concept of DPH under international humanitarian law.

The ICRC's test for determining whether a civilian is directly participating in hostilities comprises three limbs, all of which must be satisfied before direct targeting can commence. Using the 2008 armed conflict between Russia and Georgia as a lens, the following discussion examines how these limbs apply to civilians who commit cyber-attacks against a party to an armed conflict.

## *Threshold of harm*

The ICRC's Interpretive Guidance provides that '[i]n order to reach the required threshold of harm, a specific act must be likely to adversely affect the military operations or military capacity of a party to the armed conflict or, alternatively, to inflict death, injury, or destruction on persons or objects protected against direct attack'.[29]

If the effect of the conduct or the objective likelihood of the conduct is to cause 'harm of a specifically military nature' this threshold is met 'regardless of the quantitative gravity' of the adverse effects.[30] This does not just include death or destruction of military objects, but also extends to 'essentially any

---

26    Schmitt, 'Deconstructing direct participation in hostilities', 712 ff.
27    Jeremy Marsh and Scott L Glabe, 'Time for the United States to directly participate', *Virginia Journal of International Law Online* 1 (30 January 2011), 13, 20. Available at www.vjil.org/assets/pdfs/vjilonline1/1/Marsh__Post-Production_.pdf, accessed on 5 May 2017.
28    Marsh and Glabe, op cit, 14. For example, Professor Philip Alston, Special Rapporteur to the UN Human Rights Council on extrajudicial, summary or arbitrary executions, cited the *Interpretive Guidance* as the primary authority on what constitutes direct participation in hostilities in his study on targeted killings; see United Nations, *Report of the Special Rapporteur on extrajudicial, summary or arbitrary executions, Philip Alston: study on targeted killings*, Human Rights Council, UN Doc A/HRC/14/24/Add.6 (2010), paras 62–69.
29    ICRC, *Interpretive Guidance*, 47.
30    Ibid.

consequence adversely affecting the military operations or military capacity of a party to the conflict'.[31] Usefully, the ICRC's Interpretive Guidance provides examples of how this limb applies to cyber-attacks. In this context, the Guidance gives an example of 'electronic interference with military computer networks could ... suffice, whether through computer network attacks ... or computer network exploitation'.[32] The cyber-attacks against Georgia's Foreign Affairs and Defence website would almost certainly satisfy this requirement.

If the harm caused is not of a military nature, the 'specific act must be likely ... to cause at least death, injury or destruction on persons or objects protected against direct attack'.[33] Within this category there are two conditions that need to be met in order to satisfy the ICRC's threshold-of-harm requirement. First, the object of harm must be protected persons or objects, namely, civilians or civilian objects, ie not combatants or military objects. With regard to the cyber-attacks against Georgia, for example, I have already noted that civilian websites were targeted, such as the websites belonging to the Georgian Ministry of Education and private banks. Second, the nature of the harm must be such that it causes death or injury to protected persons or objects or the destruction of protected property. In relation to this second condition a key question is whether the notion of 'destruction of property' only encompasses physical damage or, in other words, damage to physical property. The position adopted by the ICRC is that the harm caused must be physical in nature. In reaching this conclusion, the Guidance relies on the definition of attack in Article 49 AP I: 'acts of violence against the adversary, whether in offence or defence'.[34] The Commentary to AP I suggests that violence only encompasses conduct that produces physical damage.[35] This approach therefore excludes from the notion of 'attack' acts that cause damage or harm that is contained exclusively to the cyber realm, ie cyber-attacks that affect the functionality of computer networks and systems.

---

31   Ibid.
32   ICRC, op cit, 48.
33   ICRC, op cit, 49.
34   Ibid.
35   Michael Bothe, Karl Josef Partsch and Waldemar A Solf (1982), *New rules for victims of armed conflict: commentary on the two 1977 Protocols Additional to the Geneva Conventions of 1949* (The Hague: Martinus Nijhoff Publishers), 289.

At one point, the requirement of physical harm seemed logical and appeared to strike an appropriate balance between the twin objectives of international humanitarian law, on the one hand satisfying the military needs of a state to be able to directly target individuals participating in hostilities, and on the other hand conferring legal protection upon those that deserve immunity from direct targeting.[36] Where physical violence was inflicted upon protected people or property, this was considered sufficient to justify direct targeting; such damage could be 'equated with the use of means or methods of warfare'.[37] Non-physical harm against protected persons or property was not considered sufficiently serious to justify the use of military force against those responsible. Instead, non-physical harm was perceived as causing the enemy party mere inconvenience and disruption and therefore did not justify direct targeting.[38]

However, in light of the significant developments in cyber technology, and in particular the heavy reliance that state and non-state actors now place upon computer systems and networks,[39] such an approach has been criticised as archaic.[40] Cyber-attacks against computer networks—especially those that sustain critical national infrastructure—can be regarded as comparable to kinetic attacks, causing significant harm rather than just disruption and inconvenience. In other areas of international law, we have seen interpretative reorientations of concepts to include cyber-attacks that do not produce physical damage but nevertheless adversely impact upon the functionality of computer systems and networks. Indeed, in relation to the *jus ad bellum* there now seems to be a consensus cohering around an interpretation of

---

36  On the objectives of international humanitarian law, see Michael N Schmitt, 'Military necessity and humanity in international humanitarian law: preserving the delicate balance', *Virginia Journal of International Law* 50, 4 (2010), 795.
37  ICRC, *Interpretive Guidance*, 50.
38  Niels Melzer, 'Keeping the balance between military necessity and humanity: a response to four critiques of the ICRC's Interpretive Guidance on the notion of direct participation in hostilities', *NYU Journal of International Law and Politics* 42 (2010), 831, 862.
39  The UN Secretary-General explains that cyberspace is now 'woven into the fabric of daily life'; see 69th Session of the UN General Assembly A/69/112 (30 June 2014) 4, foreword by the UN Secretary-General.
40  Cordula Droege, 'Get off my cloud: cyber warfare, international humanitarian law and the protection of civilians', *International Review of the Red Cross* 94, 886 (Summer 2012), 557.

Article 2(4) of the UN Charter, which defines the term 'force' to include cyber-attacks that affect the operation and functionality of computer systems and networks that sustain critical national infrastructure.[41]

Commentators have suggested that, in order for international humanitarian law to keep abreast of technological developments, the meaning of the term 'destruction' should be adjusted to include cyber-attacks against computer networks and systems.[42] At present, however, there seems little state practice to support this broader reading of the threshold of harm criterion and such an approach should be regarded as *lex ferenda*, representing an attempt to progressively develop the law in this area, rather than *lex lata*, the law as it currently stands. The upshot of this is that, because the cyber-attacks against Georgian civilian computer systems and networks did not produce physical harm, they would fall below the threshold of harm that is required by international humanitarian law to determine that a civilian is directly participating in hostilities.

## *Direct causation*

For conduct to qualify as DPH, the ICRC's Interpretive Guidance requires that, in addition to the requisite threshold of harm being attained, the conduct must directly cause that harm: '[i]n order for the requirement of direct causation to be satisfied, there must be a direct causal link between a specific act and the likely harm to result either from that act, or from a coordinated military operation of which that act constitutes an integral part'.[43]

This provision requires us to distinguish between specific hostile acts on the one hand and contributions to the 'general war effort' or to 'war sustaining activities' on the other.[44] Whereas the former satisfy the test for direct causation, the latter do not. In short, the Guidance distinguishes 'between direct and indirect causation of harm'.[45] In this context, 'direct causation should

---

41  Michael N Schmitt (ed) (2013), *Tallinn Manual on the international law applicable to cyber warfare* (Cambridge: Cambridge University Press), 45–52.
42  Michael N Schmitt, Heather A Harrison and Thomas C Wingfield (2004), 'Computers and war: the legal battlespace', background paper prepared for Informal High Level Expert Meeting on Current Challenges to International Humanitarian Law, Cambridge, 25–27 June 2004, 5.
43  ICRC, *Interpretive Guidance*, 51.
44  Ibid.
45  ICRC, op cit, 52.

be understood as meaning that the harm ... must be brought about in one causal step'.[46] In relation to kinetic weapons, this means the hostile act directly causes the resulting damage: pulling the trigger of a gun, for example. The requirement of one casual step would mean, however, that the assembling and storing of weapons would be insufficient to amount to direct causation. For the ICRC, such conduct merely builds upon or develops general military capacity; it does not cause harm. In the words of the ICRC, assembling and storing weapons 'may be connected with the resulting harm through an uninterrupted causal chain of events ... [but] unlike the planting and detonation of that device, [they] do not cause the harm directly'.[47]

In many situations, cyber-attacks will satisfy the direct causation threshold. There is little difference between an individual who pulls the trigger of a gun that results in injury or death and another who presses the key on a keyboard and causes important military websites to go offline; in both instances the resulting harm is brought about in one causal step. Take for example DDoS attacks, which have emerged as the weapon of choice for those seeking to cause harm to an adversary in cyberspace and which were widely used against Georgia during its armed conflict with Russia. The Tallinn Manual explains that DDoS attacks provide an 'unambiguous'[48] example of a cyber-attack that causes damage directly and thus meets the direct causation threshold. The reason for this is because, once a botnet[49] is created or acquired, all it takes is the touch of a computer key to instruct/command the botnet to flood the target website with requests for information and cause damage. In relation to the Georgian conflict, the DDoS attacks and acts of website defacement against cyber infrastructure supporting military operations would satisfy the requirement of direct causation.

This notwithstanding, it is important to recognise that, because of the multi-layered structure of cyberspace, combined with the increasingly complex algorithms that underpin cyber operations, in many instances the damage caused by cyber-attacks will be indirect in effect. Consider the following extract:

---

46   ICRC, op cit, 54.
47   Ibid.
48   Schmitt (ed), *Tallinn Manual*, 120.
49   A 'botnet' describes a network of private computers infected with malware and controlled as a group without the owner's knowledge.

> *One of the most difficult-to-handle aspects of a cyberattack is that in contrast to a kinetic attack that is almost always intended to destroy a physical target, the desired effects of a cyberattack are almost always indirect, which means that what are normally secondary effects are in fact of central importance. In general, the planner must develop chains of causality—do X, and Y happens, which causes Z to happen, which in turn causes A to happen. Also, many of the intervening events between initial cause and ultimate effect are human reactions (eg, in response to an attack that does X, the network's administrator will likely respond in way Y, which means that Z— which may be preplanned—must take response Y into account). Moreover, the links in the causal chain may not all be similar character—they may involve computer actions and results, or human perceptions and decisions, all of which combine into some outcome.*[50]

In light of this, Turns concludes that the effects of more modern, complex cyber-attacks will often occur indirectly and are thus unlikely to 'ever meet the requirement of direct causation for DPH, which suggests that civilians could engage in CW [cyber warfare] with impunity'.[51]

The requirement of direct causation obviously sets the threshold for DPH at a high level. It would mean, for example, that civilians involved in designing computer malware and/or disseminating malware cannot be regarded as directly participating in hostilities. Instead, it is the civilian that *launches* the malware against the target that directly causes harm and thus directly participates in hostilities.[52]

---

50  William A Owens, Kenneth W Dam and Herbert S Lin (eds) (2009), *Technology, policy, law, and ethics regarding US acquisition and the use of cyberattack capabilities* (Washington, DC: National Academies Press), 127.

51  David Turns, 'Cyber warfare and the notion of direct participation in hostilities', *Journal of Conflict and Security Law* 17, 2 (2012), 279, 288.

52  According to the ICRC, 'individual conduct that merely builds upon or maintains the capacity of a party to harm its adversary … is excluded from the concept of direct participation in hostilities … [examples of non-DPH] include scientific research and design, as well as production and transport of weapons and equipment'; ICRC, *Interpretive Guidance*, 53 (footnotes omitted). Crawford likens an individual who writes and disseminates malicious code to a 'bomb maker', who is not generally regarded as directly participating in hostilities; see Emily Crawford (2015), *Identifying the enemy: civilian participation in armed conflict* (Oxford: Oxford University Press), 88.

An important caveat is that 'the resulting harm does not have to be directly caused by each contributing person individually, but by the collective operation as a whole'.[53] Thus, although some actions on their own may not directly cause the required threshold of harm they can satisfy the direct causation requirement if they constitute an 'integral part of a concrete and coordinated tactical operation that directly causes such harm'.[54] In this context, the ICRC cites as examples 'the identification and marking of targets, the analysis and transmission of tactical intelligence to attacking forces, and the instruction and assistance given to troops for the execution of a specific military operation'.[55] Civilians who assist parties to an armed conflict by using the internet to identify targets in the field or by relaying real-time intelligence about the opposing force's capabilities or movements, while not directly causing the resulting harm, can be regarded as engaging in conduct that forms a crucial (integral) element of the hostile act's successful execution and therefore satisfies the direct-causation test. In relation to those civilians who produce computer malware, although such conduct is ordinarily regarded as indirectly causing harm it may, exceptionally, satisfy the test for direct causation where the civilian identifies the cyber vulnerabilities of a specific computer system or network and then manufactures bespoke malware that is passed to another with the knowledge that it will be used in a cyber-attack against the target's cyber vulnerability.

## *Belligerent nexus*

The final part of the ICRC's Interpretive Guidance requires that the specific act in question not only directly cause the aforesaid harm or be objectively likely to directly cause such harm, but, in addition, 'must also be specifically designed to do so in support of a party to an armed conflict and to the detriment of another'.[56] What this requires is that the hostile conduct in question represents a benefit to one party of the armed conflict and, as a result, harm to the other. The idea is that the act in question is 'so closely related to the hostilities conducted between parties to an armed conflict that they constitute

---

53    Melzer, 'Keeping the Balance', 865.
54    ICRC, *Interpretive Guidance*, 54–55.
55    ICRC, op cit, 55.
56    ICRC, op cit, 58.

an integral part of those hostilities'.⁵⁷ The purpose of the belligerent nexus requirement is therefore to exclude conduct that is unrelated to the conflict, such as a civilian who exploits the chaos and lawlessness during an armed conflict to loot shops and residences.

Did the cyber-attacks against Georgia in 2008 satisfy the belligerent nexus criterion? The ICRC's Interpretive Guidance explains that 'violent forms of civil unrest, the primary purpose of which is to express dissatisfaction with the territorial or detaining authorities',⁵⁸ do not possess a sufficiently close nexus to the armed conflict. For the ICRC, although such conduct can cause harm to a party to the conflict it does not, strictly speaking, confer a benefit to the other party.

Interestingly, the Tallinn Manual casts the belligerent nexus test more broadly and suggests that it is satisfied where the conduct in question 'directly relates to the hostilities'.⁵⁹ This suggests that 'as long as there is some direct connection between the act and the hostilities, the civilian's action will be sufficient'.⁶⁰ In contrast to the ICRC's Interpretive Guidance, the Tallinn Manual does not require that it be shown that the activity in question was specifically designed to cause harm to one party *and* confer a benefit to another.⁶¹ Evidently, the Tallinn Manual's framing of the belligerent nexus standard sets the bar lower than the ICRC's approach and could potentially encompass acts of political protest.

It is difficult to discern whether the cyber-attacks committed against Georgia's cyber military infrastructure were designed to prevent the Georgian government from utilising its computer systems to send and receive information relating to military operations and, by doing so, to confer an advantage on Russia during its armed conflict with Georgia or, instead, whether the cyber-attacks were expressions of protest against Georgia's treatment of ethnic Russians in South Ossetia. While more information would be needed to make this determination, if it is the former explanation that is accurate, a belligerent

---

57 Ibid.
58 ICRC, op cit, 63.
59 Schmitt (ed), *Tallinn Manual*, 119.
60 Collin Allan, 'Direct participation in hostilities from cyberspace', *Virginia Journal of International Law* 54, 1 (2013), 173, 188.
61 Allan, op cit, 189–190.

nexus can be established, whereas if it is the latter there would be no belligerent nexus, according to the ICRC's formulation of this criterion.

## *'For such time'*

If a civilian engages in conduct that amounts to DPH, the ICRC's Interpretive Guidance explains that they can only be directly targeted 'for such time' that they engage in this activity.[62] The ICRC determines that persons can be directly targeted not just where they are committing the hostile act that constitutes DPH, but also when engaging in measures immediately preparatory to the execution of the act and when returning from the operation.[63] In practice, however, identifying precisely when DPH starts and ends is not an easy task and will 'depend on a multitude of situational factors that cannot be comprehensively described in abstract terms'.[64]

In terms of directly targeting an individual before the hostile act is committed, the key question is how extensive the preparation must be. The ICRC draws a distinction between conduct that is preparatory to 'a specific hostile act' and conduct that is 'aimed to establish the general capacity to carry out unspecified hostile acts';[65] in the former direct targeting is permissible, whereas in the latter civilian protection remains and direct targeting is prohibited. The decisive issue is whether the preparatory conduct plays 'an integral part of a specific act'[66] or, in other words, is undertaken with a 'view to the execution of a specific hostile act'.[67] If so, during this period the civilian can be regarded as directly participating in hostilities and targeting is permissible.

In the cyber context, this would mean that a civilian would not be liable to direct targeting when performing general and speculative acts of cyber reconnaissance/espionage in order to identify potential cyber vulnerabilities of an enemy. Such conduct would only render a civilian directly targetable when performed with the objective of identifying vulnerabilities in the computer

---

62   ICRC, Geneva Conventions, Article 51(3) AP I; Article 13(3) AP II.
63   ICRC, *Interpretive Guidance*, 65.
64   Ibid.
65   ICRC, *Interpretive Guidance*, 66.
66   ICRC, op cit, 68.
67   ICRC, op cit, 66.

systems and networks of an adversary in preparation for a specific cyber-attack. Similarly, a civilian who has written computer malware and is actively 'zombie-ing' computers in order to develop a botnet would be immune from direct targeting unless the botnet is being developed in preparation for a specific attack.

In relation to when an operation can be said to have ended (and thus the window for direct targeting closes), the ICRC contends that the civilian must be 'physically separated from the operation, for example by laying down, storing or hiding the weapons or other equipment used and resuming activities distinct from that operation'.[68]

Although cyberspace is not a physical domain, this standard of physical separation can be analogised to the cyber setting. For example, DPH would end once a DDoS attack has been launched and the civilian goes offline or engages in different and unrelated cyber activity. If there is a delay between the launching of a cyber weapon and its activation (as would be the case with many malicious cyber operations, such as logic bombs), DPH extends up to the point that the weapon is activated. As with civilians who lay improvised explosive devices on the physical battlefield, for example, DPH ends upon activation and does not continue until the effects of the weapon have been felt, which may be many days, weeks, months or even years later.[69]

On the physical battlefield, the ICRC's interpretation of the 'for such time' qualifier arguably strikes an acceptable balance between the principles of military necessity and humanity. In particular, the ICRC's determination that direct targeting is only permissible when measures are being undertaken that are preparatory to a specific hostile act is acceptable from the perspective of military necessity because there is likely to be a certain period of time between a civilian engaging in preparatory measures and committing the attack. This

---

68   ICRC, op cit, 67.
69   In the words of the *Tallinn Manual*, '[t]he majority of the International Group of Experts took the position that the duration of an individual's direct participation extends from the beginning of his involvement in mission planning to the point where he or she terminates an active role in the operation. In the example [of logic bombs] the duration of the direct participation would run from the commencement of planning how to emplace the logic bomb through activation upon command by that individual'; see Schmitt (ed), *Tallinn Manual*, 121.

means that that the opposing force will have a reasonable window of opportunity to identify the threat and react to it before the hostile act is launched. However, in an instantaneous environment such as cyberspace, cyber-attacks occur at lightning speed where malicious cyber operations can be conceived, the necessary tools acquired, the target identified, the act executed, and the operation terminated with the click of a mouse or the touch of a keyboard, all of which may only take a split-second. By restricting direct targeting to only that timeframe when preparatory measures are being undertaken, opposing forces will have a very short window of opportunity to target the individual representing the threat.[70]

This problem is exacerbated considerably where civilians repeatedly commit cyber-attacks that amount to DPH, a likely possibility given the ease and speed at which cyber-attacks can be committed, and the fact that attribution difficulties in cyberspace mean that those committing cyber-attacks are unlikely to be detected and held responsible. According to the ICRC's Interpretive Guidance, where civilians repeatedly directly participate in hostilities they cannot be made the object of attack during intervals in their participation even though they form a deliberate and conscious plan to repeatedly directly participate in hostilities. This is known as the 'revolving door of civilian protection'.[71] The ICRC justifies this approach on the basis that '[i]t prevents attacks on civilians who do not, at the time, represent a military threat'.[72] For the ICRC, except for where civilians are preparing for the commission of a hostile act, committing that act or have yet to physically separate themselves from it, there is no pressing security threat to the opposing party and so military necessity cannot justify direct targeting. Instead, the party to the armed conflict must suspend targeting during lulls in participation and wait until preparatory measures are once again undertaken.

---

70  'This is problematic in that many cyber operations last mere minutes, perhaps only seconds. Such a requirement would effectively extinguish the right to strike at direct participants'; Schmitt, 'Cyber-operations', 89, 90. Indeed, this is recognised by the ICRC: 'Where the execution of a hostile act does not require geographic displacement, [such as] computer network attacks …, the duration of the DPH will be restricted to the immediate execution of the act and preparatory measures forming an integral part of that act'; ICRC, *Interpretive Guidance*, 68.
71  ICRC, op cit, 70.
72  Ibid.

In the context of cyber, however, the ICRC's position would mean that even if on the basis of previous practice a party to the armed conflict can reliably predict that a civilian will commit future cyber-attacks, it can only directly target that person during each split-second that a new cyber-attack is being prepared, launched and concluded. This would provide very little or even no window of opportunity for the party to the armed conflict to directly target the individual and would mean that, in reality, it has to withstand repeated cyber-attacks that it knows are being concocted and prepared. Such an approach is arguably unsatisfactory from the perspective of military necessity because it prevents parties to an armed conflict from pursuing their legitimate security needs.[73]

## Conclusion

In contemporary warfare, it is inevitable that the strategic corporal will be confronted with civilians who exploit cyberspace to commit cyber-attacks against computer systems and networks belonging to a party to the armed conflict. Determining whether civilians that engage in such conduct can be made the object of attack hinges upon whether they can be regarded as directly participating in hostilities. While this concept is notoriously undefined in international humanitarian law documents, the ICRC has sought to provide guidance as to its content and meaning. However, the ICRC's Interpretive Guidance was formulated principally with the physical battlefield in mind, and thus its application to the cyber setting is not always clear. By assessing the application of the ICRC's Interpretive Guidance to cyber operations, the

---

73   According to the US *Law of War Manual*, '[t]he law of war, as applied by the United States, gives no "revolving door" protection; that is, the off-and-on protection in a case where a civilian repeatedly forfeits and regains his or her protection from being made the object of attack depending on whether or not the person is taking a direct part in hostilities at that exact time. Thus, for example, persons who are assessed to be engaged in a pattern of taking a direct part in hostilities do not regain protection from being made the object of attack in the time period between instances of taking a direct part in hostilities'; see United States Department of Defense (2015), *Law of War Manual* (June 2015), 231. Available at archive.defense.gov/pubs/law-of-war-manual-june-2015.pdf, accessed on 11 April 2017. See also, generally, Michael N Schmitt, 'The Interpretive Guidance on the notion of direct participation in hostilities: a critical analysis' *Harvard National Security Law Journal* 1 (5 May 2010), 34ff.

objective of this chapter has been to provide some much-needed clarification to this important area of law and thereby assist the strategic corporal in complying with their international humanitarian law and international criminal law duties.

# 8

# Creating Strategic Corporals? Preparing Soldiers for Future Conflict

## David W Lovell[1]

THE WARS AND OTHER ARMED CONFLICTS over the past century—since the time of the 'Great War for Civilisation' (which has become known as the First World War)[2]—have seen substantial changes in many key areas of military science and technique. Wars of position have been replaced by battles of manoeuvre, and, largely as a consequence, massed battles have been supplanted by the actions of small (or smaller) units; battlefields are now unlikely to be remote from larger towns and cities, and civilian casualties (sometimes deliberate, sometimes unintentional) continue to rise; technology has made weapons more lethal and more accurate, communications instantaneous, and killing often more remote and clinical. By contrast, the fundamental causes of war, at least as Thucydides presented them 2500 years ago—fear, honour and interest—have not changed; nor has the fact that taking lives and fighting for your life is traumatic for combatants themselves; and nor has the likelihood that we will continue to wage war against each other into the foreseeable future at almost any cost to our material, social and psychological well-being. The only limit we have so far recognised, with two terrible exceptions, is with the indiscriminate nature of, and potential for human extinction embodied in, nuclear weapons, and on this self-imposed limitation there is no absolute guarantee into the future.

---

1   This chapter first appeared as an article in the *ADF Journal*. The editors would like to thank the *ADF Journal* for permission to reprint the article here.

2   See, for example, Robert Fisk (2005), *The great war for civilisation: the conquest of the Middle East* (London: Fourth Estate).

In these changes over the past century, what has been asked of the soldier—and sailor, and aircrew—has also changed. In armed conflicts, we expect soldiers of all ranks to be able to operate more autonomously, to exercise considerable judgement in (and take responsibility for) their actions, to be technically proficient, and to understand the larger picture of which their efforts are merely a part. No longer are soldiers 'cannon fodder'. In front-line forces, there are fewer of them and their actions count more than in the past; they are highly trained and extensively equipped and supported; and the loss of their lives is felt—particularly in modern democracies—as a national and political tragedy. This emphasis on individual soldiers, their physical safety in the field and their physical, emotional and psychological well-being after the conflict, is matched by the increasing surveillance over their actions, especially in the field, by the established media as well as by the electronic communications technologies that have expanded into almost every aspect of our lives in recent years with extraordinary rapidity.

But soldiers are increasingly asked to do much more than fight in armed conflicts, especially over the last three or four decades. They act as peacekeepers, in often volatile situations. They act as emergency responders in natural disasters. And they act in constabulary roles in a variety of challenging areas, including drug- and people-smuggling. In all these roles, nations look to their armed forces for professional, thoughtful and effectual but restrained behaviours that do credit to their flag. The devolution of considerable authority to soldiers at the point of action; the sometimes conflicting demands the mission makes of them; the provocations they often face; and the scrutiny that they are consistently under: all demand a degree of education and training of soldiers, and of a more general preparedness, that is the subject of this chapter.

Charles Krulak's notion of the 'strategic corporal' drew attention to a number of the challenges facing soldiers in recent conflicts: the complexity of the modern battlefield and the range of tasks that need to be prioritised and addressed; the role of the more junior ranks in making important decisions within their field of operation (whether by the incapacity of officers, the inability to receive communications, or the inherently small-group approach to many operations); and the ever-present scrutiny of their actions and thus potentially mission-crippling nature of their errors being broadcast to the world. The discussions in this chapter differ from Krulak's perhaps in the extent to which the initiative, sense of responsibility and preparedness expected by Krulak of the corporal are extended to all soldiers.

This chapter begins with some reflections on the future of conflict: on the challenges, in other words, that soldiers will need to confront in the near to medium future. Krulak's notion of the 'three block war' encapsulates some of these issues, but my purpose here is to canvass the breadth of the matters of which soldiers should have some understanding. Arguing that technology will play an ever-larger role in future conflict, the chapter goes on to stress that the challenges confronting human beings are not thereby diminished, and in some ways demand even more attention from us. The third substantive section outlines some of the ways in which an appropriate level of preparedness among soldiers can be developed. My central theme is that precisely because of the difficulties of predicting the future of conflict in any but a coarse grained sense, preparing our soldiers for the unexpected challenges that will inevitably arise needs to be given as much attention as the acquisition of weapons platforms (over which nations agonise deeply and spend extravagantly).

## The future of conflict

It seems to be a Danish proverb, sometimes attributed to the physicist Niels Bohr, that 'prediction is very difficult, especially if it's about the future'. (There were no such qualms in the former Soviet Union, of course, where the future of socialism was absolutely and officially guaranteed, and the past kept changing.) But in writing of 'the future', I want to limit my horizon to the next 30 years. That, broadly speaking, is the career span of an officer cadet or midshipman entering the Australian Defence Force (ADF) today. If we look to the next 30 years, what can we expect with reasonable certainty?

To sharpen our focus further, think of the 30 years since 1984. It was not quite the year that George Orwell had predicted in his dystopian vision written in 1948, though some of its themes rang true, especially about the corruption and control of language. And Orwell's warnings about pervasive surveillance of our everyday lives are increasingly and deeply worrisome.

In 1984, the Cold War was in full swing.[3] The first Macintosh personal computer came onto the market, changing the face of personal computing forever with its use of a graphic interface.[4] Three years later, China's 'reform

---

3   See, for example, Richard H Immerman and Petra Goedde (eds) (2013), *Oxford handbook of the Cold War* (Oxford: Oxford University Press).
4   Steven Levy (1994), *Insanely great: the life and times of the Macintosh, the computer that changed everything* (New York: Viking).

and open' policy was launched by Deng Xiaoping, which has led to the spectacular economic and strategic rise of China. The Soviet-dominated Eastern Bloc collapsed in 1989 and the Soviet Union itself followed in 1991. Al-Qaeda launched its boldest attack against the US in 2001, and US forces subsequently invaded Afghanistan and then—on the same anti-terrorist pretext—invaded Iraq in 2003 and overthrew the regime of Saddam Hussein. This has opened an era of sectarian violence in the Middle East that threatens to last for generations. In the Arab world since 2010, a large number of previously secure rulers have been unseated and civil wars and other conflicts continue to destabilise the region. Though democracy was the great hope of this 'Arab Spring', the reality has proved more diverse and more troubling. So, there have been enormous political changes, most of them unpredicted.

The internet, an electronic networking system conceived in the early 1960s as a way to provide a robust, distributed communication system for US defence purposes,[5] was increasingly deployed by academia in the 1980s, and began to be commercialised in the 1990s. This technology has shaped modern communications, with the development of mobile telephony and so-called smartphones becoming available from the mid-1990s, and exploding in 2007 with the release of the first iPhone. So, there have been enormous technological changes, particularly in communications.

Weaponry has incorporated and sometimes led these changes, including the introduction of precision-guided weapons that first saw wide use in the Gulf War in 1990–1991. The threat of nuclear weapons has receded from view, but at the same time the lethality of conventional weapons has increased manyfold. In international relations, we had hopes (and some misgivings) for a 'new world order', for an 'end to history', and for the triumph of democracy. In other words, we anticipated—for 'one brief, shining moment', to borrow a musical phrase—a harmonious world. What we have seen since the late 1990s, but especially since '9-11', instead, is a world where democracy appears increasingly unattractive; where some unfree states, notably China, seem to

---

5    Critical was work done by the Defense Advanced Research Projects Agency (DARPA); for a fuller and detailed account, see Barry M Leiner, Vinton G Cerf, David D Clark, Robert E Kahn, Leonard Kleinrock, Daniel C Lynch, Jon Postel, Larry G Roberts, Stephen Wolff, 'Brief history of the internet'. Available at www.internetsociety.org/internet/what-internet/history-internet/brief-history-internet#, accessed on 11 April 2017.

have cracked the code of wealth creation, creating an attractive model for developing states; and where the abolition of the distinction between church and state, in a new Islamic caliphate, has become a cause to which thousands are prepared to take up arms, even and especially against their co-religionists. These models are now in active, and sometimes bloody, competition with each other.

The unsurprising lesson of such an overview of 30 years is that change will continue, and will continue to surprise us. And, independent of such changes, though often linked to them, we also know that conflict will continue. Conflict is an inescapable element of the human story. Many of our human institutions are creative responses to conflict, channelling competitive energies into politics, law, markets, diplomacy, and so on. But force remains the ultimate arbiter of human disputes.

What sort of wars will we fight in the next 30 years? It has been observed that wars between states themselves have declined since the end of the Second World War, and that wars of a new type, wars within states, over issues of identity, fought in unconventional ways and with unconventional financing, will predominate. Mary Kaldor is rightly prominent among a number of analysts who have made such points,[6] and I will not gainsay them. Yet we should not be complacent that interstate wars are now impossible, especially on the basis of our impressive material achievements. We certainly have a lot to lose, but European states at the height of their material and cultural civilisation went into a disastrous war in 1914, and large modern cities—Coventry, London, Tokyo, Dresden, not to mention Hiroshima and Nagasaki—have in subsequent wars been devastated by aerial bombing and associated firestorms. We should not limit our thinking, or our preparation, by denying some futures as 'unthinkable'.

If we ought to acknowledge that interstate wars are not impossible, we should also be alive to the changes and challenges in guerrilla warfare. Fighting insurgents in remote environments in Afghanistan and Iraq, as we have been doing for more than a decade, does not constitute the 'textbook'. Dave Kilcullen rightly reminds us that the key megatrends—rapid population growth, urbanisation, littoralisation and global networked connectivity—will confront us with diverse operating environments for which we need different

---

6   Mary Kaldor (2012), *New and old wars*, 3rd edition (Cambridge: Polity Press).

types of capabilities and preparation. He summarises his point by anticipating an age of the 'urban guerrilla'.[7]

What we should acknowledge, at the very least, is that the conflict scenarios of the future are unpredictable within a wide arc, and will be complex.

Another point arises from the experience of the last 30 years (and of the history of conflict more generally) that is crucial but I think often overlooked or discounted in these sorts of discussions. Wars of all sorts are terrible, but they are rarely decisive. They do not, on the whole, solve problems. As Thomas Hobbes put it in the seventeenth century, there is no better 'hope to mend an ill game, as by causing a new shuffle'.[8] We must know that even if we are obliged, or choose, to fight a war the application of force is unlikely to solve the problems that led to it. Indeed, open conflict merely indicates that one equilibrium has broken down. That equilibrium may have been precarious, or unjust, or in other ways undesirable, but its destruction may unleash a Pandora's box of troubles, giving succour to the discontented, the opportunists and the spoilers. Wars do not promise ready or clean solutions. That is, in addition, because wars themselves often create new points of disagreement or injustice. We need to have clear and realistic views about what wars can achieve when we embark upon them. In his 1827 letter to Major Carl von Roeder, where he famously pointed out that war 'is the continuation of politics by different means', Clausewitz went on to state the consequence of this view: 'there can be no question of a *purely military* evaluation of a great strategic issue, nor of a purely military scheme to solve it.'[9]

In irregular war—much more than in regular war (where battles tend to be decisive)—the political dimension is key. Lawrence Freedman noted that we should not be too despondent about our capacity to deal with irregular warfare as a military problem:

---

7   David Kilcullen (2013), *Out of the mountains: the coming age of the urban guerrilla* (London: Hurst).

8   Thomas Hobbes, *Leviathan*, edited by Richard Tuck (Cambridge: Cambridge University Press, 1991), 71.

9   Cited by Peter Paret (2011) in 'The genesis of *On War*', in Carl von Clausewitz, *On War*, edited and translated by Michael Howard and Peter Paret (London: The Folio Society), xxx.

> The key point however is that the military strategy must be integrated with a political strategy. If the side we are supporting is weak it is probably because it lacks a strong political base and is prone to division ... The side with the strongest political foundations should prevail militarily.[10]

General Wesley K Clark has argued that the US intervention in Iraq in 2003 was 'a perfect example of dominating an enemy force but failing to secure the victory'.[11]

And especially if we *choose* to go to war, we must also be aware of the role of chance. Winston Churchill in 1930 advised that any

> statesman who yields to war fever must realize that once the signal is given, he is no longer the master of policy but the slave of unforeseeable and uncontrollable events. Antiquated War Offices, weak, incompetent or arrogant commanders, untrustworthy allies, hostile neutrals, malignant fortune, ugly surprises, awful miscalculations — all take their seat at the council board on the morrow of a declaration of war.[12]

So wars of the future will be, as they have been in the past: unpredictable, complex and inherently limited in their ability to provide solutions.

One further point I will hazard with a reasonable degree of confidence: it is unlikely that in the next 30 years Australia will fight a war for its existence as a sovereign state, and therefore the conflicts in which Australian soldiers will take part will be wars of choice, and will almost certainly be in coalition with our allies, and will be at some remove from our shores. All these predictions have ramifications for equipment and capability, but they do not change the human factors of dealing with the experience of battle. In some respects, they deepen the complications. The ADF will, consequently, continue to be a

---

10   Lawrence Freedman, 'Regular and irregular war', *Strategic Datalink* 1 (August 2008). Available at d3n8a8pro7vhmx.cloudfront.net/cdfai/pages/348/attachments/original/ 1413946891/Regular_and_Irregular_War_-_Lawrence_Freedman.pdf?1413946891, accessed on 8 May 2017.

11   Wesley K Clark (2003), *Winning modern wars: Iraq, terrorism, and the American empire* (New York: Public Affairs), xiv.

12   Winston S Churchill (2007), *My early life: a roving commission* (London: The Folio Society), 231.

professional and not a conscript defence force. That means that we not only need to think, but we can act, to prepare ADF soldiers to the best of our ability.

## Technology and organisation

Technology has become the handmaiden of the imagination. And we can expect continuing, significant and rapid technological change over the next 30 years. But how will it affect warfare? I begin my answer with a cautionary point. The impressive military technologies of today give the very misleading impression—to both politicians and citizens alike—that modern wars can be won by technology and no longer need involve large inputs of human power or loss of life. And the reliance upon technology does not absolve the decision makers 'from hard questions of strategy and policy' (which Russell Weigley argued was a dangerous American tendency),[13] and nor should it lower the policy threshold of the use of force as a last resort.

This point having been made, let me essay some of the principal areas where our military technologies will further assist our ability to wage war.

In no particular order of priority, we may expect:

- an increased ability to cut through the 'fog of war', those issues of situational battlefield awareness that Clausewitz drew to our attention, and that Tolstoy communicated so well in the battle scenes of *War and Peace*
- an increased ability to be more effectively and precisely lethal in the application of force
- a better ability to do 'more with less', in the face of increasing challenges to national budgets, to get more lethality, more mobility and more firepower from a smaller number of weapons platforms
- an ability to be more nimble in both getting to 'the battlefield', moving around it and extracting oneself and one's wounded comrades from it if necessary
- and, finally, an ability to be better protected and better able to survive what previously would have been considered fatal wounds.

---

13   Russell F Weigley (1977), *The American way of war: a history of United States military strategy and policy* (Bloomington, IN: Indiana University Press), 416.

These clusters of abilities will be variously addressed and implemented by new and developing technologies. All of them will continue to develop as they have developed across the history of organised warfare for centuries. What is different, perhaps, is the attention, seriousness and (consequently) funding they will receive, and the likely rapidity with which they will advance. The best technical and theoretical minds applied themselves to advances in warfare in the twentieth century, at Bletchley Park, Los Alamos and elsewhere, and this will doubtless continue.

While this organised human activity is fascinating, I confess that I don't find the technologies all that interesting in themselves. Identifying problems and devising fixes are what humans have become extraordinarily good at over the past two or three hundred years. Max Weber called it *Zweckrationalität*, instrumental or goal-oriented rationality, and argued that it had become a dominant characteristic of modernity.[14]

Technology is not an unalloyed good; it has the potential for unintended consequences. The use of precision-guided weapons might degrade the barriers against using nuclear weapons, or enemies might use pernicious tactics to strike back (such as using human shields, or Iraq's burning of Kuwaiti oil fields in 1991). The technology that allows people to aim and fire weapons remotely can mean that killing is not felt to be real, diminishing restraints. The increasing technological integration of civilian and military systems means that any cyber war will likely impact citizens and civilian infrastructure (especially the increasingly ubiquitous machine-to-machine communications, or the so-called internet of things),[15] and not just military systems. (That, indeed, might be its very purpose.) Technology may also lower the threshold of conflict, by one party considering that certain sorts of technological interference constitute 'aggression'. It may also lower restraints on the idea that force should be used only as a last resort. And when soldiers are provided with the 'larger picture' that the new technology allows, they are 'likely to

---

14   Max Weber (1978), *Economy and society: an outline of interpretive sociology*, edited by Guenther Roth and Claus Wittich (Berkeley: University of California Press), 24–25.
15   For a sanguine account of M2M, see Jan Holler, Vlasios Tsiatsis, Catherine Mulligan, Stefan Avesand, Stamatis Karnouskos and David Boyle (2014), *From machine-to-machine to the internet of things: introduction to a new age of intelligence* (Amsterdam: Academic Press).

second-guess decisions made at higher levels and (in richly connected systems) have the information required to undertake initiatives their superiors may find inappropriate.[16]

Soldiers, of course, will become much more adept at using the new technologies, just as children nowadays have an almost intuitive sense of how to use smartphones and computer tablets. But soldiers will still suffer fatigue and rely on judgements, good and bad, they will be courageous and afraid, they will be daring and timid, generous and mean-spirited, and I am certain they will continue to find the taking of others' lives repugnant, even if sometimes necessary. John Keegan has rightly stressed this human dimension:

> *What battles have in common is human: the behaviour of men struggling to reconcile their instinct for self-preservation, their sense of honour and the achievement of some aim over which other men are ready to kill them. The study of battle is therefore always a study of fear and usually of courage; always of leadership, usually of obedience; always of compulsion, sometimes of insubordination; always of anxiety, sometimes of elation or catharsis; always of uncertainty and doubt, misinformation and misapprehension, usually also of faith and sometimes of vision; always of violence, sometimes also of cruelty, self-sacrifice, compassion; above all, it is always a study of solidarity and usually also of disintegration—for it is towards the disintegration of human groups that battle is directed.*[17]

Soldiers need to be trained for the use of technology, but they need to be prepared more broadly for fighting wars. The human factor is the most important factor in war: in starting wars, in fighting wars and in ending wars and rebuilding. Intrinsic to this factor is the organisation of defence itself, on which I shall dwell for a moment.

Modern warfare is essentially industrial and bureaucratic. Ironically, the ability to engage in conflict requires the highest levels of cooperation and organisation. If hierarchy and bureaucracy (in the neutral, Weberian sense)

---

16   David S Alberts (1996), *The unintended consequences of information age technologies: avoiding the pitfalls, seizing the initiative* (Washington, DC: Institute for National Strategic Studies, NDU), 36.

17   John Keegan (2008), *The face of battle* (London: The Folio Society), 277.

are the best ways of getting human beings organised to pursue certain tasks, it is not surprising that militaries should be their exemplars. But bureaucracies have their drawbacks, and it is worth mentioning three in particular that can impact on our prepared soldier's ability to function strategically in combat.

First, bureaucracies tend to be risk-averse and obsessed with control; they feel threatened by different and challenging ideas, by open debate, by the unexpected. I know, or know of, senior leaders who are not like this (and the Australian Defence leadership has in recent years been commendably active in trying to bring about cultural change within the organisation); but most of their subordinates either chafe at, or quietly endure, the confines within which they must work and think, and some—through a process of socialisation—no longer see the confines at all. The soldier or official who disrupts the bureaucratic logic of control is likely to find himself with a short career. Richard Adams expands on this theme elsewhere in this book.

I have used the masculine gender above, and it relates to my second point: that the Australian military and military bureaucracy is not a diverse culture. The ADF is largely white and male (ie predominantly male and third-generation Australian). A recent report from within the organisation argued that 'the language practices of Defence are mechanisms that thwart diversity and greater social inclusion'.[18] A more diverse workforce would better represent the Australian people that the Department of Defence serves, allowing varied perspectives and enhanced operational capability. And as a professional service, uniformed and civilian, Defence needs to be attractive as a place for people to work, and to stem the attrition of highly trained people. Nick Jans has described the ADF as consisting of 4 'tribes': Navy, Army, Air Force and Australian Public Service.[19] Part of the preparation of soldiers must be to understand better the members of those other 'tribes' with whom they will almost inevitably work in the conflicts to come, and to understand the broader community from which they are drawn.

---

18   Elizabeth A Thomson (2014), *Battling with words: a study of language, diversity and social inclusion in the Australian Department of Defence* (Canberra: Australian Government, Department of Defence), xi.

19   Nick Jans (with David Schmidtchen) (2002), *The real c-cubed: culture, careers and climate, and how they affect capability*, Canberra Papers on Strategy and Defence 143 (Canberra: ANU), 121–138.

The third issue is the ceaseless bureaucratic activity of Defence: the stress on process rather than outcomes, the hamster-wheel of extraordinary exertion, even, and especially in times of peace, inducing fatigue and straining commitment.

Therefore, when we try to imagine (and prepare for) future conflicts, we should think less of the development of incipient and even imagined technologies of killing—however ingenious, effectual and precise—and more of the qualities and attitudes that are required for the successful prosecution of a war and the ultimate resolution of the issues that led to it. For they are essential if conflict is not simply to smoulder and subsequently reignite: if the deck is not to be reshuffled once again, to echo Hobbes. How do we develop such soldiers? (And by 'soldiers', I include generically soldiers, sailors and aircrew, including officers.)

## The prepared soldier

First of all, soldiers should know, in general terms, where they stand in the scheme of Defence, and where Defence stands in the scheme of government. They should know the risks and the limitations of war as a means of resolving conflict. They need to be convinced that the conflict in which they put their lives at risk, and will likely take the lives of others, has a sound cause and a strong likelihood of success, and is not merely the product of grandiose personal ambitions, rivalries fanned by unthinking jingoism, or desperation. Like every citizen, they should be able to discern whether a war involves decisive action, with clear exit points and transparent goals related to vital interests. While they might be familiar with the geographical landscape on which they operate, they should also be aware of its cultural landscape, not just to honour in some sort of token way the cultural achievements of their enemies, or even to be aware of the taboos the breaking of which can damage their relations with the local people (especially important in a counterinsurgency conflict), but also to understand the conflict from the side of the enemy, the better to judge their seriousness and motivations, and the depth of their hostility, and, in the final analysis, why the enemy is trying to kill them.

As I have argued elsewhere,[20] the advanced study of history, of politics, of law and of literature are essential to the modern soldier, and not just to the

---

20   David W Lovell (2012), 'Educating for ethical behaviour? Preparing military leaders for ethical challenges', in David W Lovell and Igor Primoratz (eds), *Protecting civilians during violent conflict: theoretical and practical issues for the 21st century* (Farnham: Ashgate), 141–157.

circle of officers, in developing the types of understanding I have just outlined. The study of history is not about 'learning from the mistakes of the past'; rather, it allows us to see the vast range of human responses to particular situations, to consider possibilities and boundaries. Literature stimulates the soldier to imaginatively construct the feel of the battlefield, and to understand how different—but at the same time how similar—they are to others, even across age, gender, ethnic, religious and cultural divides. Politics and its sub-discipline, international relations, allows a soldier to understand the reasons for a conflict and the likelihood of a just settlement. And politics, furthermore, opens up the world of the underlying power structures of the societies in which they are operating, supplemented perhaps by social anthropology. Law reinforces the importance of sets of rules of behaviour, not just in the societies in which a soldier might be operating but in the conduct of war itself. And the discipline of ethics also has something to contribute, for while technology sometimes gives a decisive edge in battle, the human control of technology requires ethical decision-making and the ability to hold humans to account for their actions.[21]

I am not advocating the development of 'soldier-scholars', though there have always been some soldiers who value the cultivation of their broader intellect almost as much as their professional mastery. Rather, I am commending the ability to process the vast amounts of information with which we are confronted to create *knowledge*: ordered and connected information. In his nineteenth-century discussion on *The Idea of a University*, Cardinal Newman described the sort of intellect I think the soldier should have: 'one which takes a connected view of old and new, past and present, far and near, and which has an insight into the influence of all these one on another; without which there is no whole, and no centre'.[22] He called this a 'liberal education', by which he meant the development of *useful* and *relevant* knowledge, but not directly *applied* knowledge (for which training was the appropriate

---

21  See Rebecca J Johnson (2011), 'Moral formation of the strategic corporal', in Paolo Tripodi and Jessica Wolfendale (eds), *New wars and new soldiers: military ethics in the contemporary world* (Farnham: Ashgate), 239–256.

22  John Henry Newman (1852), *The idea of a university: defined and illustrated*. Available at www.newmanreader.org/works/idea/discourse6.html, accessed on 8 May 2017.

avenue). The distinction between training and education is even more relevant today.

The challenges of future conflict, in so far as we can anticipate them, also, and relatedly, mean that soldiers need to develop a leadership style that embraces and encourages colleagues and subordinates: a collective style that cares about and draws from the collective to make good decisions, and engages all its members. (Nick Jans writes about this elsewhere in this book in terms of 'shared leadership', and I think our understandings of leadership are not far apart.) The ability to develop trust in collectives, teams, is vital to the development of this leadership style. Leadership and hierarchy are not synonymous concepts: hierarchical authority does not necessarily equate with experience or good decisions. The ability of senior ranks to listen to their juniors is critical. Sociologically, this style emerges more readily from a democratic society, the removal of the aristocratic element from military leadership and the modern emphasis on merit and knowledge. A genuine discussion over strategy and tactics between different ranks that was almost unthinkable in, say, a nineteenth-century Prussian *Kriegsspiel*, is nowadays taken for granted. Hierarchy has become the last refuge of the intellectually insecure.

Because of the almost universal human injunctions against killing, and what Dave Grossman has described as the 'innate resistance to killing their fellow human beings',[23] there needs also to be an educated self-consciousness of how the act of killing will be handled mentally by those who do it, and a recognition that time for group decompression at the end of a tour of duty, and frank and intelligent responses by society at large to widespread instances of Post-Traumatic Stress Disorder from returned soldiers, needs to be developed. The reality of being in a war zone one day and the safety of home in 24 or 48 hours is challenging for soldiers to process. And increasingly this aspect of what might be called 'post-modern conflict' and its dangers are being recognised. But soldiers must first know what to expect, much as Elisabeth Kübler-Ross analysed the five stages of grief when confronted by impending death.[24] I endorse Grossman's view that

---

23   Dave Grossman (2009), *On killing: the psychological cost of learning to kill in war and society*, revised edition (New York: Little, Brown), 13.
24   Elisabeth Kübler-Ross (1970), *On death and dying* (London: Tavistock Publications).

*if society prepares a soldier to overcome his resistance to killing and places him in an environment in which he will kill, then that society has an obligation to deal forthrightly, intelligently, and morally with the result and its repercussions upon the soldier and the society.*[25]

## Conclusion

There have been many models of soldiers in the past, from the patrician soldier of ancient Rome, personified by the statesman Cincinnatus, who reluctantly took up public office and returned to his farm once the task was done (and to whom George Washington was often compared),[26] to the soldier as expendable 'pawn', or in the nineteenth-century expression: 'cannon fodder'. But the sociology of armed forces has changed. Our democratic sensibilities recommend a more cooperative hierarchy of abilities and talents, and the creation of the 'citizen-soldier'. Aristocratic hangovers lurk harmlessly in ceremonial uniforms and mess rituals, which have a merely irritating way of reinforcing the distinction between insider and outsider. The new technologies of war have empowered modern soldiers and reinforced meritocracy, but underlined the importance of soldiers' ability to partake in cooperative leadership. Their education must develop the skills—and the courage—of independent judgement; their formal education must be the start of a process of lifelong learning.

Soldiers are not simply people who go onto the battlefield and fire their weapons, or whose chief virtue is obedience. They are the spearhead of a vast organisational chain, the results of years of preparation, and they must be the very best we can manage. Their lives are better protected the better educated they are; the more informed about their mission and their enemy, the more they can participate in the leadership of their mission, and the more they can appreciate the strains of battle and how to cope with stress and death. Prepared soldiers are resilient.

The soldiers who put their lives at risk for their country today need a complex set of intellectual strengths and insights to take with them into battle along with their weapons, not just the ability to punctuate a memorandum,

---

25   Grossman, *On killing*, 287.
26   See Minor Myers (2004), *Liberty without anarchy: a history of the society of the Cincinnati* (Charlottesville, VA: University Press of Virginia).

or to write an essay. Where their enemies may be zealots in some religious or ideological cause, they need an appreciation that tolerance and diversity are worth fighting for. I grant that these desiderata represent a tall order, but without a liberal education such an order has no chance of being filled.

One further, crucial point needs to be kept in mind. None of the emphasis in this chapter on preparedness for responding to the intensified challenges of modern battlefields reduces the importance of the overarching strategic decisions which put soldiers on that field in the first place. A prepared soldier cannot substitute for a poor strategy.

# 9

# Strategic Gains without the Strategic Corporal: The Singapore Armed Forces in Afghanistan (2007–2013)

## Samuel Chan[1]

> ... the strong do what they have the power to do and the weak accept what they have to accept.
> —Thucydides, *History of the Peloponnesian War* [2]

THE PREVIOUS CHAPTERS in this collection examined the broad notion of the 'strategic corporal' from the vantage points of the professional soldier, the private military contractor and the civilian in current and future conflicts. The soldier has been the focal point, given the wider demands placed on the profession-of-arms beyond the calibrated application of violence. The seemingly ubiquitous presence of non-combatants and the media within the contemporary area of operations (AO)—frequently overseas and in a different cultural zone—further implies that the decisions of lower-echelon tacticians could have a disproportionate impact on outcomes in the field and at home. The scenario painted by General Charles Krulak of 'strategic corporals' operating within the 'three block war' should theoretically concern all expeditionary militaries. Realities, however, indicate this is not necessarily so.

---

1   The author acknowledges and thanks Ho Shu Huang for comments on an earlier version of this chapter.
2   Thucydides (1972), *History of the Peloponnesian war*, translated by Rex Warner, introduction and notes by MI Finley (London: Penguin Books), 402.

This chapter is a case study of how Singapore achieved its strategic goals while bypassing concerns associated with the 'strategic corporal'. The specific aim is a detailed examination of Singapore's six-year (2007–2013) contribution, codenamed Operation Blue Ridge (OBR), to the United Nations-mandated and NATO-led International Security Assistance Force (ISAF) in Afghanistan. This inquiry is divided into two parts. The first places OBR within the historical context of Singapore Armed Forces (SAF) deployments overseas and the primacy of the American factor in Singapore's strategic calculations. Although the dominant OBR narrative was palatable to Singaporeans, it in all likelihood played second fiddle to realpolitik considerations. The second half covers the conspicuous deployment and employment characteristics of 492 SAF personnel within the ISAF AO, where risks were minimised while concomitant benefits were optimised.

## National interests and troop deployments

Singapore is an oft-quoted success story of decolonisation after the Second World War. The city-state elected its own leaders in 1959 after 140 years as a British colony and from 1963 to 1965 formed part of the newly established Federation of Malaysia.[3] Singapore had no hinterland or natural resources besides its strategic location and motley collection of ethnicities and cultures. The metamorphosis of this *entrepôt* into a sprawling metropolis and global financial hub in the last 50 years has been nothing short of a miracle. The cornerstone of this success has been 'pragmatism', to ensure Singapore remains internationally relevant. In practical terms, this means a free-market economy, minimising corruption within public and private spheres, the practice of meritocracy 'with Singaporean characteristics', and ensuring a stable environment anchored in strong governance and national defence.

In terms of international relations, Singapore observes but does not interfere in the domestic politics of others and expects reciprocity. It does not aim to spread any form of ideology, but projects influence by being a regional innovator and investing in beneficial bilateral relationships. International law and norms are adhered to provided they reflect Singapore's cultural roots and social norms and preserve racial and religious harmony. Multilateral concerns

---

3   The Federation of Malaysia was formed in 1963 when Sabah and Sarawak (present-day 'east Malaysia') and Singapore were added to the Malaya Federation ('west Malaysia').

are preferably addressed within the ambit of regional and international groupings such as the Association of Southeast Asian Nations (ASEAN) and the United Nations (UN).

How can one describe Singapore's interstate relations? Perhaps the most appropriate is 'friendship without commitment', as Harish Chandola once depicted Singapore–India relations.[4] This is not *sui generis* but generally applicable, and rightly so. Early experiences shaped this outlook, as the late former President Sellapan Ramanathan, then speaking as Ambassador-at-large in 1998, recalled:

> [T]hree days before Saigon fell, we told the US and everyone else that if they took their people out of Vietnam, we would facilitate them. When it fell and the first load of people came, we provided them shelter at St John's Island. Tents were put up. The army provided food, all in the belief that they would be taken away later. But what did they do—they took away all the doctors, engineers and accountants. They took away everybody except the fishermen and the farmers. What could the fishermen and farmers do with us? After that, we said, you take back. So, we were seen as harsh, but our first experience of charity was a bitter one.[5]

More recently, then-Permanent Secretary of Foreign Affairs Bilahari Kausikan reiterated: 'Being nice or having friendly relations is a means. The end must be national interest.'[6]

National defence has proven sacrosanct for much of the last five decades, even though Singapore seeks friendship with all and has no identifiable enemies.[7] The emphasis on national security has preserved sovereignty,

---

4   Harish Chandola, 'Friendship without commitment', *Economic and Political Weekly* 6, 39 (25 September 1971), 2046.
5   Walter Fernandez, 'S'pore "must stand up firmly to others"', *The Straits Times*, 2 July 1998, 32.
6   Wong Sher Maine, 'I say what I think', *Challenge* (magazine of the Singapore Public Service), 18 July 2011.
7   George G Thomson, 'Britain's plan to leave Asia', *The Round Table: The Commonwealth Journal of International Affairs* 58, 230 (1968), 123; Ronnie Wai, 'More stress on personnel development', *The Straits Times*, 27 May 1982, 1; Paul Jacob, 'Educate the public on role of armed forces', *The Straits Times*, 28 April 1986, 14.

provided space for political manoeuvre, and created a stable environment for trade and investment. Key bilateral relationships are maintained through residential diplomatic presence and important military ties by the presence of a defence section at the respective embassy or high commission.[8] There is also the psyche—ingrained at least in the minds of the political and administrative leadership—rooted in a persistent sense of vulnerability. Stressing this point, however, has proven a perennial challenge given the widening contradictions between the rhetoric and perceived realities of ordinary Singaporeans.[9]

The deployment of SAF personnel overseas and their contribution to foreign policy has evolved over the years.[10] Since 1971, small numbers of Singaporean soldiers have been deployed to corners of the globe where they provided medical assistance, served as unarmed UN observers or held staff billets.[11] These were missions of choice, with no direct threats to Singapore's sovereignty or its citizens (missions of direct necessity), or with minimal political credit to be gained (missions of indirect necessity). These were undertaken as a responsible member of the international community, to gain experience in (post-) conflict zones and to benchmark the SAF with other troop-contributing nations. Missions of direct necessity were rare but successfully executed. Operation Thunderbolt in 1991 witnessed the rescue of hostages from various nationalities when Singapore Airlines flight SQ 117 was hijacked en route from Kuala Lumpur to Singapore. Operation Crimson Angel in 1993

---

8   The exceptions are Taiwan and Israel, due to political sensitivities, and Singapore's bilateral interests with China, Malaysia and Indonesia, respectively.
9   Elizabeth Nair, 'The Singapore soldier', *Pointer: Journal of the Singapore Armed Forces* 12, 2 (January–March 1986), 85–86; 'So you think we've arrived?' *The Sunday Times*, 3 January 1993, 1, 6–7; 'Nation of self-reliant people needed', *The Straits Times*, 19 August 2002, H5; Edwin Lee (2008), *Singapore: the unexpected nation* (Singapore: Institute of Southeast Asian Studies), 289–290; Kwa Chong Guan, 'A new generation rewrites history, doubts Singapore's vulnerability', *The Straits Times*, 30 January 2015.
10  See, for example, Andrew TH Tan, 'Punching above its weight: Singapore's armed forces and its contribution to foreign policy', *Defence Studies* 11, 4 (December 2011), 541–558; Yee-Kuang Heng, 'Confessions of a small state: Singapore's evolving approach to international peace operations', *Journal of International Peacekeeping* 16, 1–2 (February 2012), 119–151.
11  For example, Pakistan, the Philippines, Angola, Cambodia, Western Sahara, South Africa, Ethiopia-Eritrea, Guatemala, Iraq-Kuwait, Afghanistan and Nepal.

saw the SAF evacuate Singaporeans from Phnom Penh when unrest rocked Cambodia.

Since 1991 the deployments of SAF troops overseas have gradually evolved from a few staff officers or small teams to larger contingents with multiple rotations under the auspices of the UN and UN-mandated regional arrangements. These were increasingly missions of indirect necessity for political gain with a world power (ie the US), to show state solidarity with a victim of aggression (eg Kuwait by Iraq) or to champion safe maritime passage (eg the Gulf of Aden). Although Singapore and its citizens did not face direct threats, the political implications were such that the potential cost of inaction outweighed the cost of action. Operation Blue Heron (OBH), first as part of the International Force for East Timor (INTERFET) and later under successive UN missions (1999–2003, 2008–2012), was an indirect necessity. Over 1000 SAF personnel were deployed to the former Portuguese colony, which was annexed by Indonesia in 1975. Singapore ran the risk of offending Jakarta had it been the only neighbouring country or ASEAN member involved. However, the opposite occurred and Singapore gained more than the risks involved. Politically, it stood in solidarity with the regional and wider international community. Operationally, OBH witnessed the SAF's inaugural deployment of a platoon and subsequently a company of combat peacekeepers, which coincided with the first appointment of an SAF officer—Major General Tan Huck Gim—as UN force commander.

The next sizeable deployment of SAF personnel took place on Operation Flying Eagle after the 2004 Boxing Day tsunami wrought havoc along the Indian Ocean periphery. Army personnel spearheaded Singapore's inter-agency humanitarian assistance and disaster relief efforts in Indonesia and Thailand. The month-long mission was of indirect necessity subjected to the host nations' acceptance of goodwill and displayed the SAF's readiness to conduct joint operations at short notice. Shortly afterwards, Singapore undertook another mission of indirect necessity, as a member of America's 'coalition of the willing' in the reconstruction of post-2003 Iraq. Operation Blue Orchid (2003–2008) was mainly a naval effort to protect the Al-Basra Oil Terminal.[12] Ground troops were kept to a minimum as the insurgency gripped much of

---

12 Woon Tai Ho (2010), *Partnering to rebuild: Operation Blue Orchid: the Singapore Armed Forces experience in Iraq* (Singapore: Ministry of Defence), 24–40.

Iraq. A ground security element protected a Republic of Singapore Air Force (RSAF) C-130, which supported coalition air operations in 2004.[13] A further four army officers provided representation to Headquarters Multi-National Force-Iraq in Baghdad between 2006 and 2008.[14] The correlation between risks and the roles played by boots on the ground is clear.

This brings us to OBR, where the dominant narrative and *raison d'être* was framed within the clear and present context of global terrorism.[15] Nefarious plots to cause mass casualties and video recordings of critical infrastructure compiled by Jemaah Islamiyah (JI) operatives placed Singapore firmly within the crosshairs of the al-Qaeda affiliate.[16] The JI threat was addressed by Singapore's domestic intelligence agency—the Internal Security Department—in close cooperation with other ASEAN members, especially Indonesia and Malaysia. Singapore, however, could not ignore Afghanistan. OBR was pitched as a proactive step to meet domestic threats connected to other regions and the deployment of SAF personnel an indirect response to JI. As incumbent Deputy Prime Minister (DPM) Teo Chee Hean explained in his former capacity as Defence minister in 2011:

> *The security challenges we face today are transnational. We live in an interconnected world, where instability in another part of the world can affect the peace and security of Singapore and our region. While the SAF's primary mission remains the defence of Singapore's sovereignty and territorial integrity, safeguarding our national security interests today includes*

---

13   'A Step Closer to Peace—RSAF's C-130 Detachment to the Gulf Region', *Air Force News*, 88 (March 2004), 14–16.

14   Woon Tai Ho, *Partnering to rebuild*, 84–85.

15   Singapore Armed Forces (2013), *Two thousand two hundred and sixty-three days 2007–2013: Operation Blue Ridge—The SAF's six-year mission in Afghanistan* (Singapore: Ministry of Defence), 5, 7, 12–17; Muhammad Helmi, '2263 days 5221 km from home', *Army News*, 214 (August 2013), 11; '2263 days later: the end of our journey in Afghanistan', *Army News* 214 (August 2013), 19. The exact metric for the claim of 'longest deployment' is unknown since Operation Blue Torch—Singapore's contribution to the United Nations Iraq-Kuwait Observer Mission—took place between 1991 and 2003.

16   Republic of Singapore, Ministry of Home Affairs (2003), White Paper: The Jemmah Islamiyah arrests and the threat of terrorism, Cmd 2 of 2003, 7 January (Singapore: Ministry of Home Affairs).

*participating in international peace and security missions to help bring stability to critical regions.*[17]

Yet there is also the realpolitik explanation, as the late Mr Lee Kuan Yew, Singapore's founding Prime Minister, candidly reasoned:

*We sit down, we got to make decisions. I either support or oppose, and if I oppose I give my reasons; if I support, I give my reasons. And I said look, here's the direction you have to go. We have to go to Afghanistan. Shall we or shall we not? They want us to send a medical team to support the Australians and the Dutch in a dangerous area called Uruzgan. I said look, it's part of the insurance premium we are paying, we got to pay. You want the Americans to stay here, you want a strategic framework agreement with them, known to our neighbours, you want the logistics base to stay here, you got to pay this price. Go. I mean, you calculate. If America were going to be out in five, 10 years, do we need to pay this price? No. The British—we knew they were going to leave. But we know the Americans cannot leave. If they leave, they've lost their global influence. They know that the Pacific is the biggest area of contention in this century, not the Atlantic.*[18]

Both explanations elucidated the realities facing Singapore and served different yet complementary purposes. The first was directed at the domestic audience, for whom military matters do not usually feature at the forefront of their daily concerns. Such is the 'tyranny of peace'. Furthermore, OBR was neither debated in Parliament nor put to a vote. This is possible in part because Singaporean society is accustomed to the deployment of troops overseas but expects zero fatalities all the same. Citing the SAF's role in preventing Afghanistan from reverting to a 'terrorist safe haven' and emphasising the positive humanitarian dimension to aid Afghans following decades of conflict was certainly more palatable than highlighting the possible consequences

---

17  Jonathan Chan, 'Overseas Service Medal: recognising professionalism and sacrifices', *Army News* 185 (February 2011), 2.

18  Han Fook Kwang, Zuraidah Ibrahim, Chua Mui Hoong, Lydia Lim, Ignatius Low, Rachel Lin, and Robin Chan (2011), *Lee Kuan Yew: hard truths to keep Singapore going* (Singapore: Straits Times Press), 327–328.

of inaction. On the other hand, Lee Kuan Yew's realpolitik reasoning showed that Washington and not Kabul was firmly at the centre of Singapore's calculations. That Afghanistan posed no direct strategic interests for Singapore was alluded to by another well-known public figure.[19] The same was also said of the SAF's deployment to post-2003 Iraq.[20] Yet circumstances dictated Singapore send troops to both countries in the wake of successive American interventions.

What makes the US so critical to Singapore that the cost of inaction in Afghanistan (and, for that matter, Iraq) outweighed the associated risks? The key reason is that Singapore views America as 'a protecting and not a menacing power' whose presence in the Asia-Pacific region has kept aggression 'in check' and provided a stable environment for economic growth.[21] Singapore-US relations have developed into a close relationship over the last five decades, although it has not always been trouble-free.[22] The last 15 years have drawn both states even closer. The 2003 Free Trade Agreement was the first concluded with an Asian country, while the 2005 Singapore-US Strategic Security Policy Dialogue (which provides 'the foundation for broad-based defence cooperation') was the first concluded with a non-ally.[23] One

---

19   Comments made under Chatham House Rules during a presentation by Ambassador Karl Eikenberry, former US Ambassador to Afghanistan, titled 'The Transition to Afghan Sovereignty: Assessing Progress and Identifying Challenges' at the Institute of South Asian Studies (National University of Singapore, 19 June 2012).

20   Daljit Singh (2009), *By design or accident: reflections on Asian security* (Singapore: Institute of South East Asian Studies), 52.

21   Michael Leifer (2000), *Singapore's foreign policy: coping with vulnerability* (London: Routledge), 98–99, 102, 104; Michael Chua Teck Leong, 'Long term presence of the United States in the Asia Pacific', *Pointer: Journal of the Singapore Armed Forces* 24 4 (October–December 1998); US Department of Defense (2013), 'News transcript of Department of Defense press briefing by Secretary Hagel and Minister Ng in the Pentagon Press Briefing Room', 12 December 2013. Available at archive.defense.gov/transcripts/transcript.aspx?transcriptid=5342, accessed on 11 April 2017.

22   Richard Deck (1999), 'Foreign policy', in Michael Haas (ed), *The Singapore puzzle* (Westport, CT: Praeger Publishers), 125–149; Leifer, *Singapore's foreign policy*, 100, 106–108.

23   Elisia Yeo, 'A US-S'pore first', *Today*, 5 May 2003, 17; Lynn Kuok (2016), 'The U.S.-Singapore Partnership: A Critical Element of U.S. Engagement and Stability in the Asia-Pacific', Asian Alliances Working Paper Series, Paper 6 (July 2016). Available at www.brookings.edu/wp-content/uploads/2016/07/Paper-6.pdf, accessed on 26 May 2017.

vantage point views these as agreements between 'security partners, not allies'.[24] Yet local academics proffered different perspectives. Kuik Cheng-Chwee saw Singapore as a *de facto* security ally' of the US.[25] Tan See Seng similarly opined that the FTA and SSPD 'further expands their already considerable bilateral economic, political and security ties, making them allies in nearly every which way but in name'.[26]

Independent of the official status of US-Singapore relations, one certainty has been the critical nature of American military benefits in the SAF's evolution. Military-to-military cooperation has given Singapore the most potent air force in Southeast Asia, access to advanced weaponry, vast training grounds and a combat-hardened partner. Singapore has hosted a permanent American military presence for the last 25 years, and assets make frequent visits to Paya Labar Airbase and Changi Naval Base. Besides the hardware and software, American education has also aided the career development of Singapore's senior political and military leaders. At the time of writing, four cabinet ministers and 13 of 29 (44.8 per cent) present and former members of the SAF's elite nucleus—the Chiefs of Defence Force and respective service chiefs—received formal military *and* civilian education in America. This widens to 24 of 29 (82.8 per cent) if one considers those who received *either* military or civilian education. This reflects a deliberate policy to educate the SAF's 'best and brightest' in the world's most powerful country. The importance of such experiences goes beyond world-class education and valuable networks. They reinforced America's positive standing among Singapore's leaders and further strengthened Singapore-US ties within and beyond the military spheres.

## The price

If Singapore is not a charity then it must be recognised that neither is Uncle Sam. Access to vast training grounds from which the SAF has 'gained

---

24   'Singapore and the US: security partners, not allies', *Strategic Comments* 19, Comment 24 (August 2013), viii–ix.
25   Kuik Cheng-Chwee (2009), 'Shooting rapids in a canoe: Singapore and great powers', in Bridget Welsh, James Chin, Arun Mahizhnan and Tan Tarn How (eds), *Impressions of the Goh Chok Tong years in Singapore* (Singapore: National University of Singapore Press), 159.
26   Tan See Seng, 'America the indispensable: Singapore's view of the United States' engagement in the Asia-Pacific', *Asian Affairs: An American Review* 38, 3 (2011), 156.

immensely', joint exercises to benchmark themselves against the world's best, training and education courses from pre-commissioning to war college, sales of advanced weaponry, technical cooperation and a snug defence relationship all come at a cost.[27] It was clear Singapore had to support coalition efforts in Afghanistan, not merely though words but with matching deeds as a troop contributor. Singapore, however, would not simply acquiesce to any request for boots on the ground. The risk–return trade-off was considered carefully, given that OBR was not a mission of direct necessity. This meant minimising any likelihood of death or injury, both mental and physical. OBR was also not an open-ended commitment, and keeping a small footprint provided Singapore with the flexibility to effect a rapid drawdown to conclude its involvement when required.

In light of such constraints, Singapore's strategic goals were clear: maximise political capital with Washington, gain operational experience while minimising risks to troops on the ground, and maximise positive publicity to maintain society's confidence in the SAF. Singapore would take carefully planned and small steps to meet such national interests but it would not be a perfunctory effort.[28] In 2010, DPM Teo conveyed that: 'Our contributions in Afghanistan are not large, but they are in niche areas where we can make an operationally useful contribution to the coalition effort.'[29] These niche contributions commenced with five-man dental and engineering teams in 2007. They were followed by medical contingents, staff officers at various headquarters and the inaugural deployments of an Unmanned Aerial Vehicle (UAV) team, imagery analysts, artillery radars and military institutional trainers (MITs). Those who met the civilian population were in 'feel good' roles (ie engineers and medical) that served to cultivate a positive image of Singapore. Logisticians based in Kuwait ensured SAF personnel in Bamiyan, Kabul, Kandahar and Uruzgan were well supplied at all times.

Once the question of what Singapore would contribute was answered, there was a need to address the question of 'who to send'. The total mobilised

---

27  Jeremy Au Yong, 'Huge gains for SAF by training in US: Dr Ng Eng Hen', *The Straits Times*, 15 December 2013.
28  Chia Han Sheng, 'DPM Teo visits SAF troops in Afghanistan', *Army News* 171 (October–November 2009), 5.
29  Jonathan Chan, 'Helping to rebuild Afghanistan', *Army News* 177 (June 2010), 9.

strength of the SAF is approximately 350 000, but this figure consists of 20 000 regulars, 30 000 full-time national servicemen (NSFs, or 'conscripts'), and 300 000 national servicemen (NSMen, known colloquially as 'reservists'). The force is meant to deter potential aggressors who seek to wage war on Singapore. Anything short of a direct armed conflict and the numbers available for overseas deployments shrink dramatically. This was not always the case. In the 1990s, national servicemen were actively encouraged to 'volunteer' for overseas deployments. A 30-strong medical team of regulars, NSFs, and NSMen braved Scud rocket attacks on over three dozen occasions during Operation Nightingale as they reinforced a British field hospital stationed in Saudi Arabia during the First Gulf War. In Operation Blue Torch, NSMen comprised a quarter (or more) of the 88 officers deployed in 14 SAF observer teams over the 12-year (1991–2003) period in support of the UN Iraq-Kuwait Observer Mission. The narrative then was that deployments built rapport and strengthened bonds between the citizen-soldier and the professional soldier.[30] Those were perhaps the halcyon days of national servicemen on overseas missions.[31] This was certainly true for OBR, where regulars accounted for 489 of the 492 personnel deployed.[32]

A closer examination of rank distribution (Table 1) also revealed that OBR was composed only of personnel with leadership responsibilities. Enlistees from private to corporal first class were conspicuously absent. The most inexperienced personnel deployed were junior officers and specialists who made up slightly more than a quarter (28.5 per cent) of the OBR contingents. It would seem that the first step to rendering the 'strategic corporal' a non-issue was simply to leave the lower-echelon tacticians at home. This was followed by restricting the numbers of junior and relatively inexperienced personnel. Such policies placed great personnel stresses on certain units. For

---

30  'First reservist in UN mission', *Pioneer* (June 1993), 11.
31  Tim Huxley (2000), *Defending the Lion City: the armed forces of Singapore* (St Leonards, NSW: Allen & Unwin), 256–257; Goh Kee Nguan (2004), *The Singapore Army moving decisively beyond the conventional*' unpublished MSS thesis, USAWC Strategy Research Project, Carlisle Barracks, PA, 12–13.
32  Three national servicemen—Major (Dr) Philip Lau (trauma surgeon), Major (Dr) Tan Wah Tze (anaesthetist) and Major (Dr) Matthew Cheng (orthopaedic surgeon)—possessed specialised medical skills and deployed to Uruzgan for 61 days. See Chan, 'Helping to rebuild Afghanistan', 6.

example, the 24th Battalion, Singapore Artillery, which operates the army's artillery hunting radars (ARTHUR) deployed 80 per cent of its regulars over a 15-month deployment.[33]

Table 1: Rank composition of personnel on OBR[34]

| Rank and equivalent | Number | Category | Category total | Proportion of OBR total (%) |
|---|---|---|---|---|
| Colonel (COL) | 7 | Senior Officers | 137 | 27.8 |
| Senior Lieutenant Colonel (SLTC) | 8 | | | |
| Lieutenant Colonel (LTC) | 45 | | | |
| Major (MAJ) | 62 | | | |
| MAJ (DR) | 15 | | | |
| Captain (CPT) | 71 | Junior Officers | 77 | 15.7 |
| CPT (DR) | 1 | | | |
| Lieutenant | 5 | | | |
| Senior Warrant Officer | 1 | Warrant Officers | 105 | 21.3 |
| Master Warrant Officer | 10 | | | |
| First Warrant Officer | 40 | | | |
| Second Warrant Officer | 43 | | | |
| Third Warrant Officer | 11 | | | |
| Master Sergeant | 29 | Senior Specialists | 110 | 22.4 |
| Staff Sergeant | 81 | | | |
| First Sergeant | 21 | Junior Specialists | 63 | 12.8 |
| Second Sergeant | 37 | | | |
| Third Sergeant | 5 | | | |
| Total | 492 | Total | 492 | 100 |

---

33　Chan, 'Overseas Service Medal'.
34　Singapore Armed Forces, *Two thousand two hundred and sixty-three days*, 154–163; Singapore Armed Forces Act (Chapter 295) Regulation 2(1) Singapore Armed Forces (Ranks of Servicemen) (Amendment) Regulations 2012.

After niche areas were identified and personnel shortlisted, it was imperative to prepare them well. Each soldier, regardless of rank, knew the importance of their individual role and of their role as a diplomat. They were cognisant that they had a job to do and do well, for their actions could have ramifications for Singapore's image within both the ISAF community and the indigenous community. To aid their preparation, comprehensive two-week pre-deployment training (PDT) was conducted by the army's elite Singapore Guards formation, covering geopolitical history, cultural norms, basic Dari and Pashto, and specific tactical training.[35] The conscientious attention paid off handsomely, as one MIT explained: 'We had to understand their culture, language and religious beliefs so as to build a good relationship with them and get our points across.'[36] The PDT proved tremendously helpful as cultural nuances were repeatedly highlighted and cultural taboos strictly avoided. SAF personnel who actually met Afghans never gave their counterparts the 'thumbs up', knowing it was a vile gesture. Photographs were taken only with permission, and never of women. The 'dirty' left hand was never used on its own. The soles of boots and feet were never shown when sitting on a carpet in the traditional manner. Personnel also refrained from eating or drinking in the presence of locals during the holy month of Ramadan. The PDT, generally high levels of education, and mutual respect for different cultures in Singapore are all tangible examples of the intellectual 'strength and insights' discussed by David Lovell in an earlier chapter. This also goes some way to assuaging concerns raised by Siobhán Wills in her chapter about 'arming' deployed troops with the requisite knowledge and experiences. Indeed, SAF personnel were cognisant that the cultural, religious and ideological dimensions were as real and important as possible hostile fire.

Further steps were taken to manage risk even though the PDT package prepared personnel for worst-case scenarios. Travel beyond the confines of sprawling coalition bases was tightly controlled, which limited contravention of the law of armed conflict (LOAC), fratricide, collateral damage or the

---

35 'Army team to Afghanistan recognised for their contributions', *Army News* 152 (March–April 2008), 3; Ian Cheong and Marcus Ho, 'SAF contributes to provincial reconstruction in Afghanistan', *Army News* 162 (January–February 2009), 4; Singapore Armed Forces, *Two thousand two hundred and sixty-three days*, 154.

36 Jonathan Chan, 'OSM for 29 servicemen', *Army News* 190 (July 2011), 4.

violation of indigenous cultural norms. The SAF would, at the very worst, avoid alienating anyone they met in-theatre. Force protection was also high on the agenda and was provided to all teams venturing 'beyond the wire' and even those well-protected within the confines of coalition bases.[37] The hazards faced were repeatedly highlighted, as Dr Ng explained:

> I would receive regular reports, whether it was an sms or emails, about IEDs exploding, suicide bombings as well as rockets and mortars, landing directly, some near to our camps, some near to where our soldiers lived. Each report underscored the risks that existed every day for our soldiers there.[38]

For those who ventured beyond the wire, there was the additional risk of exposure to anti-IED jamming devices on vehicles. The same concerns also applied to the ARTHUR teams deployed in Uruzgan. The MITs also faced the possibility of 'green-on-blue' attacks as they trained 1 845 Afghan National Army (ANA) soldiers (1 634 artillerymen in Kabul and 211 sappers in Uruzgan) in partnership with American, Australian and Mongolian teams.[39] MITs stationed in Kabul bore the additional burden of risks associated with convoy movement, but no cost was too great to ensure their safety. Fifteen mine-resistant, ambush-protected vehicles were acquired and modified to protect the five MIT detachments (51 personnel) that rotated to the Afghan capital between January 2011 and September 2012.[40] No cost was too great to minimise the deep impact on morale in the SAF and scarring on wider public opinion should there be any casualties. Force protection also eradicated the need for any decision-making while under direct enemy fire.

## The risk and return

The deployed personnel gained much in terms of professional growth and personal satisfaction despite the risks associated with the Afghanistan AO.

---

37  For example, the ARTHUR team deployed within the confines of the Dutch-led Camp Holland in Uruzgan had its own security team. See Chan, 'Overseas Service Medal'.
38  Shawn Tay, 'SAF to end its Afghanistan deployments', *Army News* 209 (March 2013), 6–7.
39  Singapore Armed Forces, *Two thousand two hundred and sixty-three days*, 25, 92.
40  Teo Jing Ting, 'Trucks of survival', *Cyberpioneer*, 25 November 2013; Singapore Armed Forces, *Two thousand two hundred and sixty-three days*, 158–159.

For a military that had existed in peace for five decades, OBR provided valuable operational experiences beyond the replicable realism of any training simulator or conditions found in Singapore and foreign training grounds. The ARTHUR teams operated on 24-hour shifts for 100-odd days in-theatre, knowing that the situation was 'live' and outcomes were permanent.[41] The climate was also another challenge, as one gunner discovered:

> *We faced extreme climate there. Not only is the air dry, temperatures can reach 45° Celsius (113°F) in summer and minus 10° Celsius (14°F) in winter. This took a toll on both man and machine. We had to constantly watch out for overheating during the mission as this could lead to an equipment shutdown.*[42]

Over in the medical centre, a nursing officer related: 'In Singapore we are trained to handle combat injuries, war wounds and trauma but we have never seen or dealt with them first-hand. Our deployment to Afghanistan gave us this opportunity to hone our skills.'[43] The commander of the sole UAV Task Group deployed in 2010 also revealed how regulars benefited in the face of difficulties:

> *It was tough learning to operate seamlessly with the Imagery Analysis Team. We had to return to our fundamentals as Combat Intelligence analysts to understand mission and ground demands. Despite the challenging weather conditions, every UAV team member gained a wealth of operational experience.*[44]

---

41 Chan, 'Helping to rebuild Afghanistan', 8; Singapore Armed Forces, *Two thousand two hundred and sixty-three days*, 156.
42 Glen Choo, 'Army team clinches defence technology prize', *Army News* 194 (November 2011), 8.
43 Glen Choo and Jonathan Chan, 'Supporting peace and reconstruction in Afghanistan', *Army News* 194 (November 2011), 6.
44 Helmi, '2263 days 5221 km from home', 17; Singapore Armed Forces, *Two thousand two hundred and sixty-three days*, 157.

He further added:

*The deployment gave us the opportunity to see how our tasks fit into the bigger picture and provided very practical and vital information for the ISAF. It also enabled us to fine-tune and validate our processes and systems, and boost our servicemen's confidence.*[45]

The OBR 'box score' provided a quantitative snapshot of the OBR experience.[46] The UAV Task Group conducted 68 missions and flew 112 sorties with a total of 450 hours' flight time during its 90-odd days in-theatre. Eight rotations of imagery analysts completed 204 missions over a 28-month period (November 2010 to June 2013). The four ARTHUR teams tracked all 27 indirect fire attacks during their combined 16-month employment between September 2009 and December 2010. The 70 medical personnel deployed in five medical teams and one surgical team also handled '305 surgeries, 983 emergency room admissions, 2,619 clinic patients, 62 [evacuations] to higher-echelon medical facilities, and 18 deaths'.[47] These numbers may not hold significance among troop-contributing nations but SAF soldiers still understood the strategic relevance that Richard Adams spoke of in his earlier chapter. The relevance came with keeping the Singapore flag flying within the ISAF coalition, and the significance of their efforts to the SAF's domestic and international standing.

Even though the SAF did not employ any ground troops in combat roles, the inconvenient question of whether Singaporean forces were 'secondary parties' complicit in the deaths of Afghan civilians was raised in cyberspace.[48]

---

45  Chan, 'Overseas Service Medal'.
46  'Looking into the ARTHUR', *Army News* 208 (February 2013), 18-19; Helmi, '2263 days 5221 km from home,' 11; Singapore Armed Forces, *Two thousand two hundred and sixty-three days*, 154–63.
47  Singapore Armed Forces Medical Corps (2012), *Ideas to reality: the SAF Medical Corps 45th anniversary* (Singapore: Singapore Armed Forced Medical Corps), 114; Singapore Armed Forces, *Two thousand two hundred and sixty-three days*, 155–156.
48  Wee Teck Young, 'I am hurting too: The hurt of militarized authoritarianism in Singapore, Afghanistan and the world,' blog post, no date. Available at warisacrime.org/content/i-am-hurting-too-hurt-militarized-authoritarianism-singapore-afghanistan-and-world, accessed on 11 April 2017.

This question, however, did not resonate with society at large. Cynics could point to the public's general ignorance of OBR, but this was made possible only because of the professionalism of deployed personnel. For starters, a deep understanding of the LOAC and ethics are hallmarks of an SAF officer. If this was not so, any declaration of being 'professional' and 'operationally ready' would ring hollow and prove nothing more than self-delusion. Fortunately, realities indicate these topics have been omnipresent at each stage of a regular SAF officer's development—from officer cadet course through to Command and Staff College—and most definitely reinforced during PDT. It is such practices that enabled the SAF to declare it is 'capable of a full spectrum of operations'.[49] In fact, in one incident imagery analysts identified a group of civilians as 'friendly' during an insurgent attack on a town and averted possible collateral damage.[50] Finally, it must be reiterated that the SAF deployed its forces in niche areas, none of which involved any direct combat. Those closest to any action were the ARTHUR teams, imagery analysts and UAV pilots. Staff officers at higher headquarters were exposed to the 'big picture'. Deployed personnel from combat vocations such as infantry, armour, guards and commandos were never employed in their traditional roles of closing with the enemy through fire and manoeuvre. Deployed SAF personnel faced nothing remotely resembling Operation Absolute Agility, the hypothetical mission painted by Krulak. There was no 'three block war' for any of them.

Even though SAF personnel did not play any direct combat role, those who wore the desert camouflage uniform gained a tremendous sense of satisfaction in a job well done. A staff sergeant related his fruitful six-month deployment as part of a six-man construction engineering team in 2009:

> *Helping the people in Bamiyan, whether through enhancing security, reconstruction or simply giving out stationery to the children at the orphanage, was very meaningful. It has made my stint there very worthwhile.*[51]

---

49 'Our Army: ready, decisive, respected', *Army News* 198 (March 2012), 6.
50 Ibid.
51 Chia Han Sheng, 'Overseas mission participants honoured', *Army News* 172 (January 2010), 3; Singapore Armed Forces, *Two thousand two hundred and sixty-three days*, 154.

Another specialist, an imagery analyst, explained:

> *In Afghanistan, I felt I was performing a dual role. While I was there to help in the reconstruction efforts, I was also representing Singapore on the international stage. When a linguist told me that he was very grateful to us for helping his country get through this difficult period, I knew we had fulfilled both roles which felt very satisfying.*[52]

Beyond personal satisfaction, there was also the added element of appreciating the peace and calm prevalent in Singapore and the importance of the SAF. An officer employed as an MIT in Uruzgan recounted: 'During one of the visits to the field hospitals, I saw some children who had lost their arms due to IEDs. The image is still very vivid in my mind. To me, that reaffirmed the purpose of the SAF.'[53] Another officer employed as a staff officer (SO) with Regional Command South (RC-South) at Kandahar airfield quipped: 'You worry about your security every single day … It really made me very thankful that I've grown up in a safe, secure and very stable environment. I've learnt never to take that for granted.'[54]

For their efforts, the 492 deployed personnel were awarded the SAF Overseas Medal (with 'Afghanistan' clasp) and the NATO medal (with 'ISAF' clasp). These have become undoubtedly two of the most cherished and differentiated decorations among regulars, despite their relatively low position in the heraldic hierarchy. The latter is a decoration of international standing and, together with the former, provides variation to time-based awards or those correlated with seniority and appointments. The NATO medal allows its recipient to stand tall and proclaims service in Afghanistan. It mattered not whether an ISAF soldier was based in relative safety or faced consistent danger in volatile provinces or patrolled treacherous valleys such as Korengal, Chora or Shah-i-kot, to name only a few. The medal makes no such distinctions. Furthermore, to the outside world these places will invariably fade, etched only in the minds of those who once served there and confined to the pages of history. The mere mention of Afghanistan, however, will invariably conjure instant images of conflict and dangers for years to come.

---

52    Choo and Chan, 'Supporting peace and reconstruction in Afghanistan', 6.
53    Glen Choo, 'Serving in overseas missions with pride', *Army News* 201 (June 2012), 3.
54    David Ee, 'Singapore troops in Afghanistan set to return', *The Straits Times*, 9 February 2013.

# Strategic Gains without the Strategic Corporal

OBR also served as a biographical booster for officers destined for higher appointments with the accompanying ranks of colonel and above. Among those deployed were 14 officers in the ranks of captain to colonel and recipients of the SAF Overseas Scholarship (SAFOS). This specialised scheme has, since 1971, systematically groomed officers for senior military appointments and forms a key component of the national talent pool. Seven SAFOS recipients have served as cabinet ministers.[55] OBR was the perfect opportunity for SAFOS officers on active duty (Table 2) to gain invaluable experience and even greater respect if and when they reach the pinnacle of the SAF.

Table 2: SAFOS recipients on OBR[56]

| Current rank (rank at deployment) and name | Year awarded SAFOS | Appointment held | Duration (days) | Latest known appointment |
|---|---|---|---|---|
| Brigadier-General (then Colonel) Chia Choon Hoong | 1991 | National Contingent Commander (NCC) | 21 April to 28 October 2011 (190) | Former Chief of Staff – Joint Staff |
| Colonel Wong Yu Han | 1991 | NCC | 9 December 2010 to 4 May 2011 (146) | Former Commander, 6th Division |
| Lieutenant Colonel Pang Tzer Yeu | 1995 | National Liaison Officer | 6 October 2012 to 5 March 2013 (150) | Head, iForce Office |
| Colonel (then Senior Lieutenant Colonel) Tan Cheng Kwee | 1997 | SO ISAF Joint Command | 30 April to 29 October 2012 (182) | Former Commander, 7th Singapore Infantry Brigade |

→

---

55  Lee Hsien Loong (SAFOS 1971), George Yeo (1973), Teo Chee Hean (1973), Lim Hng Khiang (1973), Lui Tuck Yew (1980), Chan Chun Sing (1988), and Tan Chuan-Jin (1989).
56  Singapore Armed Forces, *Two thousand two hundred and sixty-three days*, 152–163.

| Current rank (rank at deployment) and name | Year awarded SAFOS | Appointment held | Duration (days) | Latest known appointment |
|---|---|---|---|---|
| Senior Lieutenant Colonel (then Lieutenant Colonel) Tan Yueh Phern | 1999 | Imagery Analysis Team Leader | 15 February to 22 June 2013 (127) | Former Head, Force Transformation Office |
| Lieutenant Colonel (then Major) Cai Geren, Clarence | 2000 | SO (intelligence) RC-South | 9 December 2010 to 22 June 2011 (195) | Former CO, 2nd Battalion, Singapore Infantry Regiment (2 SIR) |
| Colonel (then Major) Goh Pei Ming | 2001 | SO (operations) RC-South | 23 November 2010 to 3 June 2011 (192) | Former CO, 3 SIR |
| Major Tan Jian Yun, Ryan | 2001 | SO (intelligence) RC-South | 25 May to 5 December 2010 (194) | Resigned from regular service (2011) |
| Lieutenant Colonel (then Major) Xu Youfeng | 2001 | SO (operations) RC-South | 8 June to 22 December 2010 (197) | Former CO, 6 SIR |
| Major Siew Zhi Xiang, Kevin | 2002 | SO (operations) RC-South | 12 November 2011 to 30 April 2012 (170) | Resigned from regular service (2012) |
| Major (then Captain) Tan Jian Long | 2002 | MIT | 11 December 2010 to 1 May 2011 (141) | Resigned from regular service (2013) |
| Major Wong Wei Han, Gareth | 2002 | SO (operations) RC-South | 9 June to 27 November 2011 (171) | Resigned from regular service (2013) |

→

| Current rank (rank at deployment) and name | Year awarded SAFOS | Appointment held | Duration (days) | Latest known appointment |
|---|---|---|---|---|
| Lieutenant Colonel (then Major) Cai Dexian | 2003 | SO (operations) RC-South | 13 April to 13 October 2012 (183) | Former CO, 48th Battalion, Singapore Armoured Regiment |
| Major (then Captain) Lee Wen Jun, Edwin | 2005 | MIT | 2 May to 14 September 2011 (135) | SO, Defence Policy Office |

A further six SAF officers were decorated by American superiors with a third medal in recognition of their meritorious services. Four received the Army Commendation Medal and one the Joint Service Commendation Medal.[57] The highlight was undoubtedly the Bronze Star Medal awarded to then-Major Cai Dexian, who served with Headquarters RC-South. This decoration is second only to the Legion of Merit, traditionally bestowed on the SAF's two-star service chiefs and the one-star Defence Attaché at the Singapore Embassy in Washington. For Major Cai, OBR meant challenging '16-hour days and seven-day weeks' that were only ameliorated by hour-long internet chats with his wife each evening, weekly phone calls to his parents, and monthly packages from Singapore. He even had the opportunity to hear first-hand from locals '[o]n rare forays off-base'.[58] The city-state could hardly contain its excitement over the distinction. The official broadsheet, *The Straits Times*, proudly proclaimed: 'For his dedicated service, Maj[or] Cai was awarded the US Bronze Star, the American military's fourth highest combat decoration, before his return—the first Singaporean to be so honoured.'[59] The Singapore Army's official newsletter, *Army News*, similarly celebrated:

---

57   Singapore Armed Forces, op cit, 146.
58   David Ee, 'SAF officer's sterling Afghan service', *The Straits Times*, 23 February 2013.
59   Ibid.

> *For his excellent performance there, Major Cai was awarded the United States Bronze Star Medal, the US Armed Forces' fourth highest combat award. It was the first time an SAF solder has received this accolade from the US military—awarded to individuals in recognition of their bravery, acts of merit, or meritorious service.*[60]

While SAF personnel deployed on OBR were focused on assigned tasks in Afghanistan and Kuwait, Singapore's Ministry of Defence (MINDEF) also ensured their loved ones on the 'home front' were well looked after. Beyond the multiple layers of physical force protection in-theatre, there was also the need to ensure that psychological and emotional protection was in place. The prime consideration was to keep deployed personnel and their family members in constant contact, and MINDEF took proactive measures to assuage concerns through frequent updates. Ground realities dictated such actions, because whether a soldier or airman actually left the confines of a sprawling coalition base or even met a local face-to-face was irrelevant. The mere mention of 'Afghanistan' instantly conjured images of violence to a highly educated and well-read Singaporean public. The wife of a nursing officer honestly conveyed such sentiments upon his return: 'Generally when you hear about being deployed to Afghanistan, there's a certain fear, but now that he's back safe and sound, I'm very proud of him for representing Singapore.'[61] The spouse of another officer similarly echoed:

> *I was initially worried and apprehensive when I heard my husband was to be deployed to Afghanistan. But the SAF helped to allay my fears and concerns with a comprehensive brief on the situation and I was assured by regular contacts with my husband while he was there. Eventually I grew to share his pride in serving and representing his country internationally. It has always been his dream. Now, I am just glad to have him home safe again.*[62]

Constant communication with loved ones and knowing that the 'home front' was well cared-for proved instrumental for mission success in certain cases.

---

60   Tay, 'SAF to end its Afghanistan deployments', 8.
61   Choo and Chan, 'Supporting peace and reconstruction in Afghanistan', 6.
62   Ibid.

For example, an imagery analyst who spent 127 days away from Singapore in 2013 to 'make a difference' reportedly

> found it very tough emotionally when he could not be there for his four-year-old daughter on her birthday. Keeping a picture of his daughter by his bedside always, he shared how fortunate he was to have his wife and family as his pillar of support throughout his deployment.[63]

The importance of the 'home front' was never lost on political and military leaders. Even as he announced the conclusion of OBR, Dr Ng conveyed his gratitude and acknowledged the sacrifices made by all involved, saying:

> It has not been easy for you. You have families, you have children, and your absence has been felt. It is because you have spouses and family members who play their part. I know when I visited our people in Afghanistan and how they took it—they said that it was because they were supported by their families back home that they have the peace of mind to do the job here.[64]

Beyond strengthening bilateral relations with Washington and the job satisfaction and operational experience gained without loss of life or injury, OBR was also deemed a success thanks to positive reinforcements from coalition partners. After a visit to Uruzgan in October 2011, Dr Ng related:

> I interacted with base commanders as well as their counterparts from the Australian Defence Force and the US, and I must say that there is high regard for how professional our SAF soldiers are ... I think this has been very good for us in terms of our ability to contribute as well as our own using this opportunity to professionalise ourselves, to learn various aspects and operating others' best practices. This has been a good trip and I am very proud of our SAF troops.[65]

---

63  Helmi, '2263 days 5221 km from home', 17; Singapore Armed Forces, *Two thousand two hundred and sixty-three days*, 158.
64  Tay, 'SAF to end its Afghanistan deployments', 6–7.
65  Choo and Chan, 'Supporting peace and reconstruction in Afghanistan', 6.

A senior officer and former infantry brigade commander also proudly expressed that

> [e]very member of the coalition had only good things to share about our time here in Afghanistan; that we are a small armed force that brought niche capabilities to the table, and contributed so much to the stabilization of Afghanistan. I looked into their eyes, and heard it from the emotion in their voices. The gratitude, appreciation, friendship and camaraderie are all real. The sadness at seeing their Singaporean comrades depart for home is real. I think Singapore, and Singaporeans, made a difference in Afghanistan. Small nation, valued contribution, equal partner.[66]

A lesson learned from previous overseas deployments was that the story had to be publicly communicated and its associated benefits harvested immediately. Long before the last SAF boots departed the sandy soil of Uruzgan, returning service personnel were already splashed across recruitment posters. As OBR drew to an end, the publicity campaign kicked into overdrive with island-wide roadshows from the Central Business District and into the heartlands. Official documentaries were made, a commemorative book published, and a MINDEF webpage specifically dedicated to OBR.[67] Public outreach, depending on one's point of view, served either to 'maintain the strong support of' or 'bolster fledging support for' a conscript military. In any case, the image presented of OBR in the court of public opinion was overwhelmingly positive. This certainly helped 'career ambassadors'—the softer nomenclature for 'military recruiters'—to seize the opportunity to feature Singapore's 'Afghan' veterans under the tagline 'Faces of Steel. Stories of Strength.'

## Conclusion

The narrative of Operation Blue Ridge was framed within the clear and present threat of terrorism to Singapore, and the need to assist in the reconstruction

---

66   Chua Jin Kiat, 'Day 2263: the final chapter in our OBR journey', *Army News* 214 (August 2013), 18.
67   Republic of Singapore, Ministry of Defence (2017), 'Operation Blue Ridge', 1 March 2017. Formerly accessible at www.mindef.gov.sg/imindef/mindef_websites/atozlistings/army/Our_Stories/OBR.html. Webpage has since been removed.

of post-Taliban Afghanistan. The key consideration, however, was the need to support American efforts. This decision brought 492 Singaporean sons and daughters far from home to preserve strong Singapore-US relations. The issues associated with the 'strategic corporal' proved moot, as lower-echelon tacticians were simply not deployed. This immediately rendered moot any questions of how inexperienced soldiers and responsibilities and decisions would impact the larger picture. The majority of the 492 were senior and experienced regulars who were employed in niche areas—as staff officers, medical specialists, construction engineers, imagery analysts, institutional trainers and radar and UAV operators—where they could exercise autonomy in meeting mission requirements, and where contact with the civilian populace was minimal and personal weapons for purely defensive purposes. Each soldier understood their strategic relevance in keeping Singapore part of the ISAF coalition, and in preserving Singapore's domestic and international reputation.

The Afghanistan expedition proved extremely beneficial and successful for the Singapore Armed Forces as it maximised return-on-investment and checked off various strategic goals. Political credit was earned with Washington and in due course can be 'cashed' for public affirmations of Singapore-linked American commitment to the Asia-Pacific region, acquisition of advanced weaponry and other mutually beneficial spheres of cooperation. Operation Blue Ridge afforded deployed personnel the experiences of operating in a conflict zone, professional and personal fulfilment, and an appreciation for the sacred role of preserving Singapore's peace and prosperity. Importantly, Singapore's record of zero fatalities on overseas missions remained intact. The well-publicised success story reinforced society's faith in an 'operationally ready', albeit non-combat-tested, defence force and was another step forward in the quest to be 'Ready in Peace, Decisive in War, Respected by All'.[68] This model of contributing to niche areas out of harm's way will persist and is continuing under the SAF's newest mission as part of the international coalition against the self-styled 'Islamic State'.[69]

---

68    Glen Choo, 'Ready, decisive, respected: what does it mean to you?' *Army News* 196 (January 2012), 2–3.

69    Sharon Chen, 'Singapore becomes the first south-east Asian country to join the fight against Islamic State', *Sydney Morning Herald*, 5 November 2014.

# Epilogue:
# A Strategic Corporal's Perspective

## *Anthony Moffitt*

IT IS 100 YEARS SINCE ALBERT JACKA (VC, MC & BAR), one of Australia's greatest strategic corporals, was finally stopped at Villers-Bretonneux; it is likely both enemy and establishment breathed a collective sigh of relief. Jacka (and his 'mob') not only disproportionately impacted the enemy on the battlefield, but significantly influenced Allied battlefield and homeland morale. His tactical and strategic effects were unquestionable, and, in spite of attempts to stymie him by a recalcitrant hierarchy, Jacka performed exceptionally in officer training and indeed for the rest of the war. Jacka was an exceptional soldier, but I contend that he is not exceptional in the entirety of soldiering. While I am not in the same league as Jacka, as a strategic corporal myself it is indeed a rare privilege to be asked to contribute to this volume.

This germane collection of essays is not only a timely reevaluation of the concept but also a call to action for an outdated military paradigm. The authors' frank and thoughtful discourse is a manifesto of sometimes uncomfortable truths, which offer a signpost to an evolution of modern militaries and, perhaps audaciously, to a revolution in how we grow soldiers. In opening the book, Charles Melson sets the scene by reminding us that it has been nearly 20 years since Krulak's strategic corporal concept was first articulated, and evokes consideration of how dramatically soldiering has changed in this time. The subsequent contributions, and in particular those of Adams and Lovell, set my mind on fire around two themes that resonate throughout the book, both of which have increasingly occupied my thinking across my 25-year career of 11 deployments and close to 1 000 days of active service. The first is the significant problem of elitism in our military, and the systemic biases that it upholds. The second is the need for free equitable education for our soldiers—formal, vocational and self-determined—as the solution to smashing through those barriers towards a system sensitive to change, as a stable state. It is to these themes that I will refer in humbly providing a soldier's perspective in this epilogue.

The themes echo through the chapters not so much as a criticism but as an opportunity for an army that self-evidently seeks transformation and change through 'unleashing human potential'. Therefore, if there is any appetite whatsoever to realise the transformative power of growing strategic soldiers, we must disenthrall ourselves from some outdated values and traditions and elevate education as an inalienable right of all soldiers. Both the problem (elitism) and the solution (education) are hiding in plain sight, and I believe the right type of change will be driven through the inevitable rise and rise of the strategic soldier.

## The strategic soldier

Any adoption of the strategic corporal ideal faces barriers, none greater than the two-dimensional hierarchical construct we think, behave and operate in. My thinking has evolved to reject this non-agile and non-adaptive hierarchical structure in favour of a garden-like mental model that correctly places the soldier at the centre rather than at the bottom. Antique and two-dimensional wire diagrams are simplistic and fail to correctly explain the complex and messy 'system of systems' that is the heart of an agile and adaptive military. This also has implications for how we view new operating environments. The garden resets our language for new thinking and change, inferring that the 'administration'[1] is primarily responsible for soil condition and root health, to cultivate our soldiers to grow upwards and outwards and in a rich environment. It also optimises the top-quality fertiliser often found in various administrations.

This abstract yet practical mental model simply turns the hierarchical model on its head; the soldier to 'up' and the administration to 'down'. I deliberately offer this model to elevate the soldier to the forefront and to expunge the existing notion of soldiers as being of 'lower' ranks as both insulting and unhelpful. The employment landscape of soldiering has significantly changed, and, until recently, the military has largely escaped scrutiny in terms of occupational ethics. As it is with many modern conventions and institutions,

---

1     I believe that the term 'administration' is more befitting of modern HQs, command, hierarchy, leadership and bureaucracies.

scrutiny is overdue if we are to break down many of the old-fashioned barriers to understanding what the strategic soldier could be.

In my mind, the strategic soldier to whom we are almost entirely referring is the front-line or close-combat soldier—principally the infantryman, and to a lesser extent the field engineer, signaller and other arms corps. Given that the majority of positions in the military and broader defence sector are mostly office, warehouse and factory jobs, this small population is almost always scrutinised and punished for poor strategic outcomes, though rarely recognised for good ones. Their profound strategic potential is central to a challenging truth—that any account of negative strategic outcomes almost always leads to the non-commissioned officer (NCO) or junior officer, and will often be articulated as the consequence of poor ethical decision-making and behaviour. On the other hand, positive strategic outcomes are almost entirely accredited to the senior officer and their war-fighting and geopolitical acumen. This point appears not to be lost on Adams, and he quotes Colonel Paul Yingling, who writes tartly: 'the soldier who loses a rifle faces a more severe punishment than the general who loses a war.'[2] In contrast, academic study reminds us that an organisation's ethical and moral culture is set by the so-called leadership in that it 'starts at the top'. Perhaps Adams best shines a light into this space in drawing our attention to Norman Dixon (*On the Psychology of Military Incompetence*, 1994), who is concerned with 'officers convinced of their own superiority los(ing) all feeling for the moral basis upon which they exercise command'. Lovell too offers insightfully that 'Hierarchy (can be) the last refuge of the intellectually insecure' where any threat to culture may exist. My experience certainly confirms that two sets of rules continue to exist. Soldiers are habitually scrutinised (often punitively), while the culture-setting hierarchy is seldom held to account.

So, with the most to lose and least to gain, I believe it reasonable to offer that it is the infantry and other combat soldiers who set the cultural and ethical benchmarks by which we act as a military; certainly, any contravention of this impacts our reputation the most. Yet what do we invest in habitual and sustained education to support this? Comparatively little, as it is the *corpus parente* that are availed of almost the entirety of such education and developmental opportunities. This dated status quo must be corrected if we are to evolve from a mediocrity to the meritocracy we aspire to.

---

2   See Chapter 3.

# Epilogue: A Strategic Corporal's Perspective

The demonstrable increase in contemporary soldiers' intellect and physical, technical, and modern social abilities gives a palpable sense that the arrival, indeed the rise and rise, of the strategic corporal is now beyond a concept and is in fact occurring. A grass-roots movement no less. The transfer of 'tactics, techniques and procedures' (TTPs) and equipment from special operations forces to conventional combat units may ultimately lead to smaller and more highly trained teams led by NCOs. It seems increasingly likely that it will be to those NCOs and more specialised combat forces that we will turn to bridge the tactical-strategic meld where the tactical and strategic are intractably interdependent. Perhaps good soldiers can make up for poor strategy to some extent; however, good strategy cannot make up for poor soldiers. It is thus vital that NCOs be strategically empowered.

However, there are impediments, as Adams correctly identifies, most notably a system rife with barriers to the amelioration of our strategic soldiers and breaking down conscious and unconscious biases that protect those 'cliquish rackets (and "psycho-technology" that) provide sanctuary for those too senior to fail'.

And so it is to the first of my themes: the disease of elitism.

## Elitism and other barriers to the strategic soldier

Adams correctly identifies a need 'to evolve, to become less bureaucratic, and to intentionally foster conscientious, independently-minded and responsible soldiers'. Our dated and suffocating bureaucracy is stifling and merely keeps soldiers 'in their place'. In her paper on the strategic corporal, quoted several times in this volume, Major Lynda Liddy claims that strategic soldiers have been a feature of the Australian Army since the 1950s.[3] Possibly the result of confirmation bias from a detached administration, this is a claim that is foreign to my experience. So-called strategic soldiers are often maligned as 'single-issue zealots' or find themselves mired in governance from bullying HQs. The reality is that zealous soldiers effect the most change, especially in the design and development of combat operations, where strategic effects are actualised. One might say that high-performing soldiers are so *because* they are zealous. Unfortunately, it appears that inflexible military hierarchies are

---

3   Lynda Liddy, 'The strategic corporal: some requirements in training and education', *Australian Army Journal* 2, 2 (2005), 139–148.

responsible for many of our highest-performing soldiers and new officers leaving service prematurely.[4]

Liddy's unconscious bias also appears in her definition of a 'strategic soldier' in offering that soldiers 'can' achieve a strategic impact, a slightly condescending tone in my mind. Surely, if we are to promote strategic soldiers, the language should be more enabling, ie substituting 'can' with 'will ... have strategic and political consequences'. In respectfully challenging Liddy, it is only fair that I propose my own definition:

> *A strategic soldier is a quiet, intelligent professional who is globally aware, culturally sensitive and who will think and behave in the interests of his or her teammates and the national interest.*

The psychology of the language is critical, and it is these deeper levels of unconscious bias that I believe we must reform. So too must the administration, in supporting change, conduct uncomfortable and courageous examinations of itself, and in particular shine a light on elitism.

Adams correctly suggests that 'autonomous, purposeful and astute soldiers emerge ... in spite of the presently dominant culture and not because of it'. I agree, and contend that elitism is at the heart of this culture, manifest in organisational behaviours such as segregation, award entitlements, bullying and othering, arbitrary privilege, narcissistic control, autocratic centralisation and plagiaristic impunity. There are in fact places where I am not welcome, indeed where I am banned. These physical, psychological, social and philosophical barriers are hiding in plain sight. Our eighteenth-century hierarchical model (appropriate for the time) is based on a poorly educated rank and file, fitting for predictable, commandable and controllable set-piece warfare. However, it is no longer relevant or indeed helpful in the twenty-first century.

I consent to a notion that soldiers largely exchange their human rights upon enlistment, and even that we are instruments of military and political objectives. But this should not come at the expense of professional development

---

4   Casey Wardynski, David S Lyle and Michael J Colarusso (2009), 'Towards a US Army officer corps strategy for success: A proposed human capital model focused upon talent', report, US Army Strategic Studies Institute, April 2009. Available at ssi.armywarcollege.edu/pdffiles/pub912.pdf, accessed on 11 April 2017.

commensurate with the responsibility and accountability that administrations regularly push up to our fighting soldiers. My position is no doubt challenging and confronting to some, but I strongly believe that elitism contemporaneously stands line abreast with sexism, racism and classism, and should follow in their footsteps if indeed we are to adopt an approach of cultivating strategic soldiers. This must be a whole-of-life, human-performance-based approach with a strong emphasis on education.

## The solution

The solution to addressing barriers such as elitism, or least a large part of it, is education—an exceptionally simple solution. More specifically, I am contending for free, equitable and self-determined educational opportunities for all soldiers from the commencement of their careers. In 'stepping out of our soldier's sun', I challenge the administration to adopt the over-quoted 'soldiers-eat-first' mindset to education. From year 12 to Master's degree, a mature approach would include blended formal and informal education, with a high emphasis on diverse and self-determined learning methods. This theme lies just below the surface throughout this book, daring here and there to spring into bloom. Most notably, Lovell asks us how we might better prepare our soldiers for service. I think this should be extended to how we simultaneously prepare them for life beyond soldiering. This is especially pertinent to those aforementioned soldiers on whom we rely to bear the brunt of combat and closing with the enemy.

Modern military forces spend hundreds of millions of dollars on hardware and materiel capability, reinforcing the illusion that wars will be won with technology and decreasing human inputs. In comparison, when we consider the pound-for-pound effects and returns, paltry sums are spent on combat soldiers. To borrow a well-circulated phrase: 'we spend all the money on what we put on and around our soldiers, but little on what we put in them.' I concede that the provision of messing and gym facilities are satisfactory; however, cognitive performance programmes that purport to build resilience are almost entirely reactive (to mental health concerns) rather than proactive (to nurture independent decision-making and intuition) and there is little or no emphasis on a soldier's education. Given that our front-line soldiers are significantly more likely to be killed or injured, become ill or traumatised, or suffer acute and chronic mental health issues, isn't it reasonable to suggest that we should be spending much more on them? And this is to significantly understate the profound impacts of service on partners and children. Current approaches are reactive and, frankly, clumsy, messy and too often too late. We must prioritise humans over hardware. Imagine for a moment if we invested billions in our soldiers' learning—a truly 'nation building' investment that would thunder down the ages.

In a rare departure with Lovell, I do advocate 'the development of "soldier-scholars"'. I think this concept provides for an evolution from current Gomer Pyle stereotypes to the intellectual soldier. The modern NCO in the army does more than manoeuvre a force over predetermined terrain and direct kinetic effects. They habitually engage and communicate with locals; facilitate hearts and minds; profile enemy forces; analyse intelligence and highly technical information; conduct diplomacy; lead and manage change; undertake project management; are sensitive to geopolitical influences; negotiate and strategise; manage human resources; and have a sound understanding of finance, statistical analysis and even business analytics. There is so much more to these military entrepreneurs that we underappreciate. The current system does little to support our soldiers to be educated in modern ways, which underpins transition problems—a topic for another time.

## Education

A soldier's 'learning' is almost entirely experiential and employment-specific, and is therefore often quite narrow. Consequence- and assessment-based (sometimes only for the purposes of 'arse-covering'), the system teaches compliance-based, and often tactically unsound, practices. It promotes a culture of fear and psychological avoidance. This approach seems anathema to the expressed aspiration of military forces being 'learning organisations', which we cannot be if our soldiers are in the states of fear, anxiety or avoidance common in past practices. Thankfully there are signs of grass-roots movements that are changing these approaches by encouraging enriched environments that promote positive states of psychological approach and autonomous, astute soldiers.

And so to Lovell's important question: how do we develop such soldiers in matters of law, international relations, politics, ethics, culture and the media? The answer is simple, its implementation merely a matter of resources and will. Imagine (in the Australian context in which I write) NCOs attending institutions like the Australian Defence Force Academy as a matter of course; equity-based study funding models; an ANZAC Bill along the lines of the GI

## Epilogue: A Strategic Corporal's Perspective

Bill; legislating for compulsory university places for soldiers; and the expansion of all representational duties and positions to include the professional soldier. The list is endless, and easy to realise, and the potential benefits are beyond what we can now imagine. This cultural shift will not be achieved by trickle-down directives; rather, it will be achieved by nurturing the soil and roots, empowering individuals to design their own pathways. I know it works. I am completing a Master's in Psychology and recently registered as a psychologist. This has been achieved mostly in spite of Defence support and thus has taken 12 years. It has contributed immensely to my performance as a soldier, leader and father. I believe this approach is exactly what Lovell is attempting to articulate towards the end of his chapter, where he identifies Cardinal Newman's idea of the 'liberal education' where 'useful and relevant (and, I believe, applied) knowledge' can be integrated. It has been my experience that this integration has been enormously beneficial to my service, which is slightly at odds with Lovell's contention that the 'distinction between training and education is even more relevant today'. However, it is entirely in accord with his assertion that soldiers' formal education 'must be the start of a process of lifelong learning' and agree that their lives are better protected, and their performance enhanced, the better educated they are.

There are critics. 'Soldiers don't have time'—many soldiers waste weeks sitting around on major exercises, being 'warm bodies' for administrators to play with; 'it will cost too much'—it is not a cost, it is an investment, and may indeed save in areas such welfare support; 'soldiers will study and leave'—so what?, but not the reality; and astonishingly, I have heard some offer that 'we don't need educated soldiers'—this deserves silence.

I will leave definitions of education, training and development for more qualified authors; however, I would ask all readers to consider that an erudite and empowered soldier will provide the greatest insight and input into design and development of any framework. To *be* erudite and strategic, a soldier must *feel* erudite and strategic, which is as much about personal permission and ownership as it is about education and development.

I strongly believe that through self-determined education, the provision of enriched environments and a culture built on equity, we will grow strategic corporals. Let us resist the old habits of segregation and bring them into the three block tent, where they have so much to offer in preparing for a future that will inevitably place them front and centre. Let us seek a greater, more self-determined and expansive model of education for our soldiers.

Let us adopt enriched mindsets and build modern frameworks that support our soldiers with appropriate resourcing and will. Humans are messy, complex and multi-dimensional, and garden-like. And so we must become comfortable in this complexity, and build complex approaches to engage with the complex environments and situations of the future.

## Conclusion

Our soldiers are highly intelligent, perhaps the smartest in history, and this may be accelerating. Strategic corporals, who number in their thousands, need, and indeed deserve, champions. It is these men and women who suffer the heaviest burdens of warfare, burdens they, along with their families, also carry with them when they transition into civilian life. The champions of our strategic soldiers will require courage if they are to rally against the 'zero-defect' and 'micro-management' mentality of the administration cited by Krulak (1999). In so doing, they will empower our soldiers by allowing them to take more control of, and responsibility for, their own learning as professionals, supported by an administration that perhaps 'knows its place'.

It will be messy and complex, but (like human beings) warfighting itself is messy and complex, as is deep processing of information, inclusive of failures and mistakes. Growing resilient and free critical thinkers rather than homogenous yes-men will not occur in sterile, directed environments. Perhaps Nassim Taleb's notion of the 'antifragile' (that which gains from shock and disorder) is helpful in this context.[5] This can be achieved through a self-directed self-exploration in concert with, not dominated by, conventional professional military education approaches.

I will leave my closing comments by repurposing the words of Sir Ken Robinson, perhaps an unwittingly important voice on how we might grow strategic soldiers: 'Just below the surface of the systemic barriers of our organisation lie a dormant capability, waiting for the right conditions to come about. This organic system, like any other, when the conditions are right, will inevitably grow in exciting and unknowable ways. Given opportunities to be creative, innovative, to act and think independently and autonomously, given responsibility our soldiers will spring to life; they will astonish you. The

---

5   Nassim Nicholas Talib (2014), *Antifragile: things that gain from disorder* (New York: Random House).

real role of the administration in a modern military is not one of command and control; rather, it is of climate control. And if this is achieved our soldiers, and our military with them, will grow in ways we cannot imagine.'⁶

---

6   This is a paraphrase of a part of Sir Ken Robinson's talk, 'How to escape education's death valley', TED Talk, April 2013. Available at www.ted.com/talks/ken_robinson_how_to_escape_education_s_death_valley?language=en (TED, 2013), accessed on 8 May 2017.

# References

## Articles

'A step closer to peace—RSAF's C-130 detachment to the Gulf region'. *Air Force News* 88 (March 2004).

*Africa Review*. 'Côte d'Ivoire "warlord" commanders plunder cocoa exports: UN', 29 April 2013. Available at www.africareview.com/News/Cote-dIvoire-warlord-commanders-plunder-cocoa-exports-UN-/-/979180/1761296/-/14ckv74z/-/index.html. Accessed on 11 April 2017.

Allan, Collin. 'Direct participation in hostilities from cyberspace'. *Virginia Journal of International Law* 54, 1 (2013), 173–193.

'Army team to Afghanistan recognised for their contributions'. *Army News* 152 (March–April 2008).

Au Yong, Jeremy. 'Huge gains for SAF by training in US: Dr Ng Eng Hen'. *The Straits Times*, 15 December 2013.

Avolio, Bruce J, Fred O Walumbwa and Todd J Weber. 'Leadership: current theories, research, and future directions'. *Annual Review of Psychology* 60 (2009), 421–449.

Baran, Benjamin and Cliff Scott. 'Organizing ambiguity: a grounded theory of leadership and sense-making within dangerous contexts'. *Military Psychology* 22, Suppl 1 (2010), S42–S62.

Bienefeld, Nadine and Grote Gudela. 'Teamwork in an emergency: how distributed leadership improves decision-making'. *Proceedings of the Human Factors and Ergonomics Society Annual Meeting* 55 (2011), 110–114.

Bigley, Gregory and Karlene Roberts. 'The incident command system: high-reliability organizing for complex and volatile task environments'. *Academy of Management Journal* 44, 6 (2001), 1281–1299.

Boin, Arjen and Paul 't Hart. 'Organising for effective emergency management: lessons from research'. *The Australian Journal of Public Administration* 69 (2010), 357–371.

Bryant, David J. 'Rethinking OODA: toward a modern cognitive framework of command decision making'. *Military Psychology* 18, 3 (2006), 183–206.

Burke, C Shawn, Kevin C Stagl, Cameron Klein, Gerald F Goodwin, Eduardo Salas and Stanley M Halpin. 'What type of leadership behaviors are functional in teams? A meta-analysis'. *The Leadership Quarterly* 17, 3 (2006), 288–307.

Carter, Ashton B. 'Running the Pentagon right: how to get the troops what they need'. *Foreign Affairs* 93, 1 (January/February 2014), 101–112.

Chan, Jonathan. 'Helping to rebuild Afghanistan'. *Army News* 177 (June 2010).

———. 'Overseas Service Medal: recognising professionalism and sacrifices'. *Army News* 185 (February 2011).

———. 'OSM for 29 servicemen'. *Army News* 190 (July 2011).

Chandola, Harish. 'Friendship without commitment'. *Economic and Political Weekly* 6, 39 (25 September 1971).

Chen, Sharon. 'Singapore becomes the first south-east Asian country to join the fight against Islamic State'. *Sydney Morning Herald*, 5 November 2014.

Cheong, Ian and Marcus Ho. 'SAF contributes to provincial reconstruction in Afghanistan'. *Army News* 162 (January–February 2009).

———. 'Overseas mission participants honoured'. *Army News* 172 (January 2010).

Chia, Han Sheng. 'DPM Teo visits SAF troops in Afghanistan'. *Army News* 171 (October–November 2009).

Chiswick, Linton. 'Cyber attack casts new light on Georgia invasion'. *The Week* (UK), 15 August 2008.

Choo, Glen. 'Army team clinches defence technology prize'. *Army News* 194 (November 2011).

———. 'Ready, decisive, respected: what does it mean to you?' *Army News* 196 (January 2012).

———. 'Serving in overseas missions with pride'. *Army News* 201 (June 2012).

Choo, Glen and Jonathan Chan. 'Supporting peace and reconstruction in Afghanistan'. *Army News* 194 (November 2011).

Chua, Jin Kiat. 'Day 2263: the final chapter in our OBR journey'. *Army News* 214 (August 2013).

Chua, Michael Teck Leong. 'Long term presence of the United States in the Asia Pacific'. *Pointer: Journal of the Singapore Armed Forces* 24, 4 (October–December 1998).

Connaughton, Stacey, Marissa Shuffler and Gerald F Goodwin. 'Leading distributed teams: the communicative constitution of leadership'. *Military Psychology* 23, 5 (2011), 502–527.

Cosgrove, Peter. 'The night our boys stared down the barrel'. *The Age*, 21 June 2000.

Darcy, Shane (2016). 'Direct participation in hostilities'. *Oxford Bibliographies*. Available at oxfordbibliographies.com/view/document/obo-9780199796953/obo-9780199796953-0137.xml?rskey=3jCnSY&result=50. Accessed on 11 April 2017.

DeRue, D Scott. 'Adaptive leadership theory: leading and following as a complex adaptive process'. *Research in Organisational Behavior* 31 (2011), 125–150.

Dorn, A Walter and Michael Varey. 'Fatally flawed: the rise and demise of the "three-block war" concept in Canada'. *International Journal* (Autumn 2008), 967–978. Available at walterdorn.net/pdf/ThreeBlockWar-FatallyFlawed_Dorn-Varey_IJ_Aut2008.pdf. Accessed on 9 April 2017.

———. 'The rise and demise of the "three block war"'. *Canadian Military Journal* 10, 1 (2009), 38–44.

Droege, Cordula. 'Get off my cloud: cyber warfare, international humanitarian law and the protection of civilians'. *International Review of the Red Cross* 94, 886 (Summer 2012), 533–578.

Ee, David. 'Singapore troops in Afghanistan set to return'. *The Straits Times*, 9 February 2013.

———. 'SAF officer's sterling Afghan service'. *The Straits Times*, 23 February 2013.

Farrell, Theo. 'Improving in war: military adaptation and the British in Helmand Province, Afghanistan, 2006–2009'. *The Journal of Strategic Studies* 33, 4 (August 2010), 567–594.

Fastabend, David A and Robert H Simpson. 'Adapt or die: the imperative for a culture of innovation in the United States Army'. *ARMY Magazine* 54, 2 (February 2004), 15–22.

Fernandez, Walter. 'S'pore "must stand up firmly to others"'. *The Straits Times*, 2 July 1998.

'First reservist in UN mission'. *Pioneer* (June 1993).

'Forum: direct participation in hostilities: direct participation in hostilities: perspectives on the ICRC Interpretive Guidance'. *NYU Journal of International Law and Politics* 42, 3 (Spring 2010).

France24. 'UN accused of covering up report into alleged sex abuse by French troops', 29 April 2015. Available at www.france24.com/en/20150429-un-accused-covering-report-french-troops-sex-abuse. Accessed on 11 April 2017.

Freedman, Lawrence. 'Regular and irregular war'. *Strategic Datalink* 1 (August 2008). Available at d3n8a8pro7vhmx.cloudfront.net/cdfai/pages/348/attachments/original/1413946891/Regular_and_Irregular_War_-_Lawrence_Freedman.pdf?1413946891. Accessed on 8 May 2017.

Gladstone, Rick. 'U.N. chief served papers in suit by Haitian victims, lawyers say'. *The New York Times*, 20 June 2014. Available at www.nytimes.com/2014/06/21/world/americas/un-chief-served-papers-in-suit-by-haitian-cholera-victims-lawyers-say.html?_r=0. Accessed on 11 April 2017.

Goldsmith, Jack. 'The Third Annual Solf-Warren Lecture on International and Operational Law'. *Military Law Review* 205 (2010), 192–203.

Gray-Block, Aaron. 'Gbagbo, Ouattara forces engaged in war crimes: ICC'. Reuters, 23 June 2011. Available at www.reuters.com/article/2011/06/23/us-ivorycoast-icc-idUSTRE75M76620110623. Accessed on 11 April 2017.

Hayes, Peter AJ and Mary M Omodei. 'Managing emergencies: key competencies for incident management teams'. *Australian and New Zealand Journal of Organisational Psychology* 4 (April 2011), 1–10.

Heifetz, Ronald and Donald Laurie. 'The work of leadership'. *Harvard Business Review* 75, 1 (January–February 1997), 124–134.

Helmi, Muhammad. '2263 days 5221 km from home'. *Army News* 214 (August 2013).

——. '2263 days later: the end of our journey in Afghanistan'. *Army News* 214 (August 2013).

Heng, Yee-Kuang. 'Confessions of a small state: Singapore's evolving approach to international peace operations'. *Journal of International Peacekeeping* 16, 1–2 (February 2012), 119–151.

Hollis, Duncan. 'Cyberwar case study: Georgia 2008'. *Small Wars Journal* 7, 1 (2011).

Human Rights Watch. 'Côte d'Ivoire: military promotions mock abuse victims', 5 August 2011. Available at www.hrw.org/news/2011/08/05/cote-divoire-military-promotions-mock-abuse-victims. Accessed on 1 April 2017.

——. 'South Sudan's new war: abuses by government and opposition forces', 7 August 2014. Available at www.hrw.org/node/126088. Accessed on 11 April 2017.

Jacob, Paul. 'Educate the public on role of armed forces'. *The Straits Times*, 28 April 1986.

Kilcullen, David J. 'New paradigms for 21st-century conflict'. *eJournal USA: Foreign Policy Agenda* 12, 5 (May 2007), 39–45.

King, Simon. 'Strategic corporal or tactical colonel? Anchoring the right variable'. *Defence & Security Analysis* 19, 2 (2003), 189–190.

Klein, Katherine J, Jonathan C Ziegert, Andrew P Knight and Yan Xiao. 'Dynamic delegation: shared, hierarchical, and deindividualized leadership in extreme action teams'. *Administrative Science Quarterly* 51, 4 (2006), 590–621.

Krulak, Charles C. 'The strategic corporal: leadership in the three block war'. *Marine Corps Gazette* 83, 1 (January 1999).

Kwa, Chong Guan. 'A new generation rewrites history, doubts Singapore's vulnerability'. *The Straits Times*, 30 January 2015.

Liddy, Lynda. 'The strategic corporal: some requirements in training and education'. *Australian Army Journal* 2, 2 (2005), 139–148.

Lindsay, Douglas R, David V Day and Stanley Halpin. 'Shared leadership in the military: reality, possibility, or pipe dream?' *Military Psychology* 23, 5 (2011), 528–549.

'Looking into the ARTHUR'. *Army News* 208 (February 2013).

Marsh, Jeremy and Scott L Glabe. 'Time for the United States to directly participate'. *Virginia Journal of International Law Online* 1 (30 January 2011), 13, 20. Available at www.vjil.org/assets/pdfs/vjilonline1/1/Marsh__Post-Production_.pdf. Accessed on 5 May 2017.

McFate, Sean. 'Outsourcing the making of militaries: DynCorp International as a sovereign agent'. *Review of African Political Economy* 35, 118 (2008), 645–654.

McMahan, Jeff. 'Collectivist defenses of the moral equality of combatants'. *Journal of Military Ethics* 6, 1 (2007).

# References

Melzer, Niels. 'Keeping the balance between military necessity and humanity: a response to four critiques of the ICRC's Interpretive Guidance on the notion of direct participation in hostilities'. *NYU Journal of International Law and Politics* 42 (2010), 831–916.

Milgram, Stanley. 'Behavioural study of obedience'. *Journal of Abnormal and Social Psychology* 67, 4 (1963).

Nair, Elizabeth. 'The Singapore soldier'. *Pointer: Journal of the Singapore Armed Forces* 12, 2 (January–March 1986), 85–86.

——. 'So you think we've arrived?' *The Sunday Times*, 3 January 1993, 1, 6–7.

——. 'Nation of self-reliant people needed'. *The Straits Times*, 19 August 2002, H5.

'Our Army: ready, decisive, respected'. *Army News* 198 (March 2012).

Pitt, Martin and Michael Bunamo. 'Excellence in leadership: lessons learned from top-performing units'. *Air & Space Power Journal* 22 (Spring 2008), 44–48.

Ramthun, Alex J and Gina S Matkin. 'Leading dangerously: a case study of military teams and shared leadership in dangerous environments'. *Journal of Leadership & Organisational Studies* 21, 3 (2014).

Reid, Captain James B, USMC. 'Educating the strategic corporal: restructure the course for better mental preparation'. *Marine Corps Gazette* 93, 3 (March 2009).

Sambrook, Clare. 'G4S private army of Gurkhas wins medals for gallantry in Kabul', 3 September 2014, OpenDemocracyUK. Available at www.opendemocracy.net/ourkingdom/clare-sambrook/g4s-private-army-of-gurkhas-wins-medals-for-gallantry-in-kabul. Accessed on 23 May 2017.

Schmitt, Michael N. 'Deconstructing direct participation in hostilities: the constitutive elements'. *NYU Journal of International Law and Politics* 42 (2010), 679, 720.

——. 'Military necessity and humanity in international humanitarian law: preserving the delicate balance'. *Virginia Journal of International Law* 50, 4 (2010).

——. 'The Interpretive Guidance on the notion of direct participation in hostilities: a critical analysis'. *Harvard National Security Law Journal* 1 (5 May 2010), 5–44.

——. 'Cyber operations and the *jus in bello*: key issues'. *International Law Studies* 87 (2011), 89–110.

Sheeran, Scott P. 'A constitutional moment?: United Nations peacekeeping in the Democratic Republic of Congo'. *International Organizations Law Review* 8, 55 (2011).

'Singapore and the US: security partners, not allies'. *Strategic Comments* 19, Comment 24 (August 2013).

Singer, Peter W. 'Outsourcing war'. *Foreign Affairs* (March/April 2005), 119–132.

Stockdale, James Bond. 'Taking stock'. *United States Naval War College Review* 31, 2 (1978), 1–2.

Storr, Jim. 'A command philosophy for the information age: the continuing relevance of mission command'. *Defence Studies* 3, 3 (Autumn 2003).

Stringer, Kevin D. 'Educating the strategic corporal: a paradigm shift'. *Military Review* 89, 5 (September–October 2009), 87–95.

Tan, Andrew TH. 'Punching above its weight: Singapore's armed forces and its contribution to foreign policy'. *Defence Studies* 11, 4 (December 2011), 541–558.

Tan, See Seng. 'America the indispensable: Singapore's view of the United States' engagement in the Asia-Pacific'. *Asian Affairs: An American Review* 38, 3 (2011).

Tay, Shawn. 'SAF to end its Afghanistan deployments'. *Army News* 209 (March 2013).

Teo, Jing Ting. 'Trucks of survival'. *Cyberpioneer*, 25 November 2013.

Thomson, George G. 'Britain's plan to leave Asia'. *The Round Table: The Commonwealth Journal of International Affairs* 58, 230 (1968).

Turns, David. 'Cyber warfare and the notion of direct participation in hostilities'. *Journal of Conflict and Security Law* 17, 2 (2012), 279–297.

Wai, Ronnie. 'More stress on personnel development'. *The Straits Times*, 27 May 1982.

Walker, Peter. 'Georgia declares "state of war" over South Ossetia'. *The Guardian*, 9 August 2008. Available at www.theguardian.com/world/2008/aug/09/georgia.russia2. Accessed on 11 April 2017.

Wee, Teck Young. 'I am hurting too: the hurt of militarized authoritarianism in Singapore, Afghanistan and the world', blog post, no date. Available at warisacrime.orgcontent/i-am-hurting-too-hurt-militarized-authoritarianism-singapore-afghanistan-and-world. Accessed on 11 April 2017.

Whitlock, Craig. 'US trains African soldiers for Somalia mission'. *The Washington Post*, 13 May 2012.

Wong, Sher Maine. 'I say what I think'. *Challenge* (magazine of the Singapore Public Service), 18 July 2011.

Yammarino, Francis J, Eduardo Salas, Andra Serban, Kristie Shirrifs and Marissa Shuffler. 'Collectivistic leadership approaches: putting the "we" in leadership science and practice'. *Industrial and Organizational Psychology* 5, 4 (2012), 382–402.

Yeo, Elisia. 'A US-S'pore first'. *Today*, 5 May 2003.

Yingling, Paul. 'A failure in generalship'. *Armed Forces Journal*, 1 May 2007. Available at armedforcesjournal.com/a-failure-in-generalship/. Accessed on 11 April 2017.

## Books

Alberts, David S (1996). *The unintended consequences of information age technologies: avoiding the pitfalls, seizing the initiative* (Washington, DC: Institute for National Strategic Studies, NDU).

Arendt, Hannah (2006). *Eichmann in Jerusalem: a report on the banality of evil* (New York: Penguin).

Avant, Deborah (2005). *The market for force: the consequences of privatizing security* (Cambridge: Cambridge University Press).

# References

Baker, Deane-Peter (2010). *Just Warriors Inc.: the ethics of privatized force* (London: Continuum).

Bothe, Michael, Karl Josef Partsch and Waldemar A Solf (1982). *New rules for victims of armed conflict: commentary on the two 1977 Protocols additional to the Geneva Conventions of 1949* (The Hague: Martinus Nijhoff Publishers).

Churchill, Winston S (2007). *My early life: a roving commission* (London: The Folio Society).

Clark, Wesley K (2003). *Winning modern wars: Iraq, terrorism, and the American empire* (New York: Public Affairs).

Cowper-Coles, Sherard (2011). *Cables from Kabul* (HarperPress, Epub).

Crawford, Emily (2015). *Identifying the enemy: civilian participation in armed conflict* (Oxford: Oxford University Press).

Crawford, Emily and Alison Pert (2015). *International humanitarian law* (Cambridge: Cambridge University Press).

Creveld, Martin van (1991). *Technology and war: from 2000 BC to the present*. Revised edition (New York: The Free Press).

Dixon, Norman (1994). *On the psychology of military incompetence* (London: Pimlico).

Du Picq, Colonel Charles Ardant (2006). *Battle studies: ancient and modern*. Translated by JN Greely and RC Cotton (Milton Keynes: Bibliobazaar).

Dunigan, Molly (2011). *Victory for hire: private security companies' impact on military effectiveness* (Stanford: Stanford University Press).

Ewans, Martin (2005). *Conflict in Afghanistan: studies in asymmetric warfare* (London: Routledge).

Fisk, Robert (2005). *The great war for civilisation: the conquest of the Middle East* (London: Fourth Estate).

Forbes, John RS (2006). *Justice in tribunals*. 2nd edition (Annandale, NSW: The Federation Press).

Foucault, Michel (1995). *Discipline and punish: the birth of the prison* (New York: Vintage).

Fukuyama, Francis (2006). *The end of history and the last man* (New York: The Free Press).

Gabriel, Richard (1982). *To serve with honour: a treatise on military ethics and the way of the soldier* (Westport, CT: Greenwood Press).

Grossman, Dave (2009). *On killing: the psychological cost of learning to kill in war and society*. Revised edition (New York: Little, Brown).

Han, Fook Kwang, Zuraidah Ibrahim, Chua Mui Hoong, Lydia Lim, Ignatius Low, Rachel Lin and Robin Chan (2011). *Lee Kuan Yew: hard truths to keep Singapore going* (Singapore: Straits Times Press).

Heinlein, Robert A (1987 [1959]). *Starship troopers* (New York: Ace Books).

Henckaerts, Jean-Marie and Louise Doswald-Beck (2005). *Customary international humanitarian law*. Volume 1 (Cambridge: Cambridge University Press).

Hobbes, Thomas (1991). *Leviathan*. Edited by Richard Tuck (Cambridge: Cambridge University Press).

Holler, Jan, Vlasios Tsiatsis, Catherine Mulligan, Stefan Avesand, Stamatis Karnouskos and David Boyle (2014). *From machine-to-machine to the internet of things: introduction to a new age of intelligence* (Amsterdam: Academic Press).

Hopkins, Andrew (2005). *Safety culture and risk: the organisational causes of disasters* (Sydney: CCH Australia).

Huntington, Samuel P (1981). *The soldier and the state: the theory and politics of civil-military relations* (Cambridge, MA: the Belknap Press of Harvard University).

Huxley, Aldous (2004). *Brave New World and Brave New World Revisited* (New York: HarperCollins).

Huxley, Tim (2000). *Defending the Lion City: the armed forces of Singapore* (St Leonards, NSW: Allen & Unwin).

Immerman, Richard H and Petra Goedde (eds) (2013). *Oxford handbook of the Cold War* (Oxford: Oxford University Press).

Jans, Nicholas with Stephen Mugford, Jamie Cullens and Judy Frazer-Jans (2013). *The Chiefs: a study of strategic leadership* (Canberra: Australian Defence College). Available at www.defence.gov.au/ADC/Publications/Chiefs/TheChiefs.pdf. Accessed on 11 April 2017.

Kaldor, Mary (2012). *New and old wars*. 3rd edition (Cambridge: Polity Press).

Keegan, John (2008). *The face of battle* (London: The Folio Society).

Kelman, Herbert C and V Lee Hamilton (1989). *Crimes of obedience* (New Haven, CT: Yale University Press).

Kilcullen, David (2013). *Out of the mountains: the coming age of the urban guerrilla* (London: Hurst).

Kübler-Ross, Elisabeth (1970). *On death and dying* (London: Tavistock Publications).

Kuhn, Thomas (1970). *The structure of scientific revolutions* (Chicago: University of Chicago Press).

Larsen, Kjetil (2012). *The human rights treaty obligations of peacekeepers* (Cambridge: Cambridge University Press).

Lee, Edwin (2008). *Singapore: the unexpected nation* (Singapore: Institute of Southeast Asian Studies).

Leifer, Michael (2000). *Singapore's foreign policy: coping with vulnerability* (London: Routledge).

Levy, Steven (1994). *Insanely great: the life and times of the Macintosh, the computer that changed everything* (New York: Viking).

MacIntyre, Alasdair (1984). *After virtue*. 2nd edition (IN, Notre Dame: University of Notre Dame Press).

Manwaring, Max G (2012). *The complexity of modern asymmetric warfare* (Norman, OK: University of Oklahoma Press).

## References

Marston, Daniel and Carter Malkasian (eds) (2008). *Counterinsurgency in modern warfare* (Oxford: Osprey Publishing).

Mason, Philip (1954). *The guardians*. Volume 2 of *The men who ruled India* (New York: St Martin's Press).

McMaster, Herbert R (1998). *Dereliction of duty: Lyndon Johnson, Robert McNamara, the Joint Chiefs of Staff and the lies that led to Vietnam* (New York: HarperPerennial).

Moyar, Mark (2009). *A question of command: counterinsurgency from the Civil War to Iraq* (New Haven, CT: Yale University Press).

Mulisch, Harry (2005). *Criminal case 40/61: The trial of Adolf Eichmann*. Translated by Robert Naborn (Philadelphia, PA: University of Philadelphia Press).

Myers, Minor (2004). *Liberty without anarchy: a history of the society of the Cincinnati* (Charlottesville, VA: University Press of Virginia).

Newman, John Henry (1852). *The idea of a university: defined and illustrated*. Available at www.newmanreader.org/works/idea/discourse6.html. Accessed on 8 May 2017.

Owens, William A, Kenneth W Dam and Herbert S Lin (eds) (2009). *Technology, policy, law, and ethics regarding US acquisition and the use of cyberattack capabilities* (Washington, DC: National Academies Press).

Powell, Colin L with Joseph E Persico (2011). *A soldier's way: an autobiography* (New York: Random House).

Ricks, Thomas E (1997). *Making the Corps* (New York: Scribner & Sons).

Robertson, Geoffrey (2006). *Crimes against humanity: the struggle for global justice* (London: Penguin).

Roseman, Mark (2012). *The Wannsee Conference and the Final Solution: a reconsideration* (London: Folio).

Rothenberg, Gunther E (2000). *Atlas des guerres napoleoniennes: 1796–1815*. Translated by G Brzustowski (Paris: Editions Autrement).

Salmoni, Barak A and Paula Holmes-Eber (2011). *Operational culture for the warfighter: principles and applications* (Quantico, VA: Marine Corps University Press).

Scahill, Jeremy (2007). *Blackwater: the rise of the world's most powerful mercenary army* (New York: Avalon Publishing).

Schmitt, Michael N (ed) (2013). *Tallinn Manual on the international law applicable to cyber warfare* (Cambridge: Cambridge University Press).

Schröfl, Josef, Sean Cox and Thomas Pankratz (2009). *Winning the asymmetric war: political, social and military responses* (Frankfurt: Peter Lang).

Shamir, Eitan (2011). *Transforming command: the pursuit of mission command in the US, British, and Israeli armies* (Stanford, CA: Stanford Security Studies).

Shay, Jonathan (2003). *Achilles in Vietnam: combat trauma and the undoing of character* (New York: Scribner).

Simpson, Emile (2012). *War from the ground up: twenty-first century combat as politics* (Oxford: Oxford University Press, Kindle ebook).

Singapore Armed Forces Medical Corps (2012). *Ideas to reality: the SAF Medical Corps 45th anniversary* (Singapore: Singapore Armed Forces Medical Corps).

Singh, Daljit (2009). *By design or accident: reflections on Asian security* (Singapore: Institute of South East Asian Studies).

Smith, Rupert (2005). *The utility of force: the art of war in the modern world* (London: Allen Lane).

Talib, Nassim Nicholas (2014). *Antifragile: things that gain from disorder* (New York: Random House).

Thomson, Elizabeth A (2014). *Battling with words: a study of language, diversity and social inclusion in the Australian Department of Defence* (Canberra: Australian Government, Department of Defence).

Thornton, Rod (2007). *Asymmetric warfare: threat and response in the twenty-first century* (Cambridge: Polity).

Threlfall, Adrian (2014). *Jungle warriors: from Tobruk to Kokoda and beyond. How the Australian Army became the world's most deadly jungle fighting force* (Sydney: Allen & Unwin).

Thucydides (1972). *History of the Peloponnesian war*. Translated by Rex Warner, introduction and notes by MI Finley (London: Penguin Books).

Toner, James (2009). *Morals under the gun: the cardinal virtues, military ethics and American society* (Lexington, KY: The University Press of Kentucky).

US Army/USMC (2007). *The US Army and Marine Corps counterinsurgency field manual* (US Army Field Manual No 3-24, Marine Corps Warfighting Publication No 3-33.5). Foreword by General David H Petraeus and Lt General James F Amos, USMC (Chicago: University of Chicago Press).

Weber, Max (1978). *Economy and society: an outline of interpretive sociology*. Edited by Guenther Roth and Claus Wittich (Berkeley: University of California Press).

Weick, Karl E and Kathleen M Sutcliffe (2001). *Managing the unexpected* (San Francisco: Jossey-Bass).

Weigley, Russell F (1977). *The American way of war: a history of United States military strategy and policy* (Bloomington, IN: Indiana University Press).

Westheider, James E (2008). *The African American experience in Vietnam: brothers in arms* (Lanham, MD: Rowman & Littlefield).

## Book chapters

Condell, Bruce and David Zabecki (eds) (2011). 'Introduction,' in *On the German art of war: Truppenführung—the German Army manual for unit command in World War II* (Mechanicsburg, PA: Stackpole Books).

# References

Deck, Richard (1999). 'Foreign policy', in Michael Haas (ed), *The Singapore puzzle* (Westport, CT: Praeger Publishers).

George, Eric (2011). 'The market for peace', in Sabelo Gumedze (ed), *From market for force to market for peace: private military and security companies in peacekeeping operations*. ISS Monograph 183, 17–38.

Gibbon, Dee (2014). 'Unexpected turbulence: the cultural, gender-based challenges facing female pilots in the Australian Defence Force', in Donna Bridges, Jane Neal-Smith and Albert J Mills, (eds), *Absent aviators* (Farnham: Ashgate), 115–146.

Hannah, Sean T, John T Eggers and Peter L Jennings (2008). 'Complex adaptive leadership: defining what constitutes effective leadership for complex organizational contexts', in George B Graen and Joni A Graen, *The knowledge-driven corporation: complex creative destruction* (Charlotte, NC: Information Age Publishing).

Johnson, Rebecca J (2011). 'Moral formation of the strategic corporal', in Paolo Tripodi and Jessica Wolfendale (eds), *New wars and new soldiers: military ethics in the contemporary world* (Farnham: Ashgate), 239–256.

Kuik, Cheng-Chwee (2009). 'Shooting rapids in a canoe: Singapore and great powers', in Bridget Welsh, James Chin, Arun Mahizhnan and Tan Tarn How (eds), *Impressions of the Goh Chok Tong years in Singapore* (Singapore: National University of Singapore Press).

Lovell, David W (2012). 'Educating for ethical behaviour? Preparing military leaders for ethical challenges', in David W Lovell and Igor Primoratz (eds), *Protecting civilians during violent conflict: theoretical and practical issues for the 21st century* (Farnham: Ashgate), 141–157.

McGuire, Frederick L (1994). 'Army alpha and beta tests of intelligence', in Robert J Sternberg (ed), *Encyclopedia of intelligence* (New York: Macmillan).

Mileham, Patrick (2008). 'Officership: some first principles', in Stephen Deakin (ed), *'Take me to your officer': officership in the army* (London: The Strategic and Combat Studies Institute).

Paret, Peter (2011). 'The genesis of *On War*', in Carl von Clausewitz, *On War*, edited and translated by Michael Howard and Peter Paret (London: The Folio Society).

Pearce, Craig L and Jay A Conger (2003). 'All those years ago: the historical underpinnings of shared leadership', in Pearce and Conger (eds), *Shared leadership: reframing the hows and whys of leadership* (Thousand Oaks, CA: Sage), 1–18.

Pudas, Terry J and Catherine Theohary (2009). 'Reconsidering the Defense Department mission', in Hans Binnendijk and Patrick M Cronin (eds), *Civilian surge: key to complex operations* (Washington, DC: National Defense University Press).

Stephens, Dale (2011). 'The age of lawfare', in Raul 'Pete' Pedrozo and Daria P Wollschlaeger (eds), *International law and the changing character of war. U.S. Naval War College International Law Studies Series* 87 (Newport, RI: United States Naval War College).

## Documents, reports and papers

Al-Jedda v *The United Kingdom*, European Court of Human Rights, Application 27021/08 (2011).

Amnesty International (2011). 'Côte d'Ivoire: both sides responsible for war crimes and crimes against humanity', press release, 25 May 2011. Available at www.amnesty.org/en/press-releases/2011/05/cc3b4te-de28099ivoire-both-sides-responsible-war-crimes-and-crimes-against-humanity/. Accessed on 2 May 2017.

Australian Defence Force (2007). *Leadership in the Australian Defence Force*. Australian Defence Doctrine Publication 00.6, 22 March 2007 (Canberra: Australian Defence Headquarters).

—— (2012). *Campaigns and operations*, edition 2. Australian Defence Doctrine Publication (ADDP) 3.0, 12 July 2012.

Australian Government, Australian Civil-Military Centre (2012). *Partnering for peace: Australia's peacekeeping and peacebuilding experiences in the Autonomous Region of Bougainville in Papua New Guinea, and in Solomon Islands and Timor Leste* (Queanbeyan, NSW: Department of Defence).

——, Department of Defence (no date). *The Defence leadership framework: growing leaders at all levels* (Canberra: Australian Government, Department of Defence, Defence Personnel Executive).

——, Department of Defence (2011). *Review of the Defence Accountability Framework, carried out by Professor Rufus Black*, January 2011 (Canberra: Australian Government, Department of Defence).

——, National Audit Office (2009). *The Super Seasprite: the Australian Auditor General Audit Report No. 41 2008–09* (Canberra: Australian National Audit Office, Commonwealth of Australia, Attorney General's Department).

——, National Audit Office (2014). *The Air Warfare Destroyer Program: the Australian Auditor General Audit Report No 22 2013–14* (Canberra: Australian National Audit Office, Commonwealth of Australia, Attorney General's Department).

Australian Senate, Foreign Affairs Defence and Trade References Committee (2012). *Procurement procedures for Defence capital projects: final report*, August 2012 (Canberra: Commonwealth of Australia, Senate Printing Unit).

Breen, Robert and Greg McCauley (2008). *The world looking over their shoulders: Australian strategic corporals on operations in Somalia and East Timor*. Canberra: Land Warfare Studies Centre Papers 314.

Chanlett-Avery, Emma. 'Singapore: background and U.S. relations'. Congressional Research Service, RS20490, 26 July 2013. Available at www.fas.org/sgp/crs/row/RS20490.pdf. Accessed on 11 April 2017.

Commonwealth of Australia (2008). *Going to the next level: the report of the Defence Procurement and Sustainment Review, chaired by Mr David Mortimer* (Canberra: Commonwealth of Australia: Defence Materiel Organisation).

—— (2009). *Report on the strategic review of naval engineering*, 12 November 2009 (Canberra: Commonwealth of Australia).

—— (2014). *Report on abuse in Defence, prepared by the Hon Justice Roberts-Smith RFD, QC* (Canberra: Commonwealth of Australia: Attorney General's Department, Commonwealth Administrative Law Branch).

*D Georges v United Nations et al*, United States District Court, Southern District of New York (2013).

Dobell, Graeme (2003). 'The South Pacific: policy taboos, popular amnesia and political failure'. The Menzies Research Centre Lecture Series: Australian Security in the 21st Century, Canberra, February 2003. Available at web.mit.edu/12.000/www/m2009/teams/students/kennyd/australia.pdf. Accessed on 11 April 2017.

Gerras, Stephen J (2002). *The army as a learning organization*, US Army War College, May 2002. Available at www.carlisle.army.mil/orgs/SSL/DCLM/pubs/Learning%20Organization.doc. Accessed on 11 April 2017.

International Committee of the Red Cross (2009). *Interpretive guidance on the notion of direct participation in hostilities under international humanitarian law* (Geneva: International Committee of the Red Cross).

—— (2017). *Geneva Conventions and commentaries*. Available at www.icrc.org/en/war-and-law/treaties-customary-law/geneva-conventions. Accessed on 11 May 2017.

International Court of Justice (1996). *Legality of the threat or use of nuclear weapons*. Advisory Opinion, 8 July 1996. ICJ Reports, 226.

International Criminal Tribunal for the former Yugoslavia (1995). *Prosecutor v Tadić*, Jurisdiction Appeal, IT-94-1-AR72 2, October 1995.

—— (2003). *Prosecutor v Stanislav Galić*, Judgment, Case No. IT-98-29-T, 5 December 2003.

International Forum for the Challenges of Peace Operations (2010). *Considerations for mission leadership in United Nations peacekeeping operations* (Stockholm: Challenges Forum Partnership/Folke Bernadotte Academy).

Jans, Nicholas (with David Schmidtchen) (2002). *The real c-cubed: culture, careers and climate, and how they affect capability*. Canberra Papers on Strategy and Defence 143 (Canberra: ANU), 121–138.

—— (2009). *Careers in conflict 21C: the dynamics of the contemporary military career experience*. Paper presented at the Biannual Conference of the Inter-University Seminar for Armed Forces & Society, Chicago, October 2009.

—— (2014). *New values, old basics: how leadership shapes support for inclusion*. Centre for Defence and Strategic Studies, Australian Defence College, September 2014.

*Jean-Robert et al v United Nations*, United States District Court, Southern District of New York (2014).

Joint Chiefs of Staff (2013). *Counterinsurgency*. Joint Publication 3-24, 22 November 2013.

Kuok, Lynn (2016). 'The U.S.-Singapore partnership: A critical element of U.S. engagement and stability in the Asia-Pacific'. Asian Alliances Working Paper Series, Paper 6 (July 2016). Available at www.brookings.edu/wp-content/uploads/2016/07/Paper-6.pdf. Accessed on 26 May 2017.

Lanovoy, Vladyslav (2014). 'Complicity in an internationally wrongful act'. SHARES project research paper 38. Available at www.sharesproject.nl/publication/complicity-in-an-internationally-wrongful-act/. Accessed on 19 May 2017.

*LaVenture et al* v *United Nations*, United States District Court, Eastern District of New York (2014).

Leiner, Barry M, Vinton G Cerf, David D Clark, Robert E Kahn, Leonard Kleinrock, Daniel C Lynch, Jon Postel, Larry G Roberts and Stephen Wolff. 'Brief history of the internet'. Available at www.internetsociety.org/internet/what-internet/history-internet/brief-history-internet#. Accessed on 11 April 2017.

*Mothers of Srebrenica* v *The Netherlands*, The Hague District Court C-09/295247/HA ZA 07-2973 (2014).

North Atlantic Treaty Organization (2010). *Lisbon Summit Declaration, issued by the Heads of State and Government participating in the meeting of the North Atlantic Council in Lisbon*, 20 November 2010. Available at www.nato.int/cps/en/natolive/official_texts_68828.htm. Accessed on 11 April 2017.

Office of the White House Press Secretary (2015). 'Remarks by the President at the Academy Commencement Ceremony'. US Military Academy-West Point, West Point, New York, 28 May 2015. Available at obamawhitehouse.archives.gov/the-press-office/2014/05/28/remarks-president-united-states-military-academy-commencement-ceremony. Accessed on 28 April 2017.

Republic of Singapore, Ministry of Defence (2017). 'Operation Blue Ridge', 1 March 2017. Formerly accessible at www.mindef.gov.sg/imindef/mindef_websites/atozlistings/army/Our_Stories/OBR.html. Webpage has since been removed.

——, Ministry of Home Affairs (2003). White Paper: The Jemmah Islamiyah arrests and the threat of terrorism, Cmd 2 of 2003, 7 January (Singapore: Ministry of Home Affairs).

Royal Australian Navy (2008). *Report of the review of submarine workforce sustainability, 31 October 2008, undertaken by Rear Admiral RC Moffitt AO, RAN*, paragraph 7.3, 64, 65. Available at www.defence.gov.au/publications/Submarine-WorkforceSustainability.pdf. Accessed on 11 April 2017.

Rumble, Gary A, Melanie McKean and Dennis Pearce (2011). *The report of the review of allegations of sexual and other abuse in Defence: facing the problems of the past* (DLA Piper Report) (Canberra: Commonwealth of Australia). Available at www.defence.gov.au/pathwaytochange/docs/DLAPiper/Volume1.pdf. Accessed on 24 April 2017.

# References

Schmidtchen, David (2006). *The rise of the strategic private: technology, control and change in a network-enabled military*. Canberra: Land Warfare Studies Centre.

Schmitt, Michael N, Heather A Harrison and Thomas C Wingfield (2004). 'Computers and war: the legal battlespace'. Background paper prepared for Informal High Level Expert Meeting on Current Challenges to International Humanitarian Law, Cambridge, 25–27 June 2004.

Singapore Armed Forces (2013). *Two thousand two hundred and sixty-three days 2007–2013: Operation Blue Ridge—The SAF's six-year mission in Afghanistan* (Singapore: Ministry of Defence).

Talbot, Steven, Denise McDowall, Christina Stothard and Maya Drobnjak. *The Army Learning Organisation Workshop* (Canberra: Australian Government, Defence Science Technical Organisation, 2013). Available at www.dtic.mil/cgi-bin/GetTRDoc?AD=ADA591410. Accessed on 18 April 2017.

*The Public Committee Against Torture in Israel et al v The Government of Israel et al*, Supreme Court of Israel Sitting as the High Court of Justice, Judgment (11 December 2006), HCJ 769/02.

UK Government, Ministry of Defence (2011). *Defence reform: An independent report into the structure and management of the Ministry of Defence, chaired by Lord Levene of Portsoken KBE* (Levene Report) (London: The Stationery Office).

United Nations (2010). *Report of the Special Rapporteur on extrajudicial, summary or arbitrary executions, Philip Alston: study on targeted killings*, Human Rights Council, UN Doc A/HRC/14/24/Add.6.

—— (2011). *Draft articles on the responsibility of international organizations, with commentaries, adopted by the International Law Commission at its sixty-third session, in 2011, and submitted to the General Assembly as a part of the Commission's report covering the work of that session* (A/66/10).

—— (2011). *Final report of the independent panel of experts on the cholera outbreak in Haiti*, 4 May 2011. Available at www.un.org/News/dh/infocus/haiti/UN-cholera-report-final.pdf. Accessed on 11 April 2017.

—— (2013). *Rights up front: a plan of action to strengthen the UN's role in protecting people in crises. Follow-up to the report of the Secretary-General's Internal Review Panel on UN Action in Sri Lanka*, 9 July 2013.

United Nations, Department of Peacekeeping Operations (2010). 'Gender equality in UN peacekeeping operations', policy document, 26 July 2010. Available at www.un.org/en/peacekeeping/documents/gender_directive_2010.pdf. Accessed on 11 April 2017.

United Nations Peacekeeping (no date.) 'Human rights'. Available at www.un.org/en/peacekeeping/issues/humanrights.shtml. Accessed on 11 April 2017.

United Nations Political Missions (2013). *Report of the Secretary General of the United Nations, 2013*. Available at www.unis.unvienna.org/pdf/0_Regular_Updates/Political_Missions_Report.pdf. Accessed on 11 April 2017.

United Nations Stabilization Mission in Haiti (2015). 'UN Security Council visit to Haiti', 23 June 2015. Available at reliefweb.int/report/haiti/un-security-council-visit-haiti. Accessed on 11 April 2017.

US Army Corps of Engineers (2003). *Learning organization doctrine: roadmap for transformation*. Available at www.au.af.mil/au/awc/awcgate/army/learningdoctrine.pdf. Accessed on 18 April 2017.

US Department of Defense (2010). 'Fourth U.S.-Singapore strategic security policy dialogue concludes', 21 April 2010.

—— (2013). 'News transcript of Department of Defense press briefing by Secretary Hagel and Minister Ng in the Pentagon Press Briefing Room', 12 December 2013. Available at archive.defense.gov/transcripts/transcript.aspx?transcriptid=5342. Accessed on 11 April 2017.

—— (2015). *Law of war manual* (June 2015). Available at archive.defense.gov/pubs/law-of-war-manual-june-2015.pdf. Accessed on 11 April 2017.

USMC Concept and Plans Division (2009). 'The strategic corporal', 1 September 2009.

Wardynski, Casey, David S Lyle and Michael J Colarusso (2009). 'Towards a US Army officer corps strategy for success: A proposed human capital model focused upon talent', report, US Army Strategic Studies Institute, April 2009. Available at ssi.armywarcollege.edu/pdffiles/pub912.pdf. Accessed on 11 April 2017.

Woon, Tai Ho (2010). *Partnering to rebuild: Operation Blue Orchid: the Singapore Armed Forces experience in Iraq* (Singapore: Ministry of Defence).

## Theses and dissertations

Goh, Kee Nguan (2004). *The Singapore Army moving decisively beyond the conventional*. Unpublished MSS thesis, USAWC Strategy Research Project, Carlisle Barracks, PA.

Pastel, Major Teague A, USMC (2008). *Marine Corps leadership: empowering or limiting the strategic corporal?* Unpublished MMS dissertation, US Marine Corps Command and Staff College, Quantico, VA. Available at www.dtic.mil/get-tr-doc/pdf?AD=ada490868. Accessed on 18 April 2017.

Scott, TM (2006). *Enhancing the future strategic corporal* ('Future War Paper'). Unpublished MMS dissertation, USMC Marine Corps University, Quantico, VA. Available at www.dtic.mil/dtic/tr/fulltext/u2/a507697.pdf. Accessed on 18 April 2017.

References

## Other

Robinson, Sir Ken. 'How to escape education's death valley', TED Talk, April 2013. Available at www.ted.com/talks/ken_robinson_how_to_escape_education_s_death_valley?language=en (TED, 2013). Accessed on 8 May 2017.

# Index

## A
Abu Ghraib scandal 57
ACC *see* Australian Civilian Corps
accountability 36, 64, 66, 68, 174
Adams, Richard 141, 162, 174–176
adaptability 12–16, 59–62, 74–75, 83
ADF *see* Australian Defence Force
Aegis 63–64
Afghanistan 6, 18, 21, 61, 87–88, 134
 *see also* Singapore armed forces in Afghanistan
AFP *see* Australian Federal Police
Africa, contractors in 69–70
AFRICOM 69
airmobile rapid response forces 65
air warfare destroyer programme, Australia 45–46
Alexander the Great 5
*Al-Jedda* v *The United Kingdom* 103
allied forces *see* coalition allied forces
al-Qaeda 134, 152
America *see* United States
Amnesty International 101–102
Angola 57, 61–62
'antifragile' notion 180
'Arab Spring' 134
Arendt, Hannah 41–42
armed groups, definition of 114
Army Commendation Medal 167
*Army News* 167–168
artillery hunting radars (ARTHUR) (SAF) 158, 160, 161, 162, 163
'asymmetric warfare' 2, 19
 *see also* 'three block war'

*Auftragstaktik* (mission command idea) 27, 32–36
Australian Army 13n13, 20–21, 26–28, 30–31, 89–91, 175
Australian Civilian Corps (ACC) 82–83
Australian Defence Force (ADF) 27, 30, 36–38, 84, 137–138, 141–142
Australian Federal Police (AFP) 88–89
Australian National Audit Office 43–46
Australian Senate Foreign Affairs Defence and Trade References Committee 39
autonomy 5, 24–25, 38, 50–51

## B
Ban Ki-moon 95
Batalona, Wes 55–56
Battle of Fallujah 55–56
Battle of Mogadishu *see* Black Hawk Down incident
belligerent nexus test 124–126
 *see also* Tallinn Manual
bias, unconscious 176
'big data' 15–16
Binet, Alfred 11
Black Hawk Down incident 55, 65
Black, Rufus 51
Blackwater USA 55–56, 67–68
body cameras 108, 110
Bohr, Niels 133
*Brave New World Revisited* 52
Breen, Robert 27
Bronze Star Medal 167–168
bureaucracy
 centralisation 36–38

# Index

contractors 70
learning organisations 14
mission command idea
  (*Auftragstaktik*) 32–36
moral obligations 40–45, 49–51,
  53–54
obligation to act responsibly 40–43
official reports 36, 43–49, 53
organisational change 52–53
procedures 38–40
routines 38–40
'strategic corporal' concept 4, 5,
  32–34, 49–52, 175–176
training of soldiers 140–142
Bureau of Conflict and Stabilization
  Operations (US) 82

## C

*Cables from Kabul* 87–88
CACI 56–57
Cai Dexian 167–168
cameras, for monitoring and reporting
  108, 110
Campaign for the Professional Ethic
  (US Army) 21
Canada 82
*Canadian Military Journal* 79
capability, of contractors 61, 67, 69–71
  *see also* training
catalysts vs controllers 29
causation of harm, direct vs indirect
  121–124
cell phones *see* mobile phones
centralisation 36–38
Chandola, Harish 149
change, in organisations 52–53
China 133–135
cholera outbreak in Haiti 95–96, 105
church and state, distinction between 135

Churchill, Winston 137
Cincinnatus, Lucius Quinctius 145
civilian leadership 74, 75, 83
Civilian Response Corps (US) 82
civilians
  comprehensive approach to
    operations 74–76, 83–85
  Draft Articles on the Responsibilities
    of International Organizations
    (DARIO) 95, 99–102, 104
  Due Diligence Policy 2013 95, 97–99,
    102, 109
  families of deployed soldiers 168–169
  gender equality 109–110
  government employees 80–83,
    89–90
  human rights violations 95, 97–100,
    102–104, 109–110
  legal responsibilities 93–96
  non-government actors 80–83, 88,
    89–90
  Operation Blue Ridge (OBR) 10,
    148–171
  principles for civilians on operations
    89–91
  reporting on abuses against 99,
    102–104, 108
  respect for 104–106
  Rights Up Front plan of action 2014
    95, 96–97, 102, 109
  role of 73 76
  'strategic civilian' concept 74–76,
    89–91
  'strategic corporal' and 76–80, 92–93,
    106–108
  time-critical aspects 86–89
  training for 86, 88–89
  UN and 106–109
  *see also* contractors; cyber warfare

201

Clark, Wesley K  137
Clausewitz, Carl von  30–31, 136, 138
climate, impact of  161
coalition allied forces  62, 169–170
COIN *see* counterinsurgency operations
'commander's intent' *see* mission command idea
communication  1–4, 38, 132
complexity of tactical environment  6, 59, 60–62
comprehensive approach to operations  74–76, 83–85
Congo *see* Democratic Republic of Congo
consequences of soldiers' actions  4, 17
constructive approach to leadership  25
contractors
  Blackwater USA  55–56
  capability of  61, 67, 69–71
  complexity of tactical environment  59, 60–62
  distributed operations  65–67
  fluidity of tactical environment  59, 60–62
  'freedom to fail'  63, 64
  implications of employing  56–57, 59–72
  lower-level decisions  59, 62–65
  media, impact of the  59, 67–69
  'strategic corporal' concept  57–59
  as strategic enablers  69–72
  strategic outcomes  56–57, 59, 62–65
  'three block war'  57–59
  *see also* civilians
control  29, 66–67
coordination  63–64
corporate governance  28
Cosgrove, Peter  78
Côte d'Ivoire  100–102, 109

counterinsurgency operations (COIN)  6, 49–50, 75, 79
Cowper-Coles, Sherard  87–88
credit for collective success  27–30
*Criminal Case 40/61*  42
criminal law  111
cultural differences  3, 6, 15, 19–21, 141, 142, 159
culture of institutions  62–63, 97, 108
cyber warfare
  belligerent nexus test  124–126
  definitions  113–115
  direct participation in hostilities (DPH)  111–113, 117–130
  direct vs indirect causation of harm  121–124
  'for such time'  126–129
  Georgian conflict in 2008  115–116, 119, 121, 122, 125–126
  international humanitarian law  111–118, 120, 121, 129, 130
  threshold of harm  118–129
  training of soldiers  139

# D

Danish proverb  133
DARIO *see* Draft Articles on the Responsibilities of International Organizations
DDoS (Distributed Denial of Service) attacks  116, 122, 127
decision-making in field  1–3
decolonisation  148–149
Defence Procurement and Sustainment Review  45
democracy  134–135
democratic leadership vs shared leadership  24
Democratic Republic of Congo  95, 97–98, 109

Deng Xiaoping 134
*Dereliction of Duty* 40–41
Diogenes of Sinope 5
directing 30
directive control
    *see* mission command idea
direct participation in hostilities (DPH) 8, 111–113, 117–130
direct vs indirect causation of harm 121–124
disaster relief 3–4, 73–74
discipline 66–67 *see also* obedience
Distributed Denial of Service (DDoS) attacks 116, 122, 127
distributed operations 65–67
diversity 141 *see also* cultural differences
Dixon, Norman 49, 174
DLA Piper Report 47–49
Dobell, Graeme 90–91
Dorn, Walter 79
DPH *see* direct participation in hostilities
Draft Articles on the Responsibilities of International Organizations (DARIO) 95, 99–102, 104
Due Diligence Policy 2013 95, 97–99, 102, 109
Du Picq, Charles Ardant 34
DynCorp 63–64

# E

East Timor campaign, 1999 20–21
education *see* training
ego-separation 29–30
Eichmann, Adolf 41–42
*Eichmann in Jerusalem* 41–42
elitism 11–12, 172–173, 175–177
EO *see* Executive Outcomes
ethical issues 3, 21, 60–62, 163
    *see also* moral obligations

European Court of Human Rights 103
Executive Outcomes (EO) 57, 61–62, 63
exploring, as activity of leadership 30

# F

failure 63, 64
    *see also* 'zero-defects mentality'
families of deployed soldiers 168–169
FARDC *see* Forces Armées de la République Démocratique du Congo
Farrell, Theo 52
Fastabend, David A 14
flexibility 12–16, 59–62, 74–75, 83
Flowers, Robert B 12
fluidity of tactical environment 59, 60–62
Fofié, Martin Kouakou 101
Forbes, John RS 49
Forces Armées de la République Démocratique du Congo (FARDC) 97–98
Foreign and Commonwealth Office, Stabilisation Unit 82
foreign policy, Singapore 148–155
'for such time' 126–129
Foucault, Michel 37
'fourth generation warfare' 19
    *see also* 'three block war'
Freedman, Lawrence 136–137
'freedom to fail' 63, 64

# G

Gabriel, Richard 37
Gantz, Peter 70–71
garden-like mental model 173–174, 180
Gbagbo, Laurent 100–101
gender equality *see* sexism
Geneva Conventions, Additional Protocol I and II 113–115
Georgian conflict, 2008 115–116, 119, 121, 122, 125–126

Gerras, Stephen J 13
goal-oriented rationality (*Zweckrationalität*) 139
Goldsmith, Jack 54
government employees, role of 80–83
Grossman, Dave 144–145
guerrilla warfare 135–136
Gulf War 134, 157
Gurkha soldiers 61, 86–87

H

Haiti 95–96, 105
Heinlein, Robert A 76
Helvenston, Scott 55–56
hierarchical authority 26–27, 173–174
*History of the Peloponnesian War* 147
Hobbes, Thomas 136
'home front' 168–169
Hopkins, Andrew 37
human dimension of battles 140
humanitarian assistance 3, 21, 73–74
human rights 8, 93–106, 109–110
Huntington, Samuel 38–39
Hurricane Katrina 13
Huxley, Aldous 52

I

ICRC *see* International Committee of the Red Cross
ICTY *see* International Criminal Tribunal for the former Yugoslavia
*Idea of a University, The* 143
independence of action 35–36, 39–40
indirect vs direct causation of harm 121–124
individual soldiers, emphasis on 132
innovation 11, 52, 70 *see also* cyber warfare; technological development
institutional culture 26–31, 62–63, 97, 108
instrumental rationality (*Zweckrationalität*) 139
'integrated mission' approach *see* comprehensive approach to operations
intelligence testing 11
INTERFET *see* International Force for East Timor
international armed conflict, definition of 113
International Committee of the Red Cross (ICRC) 8, 81, 111–130
*see also* Interpretive Guidance
international criminal law 8, 97, 111, 130
International Criminal Tribunal for the former Yugoslavia 117
International Force for East Timor (INTERFET) 78, 151
international humanitarian law 8, 96, 97, 98, 99, 102, 111–118, 120, 121, 129, 130
international relations, Singapore armed forces 148–155
International Security Assistance Force (ISAF) 148, 159, 162, 164, 171
internet 134
interoperability 63–64
Interpretive Guidance (ICRC)
belligerent nexus test 124–126
direct participation in hostilities (DPH) 111–130
direct vs indirect causation of harm 121–124
'for such time' 126–129
threshold of harm 118–129

# Index

interstate wars, possibility of 135–136
Iraq 6, 7, 18, 20, 55–57, 61, 63, 65, 66–67, 68, 69, 134, 135, 137, 139, 151–152, 154, 157
ISAF *see* International Security Assistance Force
Israeli Supreme Court 117

## J

Jacka, Albert 172
Jans, Nick 141
Jefferson, Thomas 108
Jemaah Islamiyah (JI) 152
Joint Service Commendation Medal 167
judgement, of soldiers 7, 15, 37, 42, 51, 132, 140, 142, 145
junior commanders 19–22, 59, 62–65, 87
*Justice in Tribunals* 49

## K

Kaldor, Mary 135
Kausikan, Bilahari 149
Keegan, John 140
Kempner, Robert 44
Kilcullen, David 4, 135
killing and its impact on soldiers 144–145
King, Simon 17n21
Krulak, Charles C 1–3, 7, 19, 32–33, 57–59, 62–63, 76–77, 92
Kübler-Ross, Elisabeth 144
Kuhn, Thomas 38
Kuik Cheng-Chwee 155

## L

LAC *see* Liberia Agriculture Company
leader-centric leadership 23–24

leadership style 6, 74–75, 144
*see also* shared leadership
learning organisations 10–16
*see also* training
*Learning Organization Doctrine: Roadmap for Transformation* 12–13
Lee Kuan Yew 153–154
legal issues 3, 6, 60–62, 66, 93–96, 111–115, 117
Levene, Lord 46–47
Liberia 104–107
Liberia Agriculture Company (LAC) 105–107
Liddy, Lynda 14, 16–17, 20, 175–176
life beyond soldiering 177, 179, 180
Lindsay, Douglas R 23, 27
local culture 3, 6, 19–21 *see also* cultural differences
logistics 70–71
long-term thinking 4
Lovell, David W 159, 174, 177–179
lower-level decisions 19–22, 59, 62–65

## M

MacIntyre, Alasdair 38
managing 24, 30
*Marine Corps Gazette* 49, 76
McCauley, Greg 27
McMahan, Jeff 40
McMaster, Herbert R 40–41
medals 61, 164, 167–168
media, impact of the 4, 19, 59, 67–69, 78, 132, 147
mediation skills 4, 21
meta-cognition 29
micro-management 14, 63, 64–65, 180
*Military Law Review* 54
MINDEF *see* Ministry of Defence
mindfulness 26

Ministry of Defence (MINDEF), Singapore 168–169
mission command idea (*Auftragstaktik*) 27, 32–36
mobile phones 108, 134
Moffitt Review 46
monitoring human rights violations 99, 102–104, 108, 110
MONUC (now MONUSCO) 95, 97–98, 109
moral obligations 40–45, 49–51, 53–54 *see also* ethical issues
Mortimer Review 45
MPRI 63–64, 68–69, 70, 71
Mulisch, Harry 42

## N
Napoleon Bonaparte 11–12
Napoleonic Wars 33
NATO (North Atlantic Treaty Organization) 85
NATO medal 164
natural disasters 73, 132
NCOs *see* non-commissioned officers
negotiation skills 4, 21
Newman, John Henry 143, 179
Ng Eng Hen 160, 169
NGOs *see* non-government organisations
Nisour Square incident 56, 68
non-commissioned officers (NCOs) 1, 8, 15, 17, 21, 22, 31, 49, 106, 174–175, 178
non-government organisations (NGOs) 80–83, 88
non-international armed conflict, definition of 113
North Atlantic Treaty Organization *see* NATO
nuclear weapons 5, 131, 134

## O
Obama, Barack 75–76
obedience 40–42, 54, 140, 145 *see also* discipline
OBH *see* Operation Blue Heron
OBR *see* Operation Blue Ridge
O'Brien, Patricia 97
officership 6, 27–31
official reports 36, 43–49, 53
Olive Group 63–64
*On the Psychology of Military Incompetence* 49
Operation Absolute Agility (fictional scenario) 57–59, 68, 69, 163
Operation Blue Heron (OBH) 151
Operation Blue Orchid 151–152
Operation Blue Ridge (OBR) 10, 147–171
Operation Blue Torch 157
Operation Crimson Angel 150–151
Operation Flying Eagle 151
Operation Nightingale 157
Operation Thunderbolt 150
Operation Vigilant Resolve 55–56
organisational learning 12, 20, 25
organised armed groups, definition of 114
Orwell, George 133
Osiel, Mark 50
Ouattara, Alassane 100–101
outsourcing *see* contractors

## P
Pastel, Teague A 14
Peace and Stabilization Operations Program (PSOPs) (Canada) 82
peacekeeping missions
 comprehensive approach 83–84
 contractors 70

# Index

Draft Articles on the Responsibilities of International Organizations (DARIO) 95, 99–102, 104
Due Diligence Policy 2013 95, 97–99, 102, 109
 gender equality 109–110
 human rights violations 95, 97–100, 102–104, 109–110
 institutional culture 97, 108
 legal responsibilities 93–96
 reporting obligations 99, 102–104, 108, 110
 respect for people 104–106
 Rights Up Front plan of action 2014 95, 96–97, 102, 109
 status of UN 106–109
 'strategic corporal' concept 3–4, 92–93, 106–108
physical vs non-physical damage 119–121
political dimension of war 136–137
*Political Missions* (report) 86
poor people, respect for 104–106
Post-Traumatic Stress Disorder 144–145
preparation *see* training
problems solved by wars 136–137
procedures 38–40, 93
'professional mind' 38–39
PSOPs *see* Peace and Stabilization Operations Program
psychological trauma 144–145
'psycho-technology' 42, 175
PTSD *see* Post-Traumatic Stress Disorder
publicity campaign, Operation Blue Ridge (OBR) 170
Pudas, Terry 83
'pussy cats with guts' approach 20

## Q

Queen's Gallantry Medal 61

## R

Ramanathan, Sellapan 149
rapid response forces 65
RedR 88
Refugees International 70–71
Regional Multi-National Force (RMNF) 57–58, 67, 69
regulatory framework *see* legal issues
Reid, James 49
reliability, of organisations 25–26
reporting
 human rights violations 99, 102–104, 108, 110
 official reports 36, 43–49, 53
*Report of the Review of Allegations of Sexual and Other Abuse in Defence* 35, 47–49
research and development 11
respect for people 104–106
responsibility of soldiers 1–7, 16, 35, 39, 40–43
*Review of the Defence Accountability Framework* 51
'revolving door protection' 128–129
Ricks, Tom 33
Rights Up Front plan of action 2014 95, 96–97, 102, 109
RMNF *see* Regional Multi National Force
Robinson, Sir Ken 180–181
routines 38–40
Russia 115–116, 134

## S

SAF *see* Singapore armed forces in Afghanistan

SAFOS *see* SAF Overseas Scholarship
SAF Overseas Medal 164
SAF Overseas Scholarship (SAFOS) 165, *165–167*
Scahill, Jeremy 55
scapegoating 36, 46
Seasprite Report 43–45
Second World War 41–42, 44
Seeckt, Hans von 35
'servant leadership' 29–30, 84
sexism 12, 16, 109–110
sexual abuse 35, 47–49, 96, 101, 103, 105, 109
shared leadership
   definition of 22
   issues for military institutions 26–31
   'strategic corporal' concept 19–22
   team performance and 22–26
   training of soldiers 144
Shay, Jonathan 40
Sierra Leone 57, 61–62, 63
Simpson, Emile 86–87
Singapore armed forces in Afghanistan (2007–2013)
   artillery hunting radars (ARTHUR) 158, 160, 161, 162, 163
   'box score' 162
   civilian deaths 162–163
   climate 161
   decolonisation of Singapore 148–149
   'home front' 168–169
   international relations 148–155
   medals 164, 167–168
   national interests 148–150
   publicity campaign 170
   rank distribution of personnel 157–158, *158*
   risks and returns 155–171
   SAF Overseas Scholarship (SAFOS) 165, *165–167*
   Singapore–US relations 153–155, 171
   'strategic corporal' concept 147–148, 163, 171
   training, pre-deployment 159, 163
   Unmanned Aerial Vehicle (UAV) team 156, 161–162, 163, 171
Singapore Ministry of Defence (MINDEF) 168–169
small-unit operations 14, 20
smartphones *see* mobile phones
Snow, CP 42
social privilege 11–12
soft skills 21
'soldier-scholars' 143–144, 178
Somalia 55
South Ossetia 115–116
South Sudan 95, 102–104
Soviet Union *see* Russia
Sri Lanka 95, 96
Stabilisation Unit, Foreign and Commonwealth Office 82
*Starship Troopers* 76
'stewardship' 27–31
Stockdale, James 53
Storr, Jim 38
*Straits Times, The* 167
'strategic corporal' concept
   background to 1–5, 57–59, 76–77, 92
   barriers to 173–177
   challenges facing soldiers 5–10
   definitions of 16–17, 176
   education 172–173, 174, 177–181
   elitism 172–173, 175–177
   importance of 180–181
   learning organisations 10–16
   questions around 17–18

# Index

strategic outcomes 17–18, 56–57, 59, 62–65
Stringer, Kevin D 15n18, 21, 28
Super Seasprite helicopter project 43–45

## T
Taleb, Nassim 180
Tallinn Manual 122, 125, 127n69
Tan Huck Gim, Eric 151
Tan See Seng 155
Teague, Mike 55–56
team performance 22–26
technological development 9, 11, 132, 134, 138–142 *see also* cyber warfare; innovation
Teo Chee Hean 152–153, 156
terrorism 4, 15, 134, 152–153
Theohary, Catherine 83
'three block war' 2–3, 19, 21, 57–59, 133, 163
threshold of harm 118–129
Thucydides 147
time-critical aspects during conflict 86–89
Tolstoy, Leo 138
training
  for civilians 86, 88–89
  of contractors 61, 67, 69–71
  future of conflict 133–138, 145–146
  history of conflict 131–132, 133–137, 145
  importance of 172–174, 178–180
  important issues in 142–146
  killing and its impact on soldiers 144–145
  learning organisations 10–16
  organisation and 140–142
  peacekeeping missions 94
  shared leadership 28–29

Singapore armed forces in Afghanistan 159, 163
soft skills 21
'soldier-scholars' 143–144, 178
'strategic corporal' concept 1, 132, 172–174, 178–180
technology 138–142
treaty law 117
Triple Canopy 63–64
*Truppenführung* (German Army manual) 32–35
Turns, David 123

## U
UAV (Unmanned Aerial Vehicle) team (SAF) 156, 161–162, 163, 171
UN *see* United Nations
Uniform Code of Military Justice 64
United Kingdom Ministry of Defence 46–47
United Nations (UN)
  Charter 100, 121
  contractors 70
  Democratic Republic of Congo 95, 97–98, 109
  gender equality 109
  model of mission leadership 74–76
  *Political Missions* 86
  SAF and 151, 157
  status of 106–109
  UNHCHR 95
  UNMIL 104–107
  UNMISS 102–104
  UNOCI 100–102
  *see also* peacekeeping missions
United States (US)
  Department of State 82
  Singapore–US relations 153–155, 171
United States Air Force 24–25

United States Army 12–13, 21, 27, 49–50, 75, 80
United States Marine Corps (USMC) 14, 49–50, 64, 75, 80
Unmanned Aerial Vehicle (UAV) team (SAF) 156, 161–162, 163, 171
urban guerrilla 136
US *see* United States
USMC *see* United States Marine Corps

## V

Varey, Michael 79
Vietnam War 40, 41
virtual battlefield *see* cyber warfare
Von Clausewitz, Carl 30–31, 136, 138
Von Seeckt, Hans 35

## W

Wannsee Conference 44
'war amongst the people' 19
   *see also* 'three block war'

Washington, George 145
*Washington Post* 68
weaponry 5, 131, 134
weather *see* climate, impact of
Weber, Max 139
Weigley, Russell 138
West, Bing 55
Whelan, Theresa 71
women 16 *see also* sexism
World War II 41–42, 44

## Y

Yingling, Paul 36, 174

## Z

'zero-defects mentality' 14, 63, 64, 180
Zovko, Jerry 55–56
*Zweckrationalität* (instrumental rationality) 139